IN MEMORY OF
Jacques Guicharnaud
(1924–2005)

NUMBER 112

Yale French Studies

The Transparency of the Text: Contemporary Writing for the Stage

Yale French Studies

Donia Mounsef and Josette Féral, *Special editors for this issue*

Alyson Waters, *Managing editor*

Editorial board: Thomas Kavanagh (Chair), Ora Avni, R. Howard Bloch, Edwin Duval, Christopher L. Miller, Donia Mounsef, Jean-Jacques Poucel, Julia Prest, Maurice Samuels, Agnieszka Tworek

Assistant editor: Scott J. Hiley

Editorial office: 82-90 Wall Street, Room 308

Mailing address: P.O. Box 208251, New Haven, Connecticut 06520-8251

Sales and subscription office:

Yale University Press, P.O. Box 209040

New Haven, Connecticut 06520-9040

Published twice annually by Yale University Press

Designed by James J. Johnson and set in Trump Medieval Roman by The Composing Room of Michigan, Inc. Printed in the United States of America by the Vail-Ballou Press, Binghamton, N.Y.

ISSN 044-0078

ISBN for this issue 978-0-300-11819-3

DONIA MOUNSEF AND JOSETTE FÉRAL

Editors' Preface: The Transparency of the Text

In recent years, interest has been ignited across disciplines in performance and performativity. However, the status of the theatrical text
and of playwriting remains unstable. Throughout the twentieth century it was argued that theatrical writing does not belong to literature
but to the stage through its potential for "mise en scène," and that its
critical tools should not proceed from literary studies. This stage-cen-
tric view has occluded textual analysis and undermined the autonomy
of the theatrical text. Far from a simple reestablishment of this autonomy, the articles in this collection address the diverse and evolving
body of work of contemporary stage writing as a creative, political, and
sociocultural space. In addition, they provide new critical tools that
take into account the text in its linguistic, aesthetic, and cultural con-
texts. Fallen from grace since the mid-twentieth century, the theatrical text, maligned by the various avant-gardes, lost its function as the
valiant regulator of representation, to become one of the many discourses that construct stage meaning. Three major factors contributed
to this fall: the suspicion of theater's capacity to express the real, the
impossibility of representing the subject, and the fundamental distrust
in language's ability to convey meaning. Paradoxically, modern theater's loss of language can only be fathomed through the same language
that it purports to critique. The desire to say the unsayable, the need to
speak the unspoken haunts contemporary writing, as Valère Novarina
astutely suggested: "What we cannot speak of, that is what must be
spoken."

Beyond the diversity of claims, themes, and styles, there is in contemporary stage writing in French a sense of urgency to decode the
world, to formulate identities, to express violence, silence, desire, isolation, love, death, grief, confinement. All these themes haunt the con-

YFS 112, *The Transparency of the Text*, ed. Donia Mounsef and Josette Féral,
© 2007 by Yale University.

temporary text with the recurrent impossibility of representing the real, of speaking the emotional depth of the subject, and translating the incommensurability of language. What constitutes a bigger damnation? What is more violent: to silence those voices or to amplify them? Caught between the need to tell a story and the skepticism of language, between the whims of the director and the impulses of acting, stage texts have become the embattled ground of language, liveness, and performance. Fragmented and fragmentary, in a whole or in pieces, made up of montage, collage, verbal remains, diffident words, the theatrical text seems to signify in diverse and ambiguous ways. Contemporary plays are often subject to the breakdown of dialogue, narrative fragmentation, splintered dramatic action, and a fractured progression of events. Contributing to this fragmentation is the fact that theater borrows from other genres (novel, film, television, and so on), inviting the director, the actor, and the spectator to journey outside the strictly textual into the domain of the performative. Such are the epic stories of Olivier Py or Armand Gatti, the sound bites of Valère Novarina, the elliptical parables of Philippe Minyana, the epic dramas of Bernard-Marie Koltès, the fables of Didier-Georges Gabily or Wajdi Mouawad, the excursions into the quotidian of Michel Vinaver or Michel Deutsch, the verbal hallucinations of Christine Angot or René-Daniel Dubois, the historical visions of Hélène Cixous and Normand Chaurette, the intertextualities of Evelyne de la Chenelière or José Pliya. These forms of writing often combine the verbal, the vocal, and the pantomimic, calling upon the stage to give them their strongest expression. They resonate in the body of the actor and in the space of representation; in that interstitial and transient space between the self and other, the one and the multiple, the individual and the city, at the interface of what is said and how it's lived.

Located at the intersection of presence and memory, duration and transience, individualism and collectivity, meaning and insignificance, poetry and the concrete, contemporary writing is scored throughout by enunciative and corporeal influences. In either their written or verbal form, stage texts quest for an absolute. Novarina's theater, for example, speaks the essence of the stage through acting, linking the speech act to the origins of the body. At other times, as in the theater of Nathalie Sarraute, words meander and entwine with multiple meanings, to become a minefield of discursive conflict. If there is one characteristic common to writing in the last thirty years, it is the fact that it speaks to the stage, it *makes a scene* that resonates in the actor's body. In fact, these texts demand a particular investment from the actor, calling for a style of acting different from the usual representation of a character's psychology. In its materiality, the text inhabits the body of actors, passes through them, compelling them to become a site of crossing of languages (as Gatti and Novarina both said), from the verbal to the spatial to the corporeal. Words are multiplied, fissured, creviced in the body of the actor that takes center stage with its voice, breath, and tone. The actor can no longer simply interpret a prescribed role but must make audible a text, vocalizing its musicality, rhythms, and tempos, like the early poet-dramatists. The playwright is likewise endowed with a new mission. Far beyond the conventional task of storytelling, he or she reinvents language, exploits its fault lines, in other words, infuses writing with performance.

It is to capture the various instances of this infusion, to delineate the various functions of the text today that this collection was designed. Without laying claim to total comprehensiveness, this volume bridges the gap between the 1960s and the turn of the millennium in terms of the evolution of theatrical writing. Taking as a starting point *Yale French Studies'* 1971 issue devoted to modern theater ("From Stage to Street," edited by Jacques Guicharnaud) that deals with the festive ritual and the events surrounding May 1968, this volume begins where that last noted volume on theater concluded. The essays are organized thematically into three sections. The first addresses issues of terminology and introduces the text/performance divide at the paradigm shift marking the end of the absurd tendency and the suspicion surrounding the term "avant-garde." The second deals with specific examples of this tension in the work of the most representative playwrights of the last twenty years (Vinaver, Koltès, Novarina, Cadiot, and Renaude). The third and final section expands the geographical and aesthetic boundaries of French drama to include an analysis of Francophone writing and translating.

The articles pose a number of provocative questions: what is it to write today for the stage, or for a particular stage, or with a particular director in mind? How does the text speak to the space of performance and in what language? What happens to the text when it purposely seeks to question its preconceived relation to the "mise en scène"? How can we define the contours, styles, and forms of writing when the reality of contemporary theater is one of fragmentation, rupture, and heterogeneity? The dual purpose of this collection is to address these questions and redefine the changing cultural and linguistic landscape of writing, and the way stage writing in particular radically questions our understanding and construction of literature and performance.

The editors would like to express their deepest gratitude to the managing editor of *Yale French Studies*, Alyson Waters, for her invaluable advice and critical insight into this volume. This collection would not have been possible without her guidance, support, and continuous devotion to this project from its inception, through its preparation for publication. Alyson deserves credit not only for seeing the volume to fruition but also for guiding us to focus the ideas and themes with unparalleled grace and generosity of spirit.

I. Avant and Après Garde

TOM BISHOP

Whatever Happened to the Avant-Garde?

So whatever *did* happen to the avant-garde? Not so long ago (at least for
those of us who actually witnessed that extraordinary explosion of creative theatrical innovation in the 1950s), the very notion of the avant-
garde, so much a part of the esthetics of French art in all its varied forms
since the middle of the nineteenth century, finally triumphed in the
theater with Eugène Ionesco, Samuel Beckett, Jean Genet, and Arthur
Adamov. *La cantatrice chauve* in 1950, followed immediately by *Les
chaises, En attendant Godot,* and the dazzling theatricality of Genet's
plays, and eventually numerous other dramatists writing in French and
then throughout Europe and the Americas, radically changed theater,
first in France and soon throughout the western world. This was an
iconoclastic avant-garde that sought to change the rules of the game,
to do away with what was left of realistic techniques after half a century of brilliant anti-realist reactions against the successful fourth-wall
realist brainwashing initiated and exemplified by André Antoine and
his Théâtre Libre in the 1890s.

And it was an immensely successful avant-garde. Word went out
from the little Left Bank playhouses that new concepts of theatricality
were undermining some of the mainstays of even the best of the playwrights of the time—Sartre, Camus, Montherlant, Anouilh: plot, character, psychology, coherent stories. The new playwrights did not offer
a common vision; what united them to some extent though was their
opposition to the status quo. Soon they were being performed in larger,
more important theaters, like the Odéon and eventually the Comédie
Française, and became *the* playwrights of the fifties and sixties. It is rare
for an avant-garde to impose itself so thoroughly and for the experi-
mentalists in revolt to become so quickly the established figures of an

YFS 112, *The Transparency of the Text,* ed. Donia Mounsef and Josette Féral,
© 2007 by Yale University.

art form. But astonishingly, that is, what happened with what came to be known for better or for worse as the "theater of the absurd."[1]

Serious playwrights could legitimately propose that after Beckett, after Ionesco, one could no longer write theater as before. Obviously, some dramatists *did* continue to write theater as before, just as many twentieth century novelists continued to produce good or bad nineteenth century novels as if Joyce, Kafka, Virginia Woolf, Beckett, Borges, and the *nouveau roman* had never existed. But for those who thought critically and creatively about the stage, the Parisian avant-garde of the 1950s had shattered the mold and made it impossible to go back to even the best of former models. But it also revealed a new, serious problem.

Ionesco, in a brilliant definition of the avant-garde, had pointed out that as soon as an avant-garde is so successful as to become the new establishment, it necessarily engenders its own opposition: another avant-garde which, in turn, seeks to destroy and replace it.[2] However, following its fifteen or twenty years of undisputed triumph, the avant-garde of the absurd yielded not to new writing but rather to the reign of the director.

To write after Ionesco was difficult, after Beckett, impossible. The towering figures, Beckett, Ionesco, Genet, remained; others faded or disappeared. A few important playwrights, like Fernando Arrabal and Michel Vinaver, have continued right to the present time creating absurdist-related yet highly idiosyncratic works. No powerful group emerged to take their place; some splendid writers did turn to the stage but at no point formed anything resembling an avant-garde movement. Among the best of these are Nathalie Sarraute, Marguerite Duras, Copi, Hélène Cixous, Valère Novarina, and somewhat later, Xavier Durringer, Bernard-Marie Koltès, Philippe Minyana, and Yasmina Reza.

The only "movement" to speak of was the brief period of success in the seventies and eighties of the *théâtre du quotidien*. Influenced by several brilliant German and Austrian playwrights, notably Franz

1. It is easy to quibble with Martin Esslin's famous title. Obviously, the concept of the absurd fits some authors better than others, and some, like Genet, not at all. Still, Esslin focused on one significant new element in the writings of the new dramatists of the fifties and if "theater of the absurd" is not a wholly satisfactory label, it is still better or more meaningful than the others, such as "new theater," "antitheater," "theater of derision."

2. *Les entretiens d'Helsinki* (Paris: Editions Michel Brient, 1961), 13–14, quoted in English in Eugène Ionesco, *Notes and Counter Notes* (New York: Grove Press, 1964), 40–41.

Xaver Kroetz, peter Handke, and Botho Strauss, a few French authors, especially Michel Deutsch and Jean-Pierre Wenzel, both working in Strasbourg, and later the very talented Parisian Tilly (no first name, like Brazilian soccer players) put a new focus, however briefly, on the text and with it, on the preeminence of the dramatist. They dealt with the things of everyday life, especially in the lives of simple, inarticulate people, implying a social critique though eschewing Brechtian didacticism. Most notably, the *théâtre du quotidien* is the first important movement on the French stage since 1900 to go against the almost continuous, century-long reaction against theatrical realism. If this new movement, late in the century, did not revert to truly outmoded, nineteenth century forms of theatricality, it certainly did not point to a new, experimental direction and it did not incarnate some new avant-garde attitude.

But of course it is doubtful whether by the end of the twentieth century, a theatrical avant-garde was still even possible in France. Many important elements conspired against it. Strangely enough, one of these was the accession to the Ministry of Culture in 1981 of Jack Lang, a long-time enthusiast of the avant-garde in all its manifestations and especially in the theater. It had, after all, been Lang who had created the seminal Nancy Theater Festival of New Theater in the seventies. Lang obtained a commitment from President François Mitterand for an unheard-of 1% of the country's budget for his ministry. Culture, the arts, and especially theater had never had it so good!

Lang gave strong support to the growing list of state supported theaters in Paris and accelerated enormously the process of decentralization that brought important companies to the rest of France. To run these many enterprises, ranging in size and importance from modest provincial cities to the Comédie Française, Lang's Ministry of Culture selected talented, innovative directors like Antoine Vitez, Patrice Chéreau, Jean-Pierre Vincent, Jean Jourdheuil, Jacques Lassalle, Marcel Maréchal, Bernard Sobel, Joël Jouanneau, and Georges Lavaudant.

Together with other directors who had made their reputation earlier (Roger Planchon, Jean-Louis Barrault, Peter Brook, Ariane Mnouchkine) they brought a lively new spirit to the theaters of France. But institutionalizing innovative creators does not necessarily make for innovative institutions—if such a notion is even conceivable. Meanwhile important foreign influences had come to play crucial roles in introducing startling theatricality, almost always at the expense of text. Following the initial, powerful impact of Jerzy Grotowski and the

Beck's Living Theater, the French public was much taken by the startling stage images of Tadeusz Kantor and Robert Wilson. Often there was little or no text and no real author. At its best, in the hands of a Wilson and a Kantor, the sheer visual impact of some of these works was not only stunning, it proved to be truly dramatic.

But not all directors possess the same power of imagination nor the same means to express it. The French directors of the eighties, on the whole, followed analogous paths, preferring classics to contemporary authors, little known works by famous authors to the best known ones, stage adaptations of works not written for the stage to existing dramatic texts. More and more theater—*French* theater, but not only French theater—lost one of its key components: a text, a play. Directors tended to compensate for this crucial loss by substituting other stage activity: dance, pantomime, movements of various sorts, organized or not, meaningful or not. "The writer for the theater today," wrote Jean-Pierre Thibaudat in 1994, "is the victim of the revolution that turned over power to the director. It left him in a position of subordination. And after being put through the mill by the staging, his frequently fragile plays are often reinterpreted, transformed, disfigured. The author is no longer God almighty. He is a worker, the specialized worker of the text."[3] And, unsurprisingly, Thibaudat concludes that this state of things led to generally devitalized writing for the stage.

If the place of the author has not returned to its former position of primacy, it has improved recently as French directors seek perhaps a more equitable distribution of attention to the various components of the work on stage, *including* the text. Patrice Chéreau, who acknowledges "crushing" the text to some extent in all of his stagings, announces his renewed interest in the text as the most important element of the theatrical activity.[4]

But even a modest return to the role of the playwright, does not necessarily mean a revivified avant-garde. It all depends on what kind of writing, what kind of text, leading to what sort of theatricality. A Pirandello, a Genet, a Beckett expressed a radical theatricality that forced directors to provide innovative stagings *required* by the written work, inscribed in it. Today one looks in vain for such a need for experimentation.

3. Jean-Pierre Thibaudat, "Tribulations de l'écriture dramatique en France" in *Le théâtre français* (Paris: Ministère des Affaires étrangères, 1994), 23 (translation mine).
4. In Thibaudat, *op. cit.*, 28–29. It was at this time that Chéreau directed the very poetic, very textual plays of Bernard-Marie Koltès.

At the start of the twenty-first century, dramatists are drawn to political and social content, ranging from French problems of immigration and integration to world-wide concerns with AIDS, terrorism, and American military domination. There is no reason why such matters cannot be expressed in theatrically experimental forms. In the sixties and seventies, the creative strength of the work of the Living Theater, Richard Schechner, Jean-Louis Barrault, notably in *Rabelais* (to name just a few) proved that the two presented no contradictions and made for a particularly dynamic avant-garde.

Now, the most theatrically stimulating works dealing with political and social concerns are undoubtedly those of the Théâtre du Soleil (for example, *Le dernier caravansérail* by Ariane Mnouchkine), yet even their highly original stagings no longer qualify as "avant-garde." They are internationally recognized as part of the best, the most inventive of contemporary French theater. But if an avant-garde is, as Ionesco rightly claimed, a frontal attack on what *is* with the intent of destroying it and replacing it with a new, radical vision, not even Le Théâtre du Soleil can be considered to be an avant garde in the twenty-first century.

One may well wonder then whether an avant-garde in the French theater today is even possible. The question came to a head at the 2005 edition of the Avignon Theater Festival, always a showcase for the new and the daring. Under the leadership of the "artiste associé" invited each year to give structure (and meaning?) to the selection of playwrights, directors, choreographers, and others—the Flemish mixed-media artist Jan Fabre, selected by the Festival's directors, Hortense Archambault and Vincent Baudriller, to animate the festival, 2005 proved to be a catastrophe for public and critics alike. The co-directors and their "artiste associé" succeeded in alienating audiences with a polemical, vulgar, ultra-violent program that sought to shock—hardly a novelty in 2005 and not successful at that. After all, after nudity, after incest, after murder, rape, or cannibalism, how can you still shock a public that is force-fed the worst horrors daily on the evening news? Jan Fabre thought that urinating on stage, for instance, would be one way.

The intellectual and esthetic poverty of this strategy may have escaped the festivals' directors who claimed to want to question the limits of theater, but it did not escape the audiences. They were less shocked than irritated and bored. Theater was elsewhere. "It will undoubtedly take some time to begin to understand what really happened at this Festival," write Fabienne Darge and Brigitte Solino in their wrap-up for *Le monde.* "But one can already analyze certain elements. . . . This festival will have been an important moment in the history of Avignon, because it has been so revealing. It is evidence of a loss of ideological landmarks (through a brutal and meaningless reproduction of violence) and of esthetic ones (through a formal research that draws on the avant-garde of the years 1960–1970 without managing to bring it to life again)."[5]

The fiasco of the 2005 Avignon festival was probably the high water mark of the irrelevancy of theater that scorns text. Yet if one might therefore now predict a gradual revalorization of the dramatic text, such a pendulum swing would probably not be a harbinger of some incipient avant-garde. The years of the revolutionary theater of the absurd followed by a period of directorial innovation shook up the establishment, as avant-gardes are intended to do. If an avant-garde has been successful (and these were) it then becomes absorbed and dominant, bringing on a new established form of theater. Eventually, this new establishment, once it becomes, in Ionesco's words, a new tyranny, will be brought down by some new avant-garde. But the French theater is not there yet. It is impossible to guess what such a new avant-garde might be; if it were imaginable it would already exist. But it does not.

A similar situation existed in the nineteen thirties. After several decades of radical reactions against the realism institutionalized by Antoine, led by such towering figures as Aurélien Lugné-Poë, Jacques Copeau, Charales Dullin, the young Cocteau, the Surrealists, Gaston Baty, and Georges Pitoëff, a period of assimilation led to Giraudoux, Montherlant, Anouilh, and Sartre. Who could have imagined while watching, say, Giraudoux's *Intermezzo* in 1933 that twenty years later, two tramps would wade through endless silences while waiting for Godot and that the Martins and the Smiths, interchangeable, two-dimensional pseudo English couples would hurl phrases, words, and syllables at one another while no soprano, bald or otherwise, made a promised appearance. Beckett, Ionesco, Genet, and all the others had to write, to create, before their attack on the French theater establishment could as much as be envisaged. Only then could their avant-garde be detected, named, performed, analyzed.

Can we imagine that no new avant-garde will eventually rise against the current theater establishment in France? Not really. But

---

5. Fabienne Darge and Brigitte Salino, "2005, l'année de toutes les polémiques, l'année de tous les paradoxes," *Le monde* (July 28, 2005): 20 (translation mine).

what will it be? And will it be successful, as was the theater of the absurd, or relatively unsuccessful with no strong long-term traces (as was the case for instance of the expressionist theater of the twenties in France)? We will need to wait and see. But when it comes, it is likely to stem from unexpected sources and take unusual directions. The concerned theater critic awaits avidly.

JEAN-PIERRE RYNGAERT

Speech in Tatters: The Interplay of Voices in Recent Dramatic Writing

"But it's not theater." In 1993, in my book *Lire le théâtre contemporain*,[1] I noted that this remark, so often overheard upon leaving a theater, seemed to sum up the attitude, at once anxious and radically opposed, of spectators (and readers) who failed to recognize dramaturgy as they understood it on the basis of Aristotle and of nineteenth-century drama. Now, almost fifteen years later, the gap has widened even more between texts obeying the old rules (though these are still in the majority) and those, such as the ones I am about to discuss, that challenge the principles of absolute drama as theorized by Peter Szondi and defined by him as "an interpersonal event in the present."[2]

Since the 1980s, French playwrights have regained a more important place in the theatrical landscape after a long period in the wilderness during the 1960s and 1970s, when one often heard it said that French writing for the stage was dead. Things changed thanks in part to the vigorous cultural policies initiated in 1981 by Jack Lang and Robert Abirached at the French Ministry of Culture. Grants, writers' residencies, subsidies for authors and producers, and workshops all helped. A certain new awareness among theater people in general has perhaps played a part, but changing attitudes are not of themselves a sufficient explanation. It is worth noting also that the almost worldwide acclaim for an author such as Bernard-Marie Koltès, and the kind of public infatuation that has surrounded Koltès's work in France,

---

1. Jean-Pierre Ryngaert, *Lire le théâtre contemporain* (Paris: Dunod, 1993).
2. Peter Szondi, *Theorie des modernen Dramas, 1880–1950* (Frankfurt am Main: Suhrkamp, 1956). English translation by Michael Hays: *Theory of the Modern Drama* (Minneapolis: U. of Minnesota Press, 1987), 45.

YFS 112, *The Transparency of the Text,* ed. Donia Mounsef and Josette Féral, © 2007 by Yale University.

14

turned a bright spotlight on an area that usually receives little by way of media attention.[3]

The number of productions may not be high enough to satisfy the writers, who still complain about being treated as mere experimenters, but, to judge by the immense growth of publication, public readings, various kinds of *mise en espace* (preliminary presentations or stagings), and specialized theaters and festivals, this sphere seems to be enjoying a distinct vogue.[4]

It is quite possible, without pointing to particular trends, to list the main articles of faith of this modernity. Any such list would include the dismantling of story-line and action, fragmented organization, a farewell (or at least an *au revoir*) to characters, the breaking up of dialogue, the death of illusion, and the end of "double enunciation" as a logical way of conveying information to the reader/spectator. To these features might be added such countervailing tendencies as the "novelization" of the theater (the subversion of the dramatic form by the novel form); its "poetrification" (a major return to lyricism); and reliance on the direct addressing of the audience.

Though countless exceptions need to be taken into account, I would suggest that there now exists—in the subsidized theater, at any rate— an implicit dramaturgical template. For fun, I recently proposed a rough sketch of such a template in the journal *Pratiques*—not a theoretical model, obviously, but a composite of traits drawn from a variety of works.

> The play in question would be devoid of action, and its dramatis personae would be vague figures rather than socially or psychologically identifiable characters; in the absence of any *nouement* there would be no dénouement either; the issues addressed would not be immediately discernible, and recognizable networks of meaning would have nothing in the least to do with a plot. Beginning and end would doubtless be abrupt, and the necessity for either quite unclear. Readers would, however, have a few tenuous narrative elements available to them, allowing them to surmise that something was being recounted to them with their participation. And, most importantly, there would be talking: an

3. Theatrical authors have even formed an association to protect their interests: Écrivains Associés du Théâtre (EAT).

4. The Théâtre Ouvert was the pioneer, but the Théâtre National de la Colline and the Théâtre du Rond-Point should be mentioned. Villeneuve-lès-Avignon has a Centre National des Écritures du Spectacle, and the Abbaye des Prémontrés in Pont-à-Mousson hosts a festival for new theatrical writing and a summer school, "La Mousson d'Été."

interplay of voices in the shape of monologues, addresses, fragmented dialogue, and speech of uncertain provenance—sometimes suggesting a chorus, sometimes conversation, sometimes an independent discourse coming from memory. A veritable whirlwind, sweeping away all the rules of turn-by-turn speaking and address, would nevertheless manage to place speech at the center of things. For talking would go on, from beyond the grave, as it were, or beyond the character. . . . No theatrical convention reinforcing the notion that all this had to do with an imitation of the real world would be indispensable; nor would parodic features signaling theatricality be in evidence: there would indeed never be any question of anything except a free, artificial space for writing that transgressed all earlier conventions. The play would thus be totally *written*—in the sense that writing, as its texture, would be its chief component and its raw material far more than any subtle conception, any reasoned construction, or even any narrative concern.[5]

All this has been described in detail, commented upon at length, attributed to various "crises" in our societies, and labeled "postmodern" or (to use Hans-Thies Lehmann's term) "postdramatic."[6] I shall not lend my voice to the chorus of those endorsing or calling for a dramaturgical tabula rasa. I see these formal departures and reinventions as signs—sometimes clumsy or excessive, sometimes truly exciting—of the rebirth of a drama which, having completed its mourning for the "old theater," is developing ways of writing that approach fiction from a different angle.

Challenging the old dependence on illusion, the new playwrights appeal to their readers and spectators to assume a position that is more dangerous, more active—more of a gamble perhaps—as a genuine participant in an aesthetic that is not so much *new* (discussion of the word "contemporary" has become tiresome) as *different*. On occasion, indeed, it is a position that involves returning to pre-dramatic traditions.

Most aspects of drama are implicated in this upheaval, but, not wishing to fall into the trap of mere inventory-taking, I shall address only the question of speech, its use, and the overthrow of the former system of enunciation. This emphasis is consistent, moreover, with Pasolini's call, in his "Manifesto for a New Theater" (1968),[7] for "a the-

5. Ryngaert, "Écritures théâtrales contemporaines. État des lieux," *Pratiques* (December 2003).

6. Hans-Thies Lehmann, *Postdramatisches Theater* (Frankfurt am Main: Verlag der Autoren, 1999). French translation by P.-H. Ledru: *Le théâtre postdramatique* (Paris: L'Arche, 2002).

7. *Pier Paolo Pasolini: Contemporary Perspectives*, trans. David Ward, ed. Patrick Rumble and Bart Testa (Toronto: Toronto U. P., 1994).

ater of the word." Similarly, Valère Novarina evokes a "theater of words" or a "theater of speech" in which all the dramaturgical categories give way to the deployment of speech and language. These developments are certainly significant enough in the French and European theater to justify serious attention.

THE PHYSIOLOGY OF THE TEXT:
A TENDENCY TO EXTREMES

An initial examination of the surface features of the new dramatic writing reveals a propensity to go to extremes, an absence of balance and proportion, and a great freedom regarding the distribution of lines (if they can still be so called), all of which fosters a new-found autonomy of the spoken word. The old formal regularity created by the rhythm of utterances, by what Jean-Pierre Sarrazac calls a fair "sharing out of voices" (*partage des voix*), and by a reasonable amount of didascalia, has given way to excess: everything seems possible once words are no longer instrumentalized and no longer serve to move the action forward. This freedom manifests itself immediately in the form of either a great abundance or an extreme rarity of words; it shows even in the choices made regarding the layout of the printed page.[8]

The "physiology" of these writings thus offers a picture full of contrasts, where the text as a whole only rarely reflects an organization or a distribution of lines based on balance or on some clear intention. Sometimes named characters with no more than a shadowy identity, or alternating voices set off solely by punctuation indicating a change of speaker, are assigned very long speeches that pile on redundancy, variations, lists, and a proliferation of texts of all kinds, even borrowed ones. In other instances speeches are very brief, fragmented, and attributed to speakers who are clearly identified but who appear in the most ephemeral way. The first of these two models is exemplified by the writing of Valère Novarina, where the page is filled by copious, diverse, and heterogeneous speeches. Noëlle Renaude's texts correspond more closely to the second model, for they are more conversational and teem with apparent banalities. Michel Vinaver had shown the way here with his interweaving of often incomplete phrases, his reliance on fragmented and elliptical dialogue, and his way of cutting up and reassembling text so as to emphasize breaks and joins.

---

8. In her most recent writings, Noëlle Renaude experiments in many ways in this area.

Of course, there is no lack of long tirades in the history of the theater, from *Phèdre* to *Hernani;* nor is stichomythia a rarity. Traditionally, however, long reflections, glosses, or commentaries partook of the logic of the characters or of the action, as did the lightning flashes of rapid-fire exchange. It is far harder to make any such claim with respect to some of the verbal torrents or radical reductions of speech length in the works under consideration. We are confronted rather by a clear desire on the part of the author to commandeer the space of speech, even if this fact continues at times to be lightly concealed by the vague identity of some character or figure.

Effusiveness of this kind first made its appearance in the monological texts characteristic of 1980s; it then became the hallmark of writing that could not abide technical constraints and rejected all rules, even unstated ones. There could now be a very great deal of talking— or very, very little. Among historical antecedents, Lucky's long discoursing in *Waiting for Godot* is seminal. It is in a completely different register, however, that Koltès's Client and Dealer in *Dans la solitude des champs de coton/In the Solitude of Cotton Fields* (1985) exchange speeches many pages in length.[9] As for the current resort to abbreviated, almost anemic dialogue vouchsafing just the occasional fragment of speech, it may reflect differing intentions. Back in the 1950s, Beckett's characters, as loquacious as they could be at times, or those of Robert Pinget, appeared to personify the fact of having "nothing to say," of being unable to articulate any logical or coherent discourse. Their meager verbal assets were commonly taken to imply an overall failure of language. In the nineteen-seventies, by contrast, brevity meant not so much nothing to say as a socially or psychologically determined difficulty saying something, as witness the work of Jean-Paul Wenzel, Daniel Lemahieu, or Michel Deutsch. Brevity now, as in such authors as Joseph Danan ou Catherine Anne, or even Yasmina Reza (*Art*), does not necessarily have any immediate discernible meaning.

Today these kinds of disproportion and excess reflect the fact that speech is no longer beholden to a logical and continuous narrative project. Freed from any obligation to carry the story forward, to present identifiable dramatic situations, speech develops in a textual space without constraints. It is not that the story is necessarily absent, but simply that it has become more discreet, and that it is up to the reader

---

9. *In the Solitude of Cotton Fields,* tr. Jeffrey Wainwright, in Bernard-Marie Koltès, *Plays: 2,* ed. David Bradley and Maria M. Delgado (London: Methuen, 2004), 192ff.

or spectator to construct it on the basis of the textual material supplied, whether that material is profuse or cryptic and elliptical. The basic question is no longer "What is the story?" The text exists for its own sake, for its own qualities, for its literariness perhaps, or even for its "theatricality," while the story develops on the surface of the language only, in fits and starts, instead of being a deep and essential structure. Since narrative economy has thus ceased to be the prime consideration, the deployment of speech obeys other principles. A great historical precursor here is Paul Claudel, a true poet of the theater, emancipated from all the "dramatic" obligations of his time, which he cited and parodied as and when he pleased. It is precisely to this poetic freedom that Valère Novarina, Olivier Py, and a few others aspire today.

HYBRIDIZATION: NARRATIVE AND DRAMA

For twenty years or more the dramatic text has been infiltrated by forms that contribute to its "novelization." This term, much employed by Bakhtin and theorized notably by Jean-Pierre Sarrazac,[10] is intended to account for a general tendency for dramatic dialogue to be contaminated by narrative features. Thus the portion of the dramatic script traditionally assigned to the speech of the characters has been replaced by kinds of language that do not belong to ordinary dialogic exchange. This tendency restricts the characters' speech more and more, and weighs it down with storytelling moments, as may be seen, for instance, in Roland Fichet's *Animal* or in Daniel Danis's *e, roman-dit*. In such writing, first- and third-person modes are obliged to operate simultaneously.

Some have seen the influence of Brechtian epic theater here. That theater, however, always shifted back and forth between moments of dialogue and genuinely epic moments—words addressed to the audience, songs, and so on—and clearly indicated each change in the nature of the text. Today, by contrast, although one cannot detect any sign of a political intent or even of an epic consciousness, characters belonging in a more or less evident way to fiction sometimes adopt a narrative way of speaking or address the audience directly. The dramatis personae thus come to include all manner of narrators, reciters, monologists, storytellers, and reporters—all manner of mediators between the fiction and the public. In *e, roman-dit*, by the Quebec writer Daniel Da-

10. See Muriel Plana, "Romanisation," in *Lexique du drame moderne et contemporain*, ed. Jean-Pierre Sarrazac et al (Belval [Vosges]: Circé/Poche, 2005).

nis, for example, the didascalian Soleil introduces facts or stories that are then actualized by the characters, whose apparent independence and measure of realism are thereby ever more diminished. For Danis redundancy is welcome, as are the contradictions that arise, say, when a character fails to execute what has been announced. This kind of competition between two systems (or two voices) gives rise to clashes that create quite distinct effects.

Sometimes, duly named and designated, representatives of the writer cast aside their masks and intervene in the fiction as the author's alter egos. A case in point is Joseph Danan's *R.S./.Z.*, where two figures appear, the Author and the Writer, who share the onerous task of confronting the figure of the killer and investigating the power that figure exercises over the public (especially after Koltès's *Roberto Zucco*).

There is nothing particularly disconcerting about these devices when the narrative aspect is clearly demarcated. Things get trickier when the dramatic and the epic are no longer distinguished, when the two registers coexist within a single fragment of text without any indication of a change of speaker or any word of forewarning. The glide from properly dramatic speech into narrative speech is typically executed with great naturalness. There are many examples in the work of Daniel Danis, for whom this procedure is de rigueur. Throughout his writings, Danis continually makes it possible for his characters to narrate while almost simultaneously engaging in dialogue with other characters. This to-and-fro, flying in the face of all theatrical conventions, gives characters the enormous power to divulge whatever they may be experiencing in the immediate moment. Certainly, this helps carry the story forward, but in a much subtler way it allows feelings to be introduced without resort to anything that might properly be called interior narrative.

In Danis's *Celle-là/That Woman* (1993), for instance, the characters are at once narrators and actors: "I walk into the smell of the house from when I was as high as a small tree with red apples," says the Son in scene 2, and the use of the present tense allows doubt to persist concerning the immediacy of this action of his, for at the time when he speaks his mother is dead and he is in fact *remembering*.[11] The same alternation of narrative and dramatized sequences characterizes *Le chant du dire-dire/Song of the Say-Sayer* (1996), and the same sudden oddnesses oc-

---

11. Danis, *Celle-là*, English version *That Woman*, tr. Linda Gaboriau (Burnaby, B. C.: Talonbooks, 1998), 12.

cur in *Le langue-à-langue des chiens de roche/In the Eyes of Stone Dogs* (2001):

To his mother Joëlle who says: "I busted my heart all day asking you to stop bugging me about a father you might have had,"[12] Djoukie responds:

> This woman whose head I'm clutching is my mother, Joëlle, and I speak these words to her: I'm going crazy, I need an answer, a certainty, any certainty. Tell me who the father I don't want to meet is, just give me the guarantee I have one. Why can't we go live on our ancestor's land, Ma? (11)

Utterances addressed to the audience are thus interpolated into the dialogical exchange, permitting the characters to emerge from the fictional realm without for all that appearing to be diminished in any way. A good many dramatists now make use of whichever speech register best suits their composition at any particular moment. Shifts are no longer announced, nor is any need felt for special characters positioned on the fringe of the fiction and dressed in a way somehow signaling the role of mediator.[13] It is as though theatrical speech were now able to work with everything available, to use whatever form of utterance is most appropriate at the time, without any theoretical justification, certainly without any need to defend such practices as properly theatrical, or even as expressive of some *literary genre*.

MORE HYBRIDIZATION: DIDASCALIA WITHIN DIALOGUE

Another level of hybridization is added in texts where the status of didascalia also changes. For more than thirty years now, didascalia have been spoken aloud during the public readings and *"mises en espace"* that have become so frequent. In a few productions of the late 1970s, texts not originally intended to be spoken by the characters were incorporated into the performance.[14] Today the practice is commonplace, and very fashionable: with or without a microphone, with or

---

12. *In the Eyes of Stone Dogs*, tr. Linda Gaboriau (Burnaby, B. C.: Talonbooks, 2004), 10.

13. On the question of the character, see Ryngaert and J. Sermon, *Le personnage théâtral contemporain: décomposition, recomposition* (Montreuil-sous-Bois: Éditions Théâtrales, 2006).

14. A benchmark here is J.-P. Vincent's late-1960s production of *Félicité* by Jean Audureau at the Comédie Française.

without a designated *diseur*, didascalia are now read during performances whether or not a dramaturgical call for them is evident, and at the risk of boring the audience. Though this practice is by no means universal, the interest of authors in didascalia has markedly increased. Writers plan them for each scene, make pronouncements upon the characters, intervene in their own person completely unconcealed, and, in short, considerably shift the longstanding rules of dramatic writing. It becomes ever harder to draw a clear distinction between those "language surfaces" (Lehmann) that are to be spoken and those that should not be.

Traditionally it falls to the dramatist, ostensibly absent from the stage, to organize the different voices by assigning speeches on the basis of the identifiers heading each set of lines. This system has functioned for so long that it appears inherent to theatrical writing. Ordinarily, the author's discreet role decrees that he or she does not figure in a play's written form as the official assigner of parts. But other conventions have begun to emerge. Consider Philippe Minyana's *Pièces*, where the writer finds himself literally in the midst of the assembled characters, as though to impose rhythm on the playing as he sees fit. Such didascalia, which are carefully wrought, would seem difficult indeed to eliminate at the time of the work's staging, for the author's own speech is as it were incorporated into that of the characters:

> 3. Little village scene (back to the roots). . . .
> *Anna says to Tac:* "Kiss me and see." *Anna's husband says:* "Sit down, Anna." *He asks Tac:* "Are you coming to the cemetery." *Tac replies:* "An idea suddenly to come here and here I am." *He laughs, he's as joyful as can be; he even says:* "Oh what joy." *Irène says:* "The villa of your mother's parents at the end on the right derelict but gated garden just the same you'll see." *Anna says:* "Since the operation dizzy spells." *Tac says:* "Anna your little dressmaker's hands my mother is dead and your daughter." *Anna replies:* "Dead yourself then you stack of bones you'll see same here except for the football field."[15]

In this context Minyana becomes a kind of animal trainer or puppet master, calling up figures according to the requirements of the memory of the main character, Tac, and reducing the referential force of the stick figures, which come to life only briefly when didascalia accord each a fleeting moment of speech as one part in a kind of chorus.

Reduplication of details sometimes creates a comical or ironic ef-

---

15. *Pièces* (Montreuil-sous-Bois: Éditions Théâtrales, 2001).

fect on the model of "I say it and I do it" (or: "he says it" and "I don't do it exactly"!).

Another new practice is the incorporation of identifiers into the text of characters' speeches, as for example in *Promenades*, by Noëlle Renaude:

> "My name is Pat," says Pat.
> "My name is Bob," says Bob.
> "We are above reality, Bob," says Pat again.
> "Our love is unique and rapturous, Pat," says Bob in response.[16]

As Renaude's use of quotation marks here indicates, she continues to distinguish clearly between two registers of utterance. This is a procedure that also brings the work closer to the conventions of the novel with respect to dialogue, not without parodic or humorous intent. The text of *Promenades* is awash in "says Pat," "says Bob," and "says Jim," and it includes such narrative statements as "On the road to the south, Pat says. . . ."

The rules of the novel would dictate that such interventions be those of the author, the author's representative, or some narrator. But we are concerned here with a piece of dramatic writing, one containing no didascalia other than these rare textual elements, not really marginal yet not falling properly speaking under the identifier of a character. Even though the decision as to who exactly will pronounce such elements, which are "extra-dialogical" but at the same time an integral part of the text, may be made only when the work is staged, that decision will in any case affect our conception of the character.

The author in *Promenades* is not technically present in the same sense as in *Pièces*, because no external voice assigns speech in a definitive manner. On the contrary, the author seems to have left complete freedom to the characters, as though it were entirely up to them to sort out the apportionment of speech and the development of the story. The net result, however, is much the same, in that in both cases the characters no longer enjoy the standing of actors in a fiction: whether they seem to be completely dependent, literally the author's creatures, or whether the author has let them operate the machinery for creating illusions (or for dismantling them), the fact is that they are no longer members of the tribe of "real" characters of Aristotelian drama.

In my view, these texts from the margin incorporated into stage per-

---

16. Noëlle Renaude, *Promenades*, (Montreuil-sous-Bois: Éditions Théâtrales, 2002).

formance partake of a new theatrical poetics that abandons the exhausting task of representing the world, whether faithfully or not, according to instructions embodied in traditional stage direction. This radical departure with respect to representation (which also implies leaving behind the unfruitful question of the unrepresentable) proposes something more than a "theater of speech" to the senses and intelligence of the spectator, something that might be described as a theater of confrontation between saying and doing.

The nature of stage directions has changed, therefore. They are no longer either prescriptive or poetic, central or marginal; they no longer merely infiltrate the stage performance, but participate directly, in a crucible where several languages at once work on the construction of forms susceptible of reconciling saying and doing, which are no longer viewed as rival or redundant principles but rather as a unity. Indeed it is not altogether clear that these elements should continue to be called stage directions, considering that neither margin nor center can be said to exist in this kind of writing.

TURBULENCE IN THE SYSTEM OF UTTERANCE

Dramatic tradition decrees that a speech should be uttered by one character and addressed unequivocally to another. In the words once assigned to Louis Jouvet, "Theater is simple—I speak to you and you reply." The system of "double enunciation" does the rest: as we well know, every dramatic speech constitutes information directed to the reader/spectator. But things are much less straightforward for texts where the sources of speech are poorly defined or absent, and where the addressee proves to be likewise uncertain. Sometimes the dialogue is modeled on conversation, weaving lines into a fabric; sometimes, to the contrary, it destroys all logical connections—with serious consequences, naturally, for the very concept of the character.

A greater freedom of utterance derives, too, from the fact that very often, as Daniel Danis states at the outset of *Cendres de cailloux/ Stones and Ashes* (1992), "the drama has already taken place," and the characters are thus not obliged to "speak" a drama as it runs its course. Nonetheless, every aspect of the player's speech is focused on the urgency of the actual moment of its utterance.

These new conversational dramaturgies vary greatly in form (Michel Vinaver, Nathalie Sarraute, Jean-Luc Lagarce, Bernard-Marie Koltès, Noëlle Renaude, Daniel Lemahieu, Christophe Huysman), but

overall their emergence signals a shift from a theater that makes characters' utterances into the instruments and vectors of a teleonomic development to a theater where all attention is concentrated upon the act
of speaking in the present. These works are no longer concerned with
shaping a univocal, linear dramatic context, but instead with exploring
and revealing diverse spaces of utterance; thus, their speakers, constructed through their own speech-acts, are liable to be characterized
by plural, polyphonic, even incompatible features that structure situations and govern relationships of variable geometry. Although utterances no longer build up monolithic identities, a pragmatic analysis of
the speech exchanged nevertheless makes it possible to make out iden-
tifying profiles, roles, and positions—all in continual interplay. The
length and type of sentences, tendencies either to monopolize or to
withdraw from the discursive sphere, and particular approaches to listening, to modalization, or to modulation—all are possible constitu-
tive traits of the interlocutors present. By playing on the assumptions
and performative effects of speech, the new dramatists do not therefore
abandon storytelling. Rather they tell stories otherwise: they use sam-
pling, dissection, suture, graft, and the hybridization of voices and utterances to deliver fragments of fiction to the spectator.

Peter Szondi highlighted the phenomenon when he challenged
what he called "the conversation play," with reference in particular to
Chekhov. Szondi deplored the fact that in conversational forms of dialogue characters are not fully implicated in what they say: "because the
conversation play hovers between people instead of uniting them, it is
not binding. . . . It has no subjective origin and no objective goal; it goes
nowhere and is not transformed into action."[17] Szondi's argument im-
plicitly defends a circularity in the relationship between the character
and his or her discourse, thus implying a principle of consistency according to which characters would always express what they are (at the
moment when they are that) and would always be what they say.
Speech is thus instrumentalized within the absolute drama as defined
by Szondi in the Aristotelian tradition. In today's de-instrumentalized
theater, by contrast, the character is a poetic creature, formed by a
process of linguistic crystallization.

The weakening of the subject behind speech may be seen as merely
the first symptom—a historical one—of a tendency that has only

17. Szondi, *Modern Drama*, 52, 53.

grown stronger with the increasing autonomy of "language surfaces." It is now no longer necessary that a consistency be discernible between the speaker and what is spoken. The gulf between them has indeed widened, and the differences become more striking in ways that largely transcend the issue of the "conversation play."

THE RETURN OF THE CHORUS

The assigning and complex harmonizing of voices in these works has led to chorus-like devices, some of which return to the very oldest theatrical traditions. Arrangements vary from text to text, even though the aims correspond to those enumerated by Mireille Losco and Martin Mégevand: "to replace the individual by the group; to strive for multiform speech; to deplore the separation of human beings and dream of community; to brave the risks of song and the seductions of rhythm."[18] A chorus does not have to be formally identified in the text for such aims to be discernible. In the work of Jean-Luc Lagarce, for instance, the "exchanges" seem to suffer the temptation of monologue, or more precisely of a choral form where successive utterances seek to revisit the speech of the other, modifying it in part, or echoing it, in a continual interplay of repetition and resumption. This may be seen in Lagarce's *J'étais dans ma maison et j'attendais que la pluie vienne* (1994), where three generations of women speak in turn, commenting on the return of the son of the house. The common traits of their manners of speaking stamp them as members of a single tribe clearly assembled under the writer's banner.

In the same author's *Juste la fin du monde* (1990), all the characters belong to the category of those who have difficulty expressing themselves, often correcting their own statements, or seeking confirmation from their interlocutors, in the shape of signs of agreement, that their words have been taken in and understood.

> SUZANNE. You shake her hand, he shakes her hand. So you're really not going to shake her hand? They aren't going to shake hands, you'd think they were strangers.
> He doesn't change. I saw him exactly like this,
> you don't change,
> he doesn't change, like this the way I imagine him, he doesn't change,
> Louis,

---

18. Sarrazac et al, *Lexique*, 40.

and with her, Catherine, with her, you [*tu*] will find your bearings all
right, you [*vous*]
will find your bearings easily, she's the same, you're going to find your
bearings. . . .[19]

In many works we encounter cumulative effects, repetitions, variations, and reprises that eventually constitute a chorus—in fact if not
in name—within the warp and weft of a play's language. Examples
range from a simple interplay of voices with no precise origin, brought
together for just a moment, to ritualized and structured dramatic passages deploying differentiated identities.

In the hands of such representatives of dramatic modernity as
Bertolt Brecht, Aimé Césaire, Max Frisch, Heiner Müller, Michel Vinaver, Peter Weiss, Michel Tremblay, or Armand Gatti, choral effects
could not be more varied in character, depending on the dramaturgist's
intentions. The same may be said of such more recent works as those
of Patrick Kerman, Daniel Danis, or Philippe Minyana.

Whether these choral effects are harmonious or "dissonant" (to bor-
row Jean-Pierre Sarrazac's term), they may be univocal or multivocal
in nature, and their functions may closely resemble or radically depart
from those of the mythical chorus, with a propensity toward commentary. Their presence is undoubtedly linked to the importance these
texts ascribe to the interplay of voices. Certain present-day choruses
probably originate paradoxically in the extreme fragmentation and re-
constitution of these voices.

From the dramaturgical point of view, current instances of a chorus
are part of the new logics of composition, for the chorus always offers
a set of lines uninvolved in the advancing of the action, stands apart
from the individualized character bound up in conflict, and presents an
opportunity for lyricism to find expression.

The relations between character and chorus are nonetheless very
variable, while the question of "kinship" or identity among the voices
of a single choral group arises just as it does with individual identities.
That question is concerned with the quality of the bonds uniting a community, and seeks to measure the social or political weight of a given
chorus. But there is an extreme point where the identity of a chorus is
in fact lacking, where it rests on nothing more than a sum of voices
brought together for no particular or apparent reason whatsoever.

19. Jean-Luc Lagarce, *Juste la fin du monde*, in *Théâtre complet* (Besançon: Les Solitaires Intempestifs, 1999–2002), vol. 3, 210.

In the works cited here as references, the founding principles of the organization of speech are put into question, beginning with speech's informative role. In some of them, for example, the characters converse as though alone among themselves, never evincing the slightest concern for the reader and peppering their exchanges with much that is merely implicit. In others, the author addresses the reader or spectator directly, short-circuiting any mediating characters. In yet others, speech bears no clear indication of any intended recipient, and it falls to performance to determine its destination. The old rule of double enunciation—the idea that dramatic discourse is addressed simultaneously to others onstage and to the audience, who are thus informed, is thus seriously manhandled, if not ignored. The whole question of the distribution of voices therefore needs to be reexamined.

It is reasonable to ask whether the center of interest has not shifted entirely to speech developing autonomously, in and for itself, speech that it is no longer essential to attribute to anyone: whether speaking as such has not become a legitimate focus of interest. What these "interlocutory writings" offer is a theater of human beings struggling with speech, and it is speech itself, with its strategies, tragedies, dramas, powers, coquetries, and pretences, that they aim to produce on the stage.

BERNADETTE BOST

Drama Out-of-Bounds: Theater of Totality

In borrowing the title *Drame de la vie*[1] from Nicolas Restif de la Bre-tonne, Valère Novarina paid discreet homage to one of the founders of what might be called the "drama of totality." Indeed, shortly after the French Revolution, the prolific writer Restif had printed a 1396-page text bearing this same title, to which he added the precision "containing an entire man": ten plays and thirteen shadow theater acts meant to stage the life of the author, punctuated by his amorous encounters.[2] If in his own text Novarina displays no autobiographical purpose, at least the text reveals its desire for capturing totality, since it gathers 2587 figures represented in acts, through words, or simply enumerated by the character Adam. A single life yielded to the life of the human race. "I've made all those who have lived until now speak," noted the playwright in the "Impératifs" series, which accompanied the writing of *Drame,* and he announced "time regained of humanity as a whole."[3]

He never ceased to summon this proliferating humanity from text to text in a series of genealogies that string together not only Adam's descendants but also his predecessors. At the beginning of *L'origine rouge,* he even goes so far as to reinvent the nomenclature of pale-ontologists: 55 links in the great chain of species between "purgato-rius" and "homo sapiens sapiens."[4] However, his project of totaliza-tion was not limited to the never-ending collection of names. Beyond its 3171 characters and endless lists of intentions, activities, functions,

1. Valère Novarina, *Le drame de la vie* (Paris: P.O.L., 1984).
2. Nicolas Restif de la Bretonne, *Le drame de la vie* (1793) (Paris: Imprimerie na-tional, 1991).
3. Novarina, *Le théâtre des paroles. Impératifs* (Paris: P.O.L., 1989) notes 186 and 207.
4. Novarina, *L'origine rouge* (Paris: P.O.L., 2000).

YFS 112, *The Transparency of the Text,* ed. Donia Mounsef and Josette Féral, © 2007 by Yale University.

29

dances, acrobatic figures, or names of rivers, *La chair de l'homme* endeavors to encompass the sum of metaphysical representations transmitted through writing since its origin. Chapter XXXV contains 288 definitions of God—including anti-definitions formulated by agnostics or non-believers—gathered by theologians, philosophers, and other learned figures over the last 3000 years, plus 70 others attributed to those close to the writer, officially recognized or casual thinkers, real or fictional.

About twelve years earlier, Bernard Chartreux had been seduced by the dizzying temptation for a totalizing seizure [*une saisie totalisante*] by experimenting, for the director Jean-Pierre Vincent, with a dramatic kind of writing that was at once documentary and liberated from all constraint. Collecting historical facts regarding the plague of London in 1665 for his allegorical play *Dernières nouvelles de la peste,* he proclaimed in a preface the necessity to "tell everything," to call attention to the names "of streets, churches, neighborhoods, people, potions," to the number "of dead, of living, of dogs, of cats, of barrels," to "those rules, edicts, forms, recipes, prayers, compilations, treaties" and to "take the whole batch, to keep everything."[5] The first scene of the play, although written entirely by Chartreux and not concerned with the compiled lists of objects and information, confirms the influence of a totalizing vision on the writer's imagination: eighteen Londoners describe their city in terms in which all of the riches of nature and culture converge, as do human labor and the elements, art and industry, in a flamboyant multiplicity of landscapes and styles. A city becomes the sum of all cities, closed yet open to unlimited space.

Chartreux then tried to tell a story through a series of documents, from the beginnings of the illness to its development and then its extinction. Novarina, however, seems to want to develop a fable only in his first play, *L'atelier volant,*[6] and after that to adopt structures based on distributions of paradigms. When he speaks of *La chair de l'homme* constructed "on four rose windows: the rose of names, the rose of philosophers, the rosette of rivers, the rose of 8,"[7] he refers, in fact, to the four most obvious episodes in the text: genealogy, definitions of God, the list of names of waterways, and accumulations of names and

---

5. Bernard Chartreux, *Dernières nouvelles de la peste* (Paris: Edilig, 1983).
6. Novarina, *L'atelier volant* (Paris: *Travail théâtral* 5, October-December 1971).
7. Novarina, *La chair de l'homme* (Paris: P.O.L., 1995). The cited definition is found on the back cover.

gestures of people gathered at a fun fair. Four litanies, none of which introduces or concludes an absent history strictly speaking, even if two among them are used at the beginning and the end of the text. Contrary to *Drame de la vie* by Restif de la Bretonne, *La chair de l'homme* owes its monumental format (526 pages) not to the opulence of an epic journey, but to the recurrence of totalizing sequences. In this sense, it might be considered an open work, a sort of superdrama or drama matrix from which representable acts or scenes were borrowed: *L'équilibre de la croix*, a significantly shortened "stage version," and *Le repas*, an adaptation of the first pages.[8]

Noëlle Renaude, an admirer of Novarina, wished to increase this openness by experimenting with the *a priori* "unlimited" dramatic writing in *Ma Solange, comment t'écrire mon désastre, Alex Roux*.[9] Originally conceived as a "theatrical serial," written in a stream of consciousness with no hesitations or corrections, to be taken on by the actor and delivered to the public in 45-minute fragments, this three volume river-play with neither subject, nor action, nor progression could continue indefinitely. "I chose to end *Ma Solange . . .* arbitrarily," said the author, "when I discovered that it was becoming a work on my own life,"[10] not like an autobiography but perhaps rather like the cathartic nature of a regurgitation of thousands of voices gathered through time: an entire world (a people?) understood, felt, internalized. This is not a construction but an infinity of moments of speech juxtaposed, an uncontrolled flow of scraps of stories, anecdotes, reflections on the self and others, connected or interwoven lamentations and interpellations through which various states of common language are exposed, French that is scrutinized or lax, spoken in dialect, stammered, muttered, even adapted to the rash statements of young children or to the clumsy articulations of the dead, since the dead themselves wish to take part in this universal concert.

If one must find a precedent to the proliferation of "statements" implemented by Renaude in this theater of voices, Raymond Roussel's

8. *L'équilibre de la croix* was produced for the first time in July 1995 at Tinel de la Chartreuse of Villeneuve-les-Avignon, during the Festival d'Avignon, and *Le repas* was first produced in November 1996 at the Centre Georges-Pompidou in Paris.

9. Noëlle Renaude, *Ma Solange, comment t'écrire mon désastre, Alex Roux* (I, II, and III). (Paris: Éditions Théâtrales, 1996 and 1997). The three volumes have since been collected into one.

10. Renaude, "Entretien croisé d'auteurs" (interview with Joseph Danan) *Alternatives théâtrales* 61 (July 1999): 42.

self-censored attempt at the beginning of the twentieth century in his monstrous play *La Seine*[11] might come to mind: it was a theatrical project that the writer rejected, forgotten in the bottom of a trunk until its discovery in 1989, whose single second act included, in its 4742 alexandrines, the sum of conversations and stories through which Parisians recounted their desires, their fears, their adventures and fantasies, boredom and passions. Before Renaude, Roussel placed prattle and confessions on equal ground, futile words and confidences that gave a glimpse of the disruptions of lives in a flash. His 200 or so "characters," simply silhouetted passers-by whose conversations served as a backdrop for the sparse exchanges of lines between the alleged heroes, were useless except for achieving this desire to seize the world, which is also the driving force behind Chartreux's and Novarina's writing.

HISTORY OF ART AND THOUGHT

The totalizing ambitions in the work of contemporary French playwrights are not only expressed in paradigmatic structures and unlimited episodes; not all of them treat the fable with disdain. On the contrary, in the work of certain playwrights, the fable acquires the scale of vast epic dramas. In this case, the precedents could be the Victor Hugo of *Cromwell* or the Paul Claudel of *Le soulier de satin* and *La trilogie Coûfontaine*. On the one hand, like *Cromwell* and *Trilogie*, they are historical dramas embracing a period; on the other, following the example of *Le soulier de satin*, they are allegorical dramas on the mental conquest of the world. Three writers are thus confronted with excess in devising "great tales" fueled by philosophy and myths.

It is nothing less than the history of modern Europe that Denis Guénoun tackled in three plays written between 1982 and 1991, which he envisaged from the outset as constituting an organic whole: *Le printemps*,[12] *La levée*,[13] and *Le pas*.[14] His project was to forge a relationship between three periods strongly "marked by the sudden appearance . . . of thinkers or artists in clusters, in bunches, whose production quickly bloomed culturally, apparently without motivation: the Italian *Quat-*

11. Raymond Roussel, *La Seine. Oeuvres III* (Paris: Pauvert, 1994).
12. Denis Guénoun, *Le printemps* (Arles: Actes Sud: 1985). Preface by Tzvetan Todorov, "Un drame du présent." First production in July-August 1985 at the Festival de Châteauvallon, directed by the author.
13. Guénoun, *La levée* (Reims: Le Grand Nuage de Magellan, 1989). First production in May 1989 at the Centre dramatique national de Reims, directed by the author.
14. Guénoun, *Le pas* (Paris: Éditions de l'Aube, 1992).

trocento, the first moments of Romanticism, and the artistic and intellectual explosion after the Great War."[15]

The events recounted in *Le printemps* unfold between January 2, 1492, the date of the entry into Grenada of the Spanish Catholic monarchs Ferdinand and Isabella who had defeated the Muslim king Boabdil, and the winter of 1541–1542: a half-century marked by the Renaissance, the Reformation, and the beginnings of the conquest of America. From one European city to the next: Grenada, Rome, Ghent, Heilsberg, Erfurt, not to mention the incursions into Cuba and Santo Domingo, 81 historical figures are encountered, among them the four major figures of Michelangelo, Martin Luther, Copernicus, and Bartolomé de Las Casas.

The time frame of *La levée* is the most compressed, from September 1792 to October 1808. While the play is delimited by two dialogues between Goethe and Napoleon in Valmy and Erfurt, the central part occurs in Dresden in 1798. This is the moment when the Romantic writers of the "Iena group" who were subject to the shock wave of the French Revolution—Novalis, Friedrich Schelling, and the Schlegel brothers—were preparing to implement a new mode of writing and thought that would privilege the intermittent, the shattered, the fragment, in their journal *L'Athenaeum*. Finally, *Le pas* is set in Berlin, Paris, New York, Hollywood, a Mexican train station, Moscow, and on the Franco-Spanish border. It has two protagonists, "Serge" and "Walter," two first names the make easily identifiable references to the film director Eisenstein and the philosopher Benjamin. Between 1929, the peak of the former's reputation, and the suicide of the latter in 1940, Europe's response to both cultural profusion and the political collapse of a civilization.

It is precisely toward this Western "civilization" for which Europe is the cradle that Denis Guénon casts his all-encompassing gaze, evaluating the role played by notable personalities, but even more importantly, by the movements of thought that advanced generations toward progress or collapse. He is not satisfied with simply recording facts, enumerating the factors of success or failure, but instead he philosophically asks the question throughout his work (one that might also be asked by our contemporaries) regarding the reasons for the "backwash": "Through what necessity does the production of novelty come

15. Guénoun, *Relation (entre théâtre et philosophie)* (Le Revest-les-Eaux: Les Cahiers de l'Égare, 1997), 45–46.

to engender the movement that repudiates it?" In *Le printemps*, for example, we witness Luther's undertaking, at first liberating in that it substitutes individual faith for the observance of rules decreed by the Church or perverted practices such as the sale of pardons, but that ends up as the "attempt at . . . standardization of a novelty too difficult to let survive on its own" (53). During the theologian's old age, his bitterly reactionary comments gave a future glimpse of the horrors of the Saint Bartholomew's day massacre. And, whereas the last character in the trilogy, Walter Benjamin, does not show the same obstinacy of thought, the collective behavior of Europeans engaged in Fascism and anti-Semitism has gotten the better of his will to survive. Even though, during his attempted escape to Spain, he invokes "the triumphant and prophetic flight" of the Hebrews in the Bible "beyond the land of the dead," the final image of the play remains that of a dying man limping in the direction of a door that may never be reached.

To the other question underlying the trilogy, that of the place of art in the consequences of History, the writer never really provides an answer, but at least he conceives the three plays as a basis for reflection on the art object as well as on theatrical forms, and more broadly, on the artistic forms put to the test during the periods he stages. The spirit of the Renaissance is expressed in Michelangelo's comments on the relationship between the bare human body and the mystery of the soul. In *La levée*, references are made to Schelling's views on the articulation of the ideal and the real. The beginning of *Pas* contains an enlightening study, borrowed from Serge (Eisenstein), on the process of montage and its effects, while the use of the fragment and recourse to the collective, anonymous *oeuvre* are commented on in the conversation between the authors of the *Athenaeum*. Guénoun recounts the major aesthetic choices, and, further, puts these modes of expression into practice himself. In *Le printemps*, he mixes the epic course of action in the Aristotelian sense of the word—that which permits the telling of heroic adventures of a community—with various dialogued scenes, a sort of hyper-dramatization that the Renaissance was "constituted of a potentially infinite plurality of *situations*" like a "multiple drama, arboreal, *open*, spreading itself to the edges of Europe (and the world) through the logic of metastases reproducible to infinity" (*Relation*, 61). This is the origin of the rich structure of a play that multiplies places and moments. Tzvetan Todorov, who wrote the preface for *Le printemps* under the title "Un drame du temps présent," emphasized this alliance of the epic and the carnivalesque, "with its mix of styles and its reversal of propriety."

Not only is a totalizing vision expressed in content but in forms. In *Le pas*, the author introduces filmed images and a variety of textual elements as a way to delineate the relationship between literature (the essay, newspapers, correspondence) and theater and cinema.

PRESENT-DAY ALLEGORIES

Whereas Guénoun did not attempt to assemble the considerable mass of texts constituted by the three plays (more than 700 pages total) into one single show, Olivier Py showed no hesitation in bringing to stage a non-stop, inordinate work like *La servante*, composed of five plays and six "dramaticules."[16] After the separate production of certain plays, the whole constituted a 24-hour run of non-stop theater at the Festival d'Avignon in July 1995. In a series of daytime and nighttime performances, each was immediately followed by the next, which gave the author's desired impression of a never-ending theater.

The structure might echo that of Greek tragedy, with its "opening" or *parodos*, its four play-episodes punctuated by brief forms serving as interventions from the chorus, and an epilogue entitled "return" in the guise of an *exodos*. But it would be more appropriate to speak of an epico-dramatic and tragicomic ensemble in which the author develops his view on theater, acting, human relationships, love and war, the meaning of life. Theater is the most obvious theme, even in the title of the series, *La servante*, the name given to the small lamp that remains permanently lit onstage after the actors have left. In certain plays, Py enlisted characters borrowed from Aeschylus, Shakespeare, and Molière: Orestes and Pylades, Romeo and Juliet, Agnes and Arnolphe. However, he shows little interest in examining the meaning these characters represented to the playwrights who wrote them. The most obvious reference to the history of theater is the recurring presence of traveling actors, the "Matamoros troupe." The task of these tumblers is both to advance the action by helping the other characters realize

16. Olivier Py, *La servante* (Arles: Actes Sud – Papiers, 1995). First production in July 1995 at the Festival d'Avignon, directed by the author. Translator's note: no precise translation exists for "*dramaticule*," but the word suggests a sort of "small theatrical unit" based on the words *drame* (drama or theater) and *particule* (particle) or *molécule* (molecule).

their destinies and to perform "games" that are supposed allegorical representations of a state of the world. Reduced to dances of death and bloody puppet shows, the transformations of their performance, from play to play, display a sinking of humanity into spectacular violence.

Injecting his multi-drama with religious symbolism, Py, following Claudel's example, did not conceal his identity as a militant Catholic writer. The "*servante*" is not only a lamp, but a religious presence that bears the name of one of the holy women, Martha. *La servante* echoes Claudel's female figures, which he compared to the Virgin Mary, the wisdom of the proverbs, and even the Catholic Church. From the prologue forward, it expresses the vision of a writer who has faith and frequently demands joy: "God shall be born from word of mouth. / . . . The angel's stubbornness shall still find virgin wood for its fire" (18). Though a pious text, *La servante* includes many pages exalting human violence or conforming to baudiness in a carnivalesque tradition that is much more evident than in Guénoun's work. The combination of a project of high spiritual content with numerous farcical scenes fits this ensemble into the heritage of the fifteenth-century French *Mystères*, which combined sacred and profane motifs and referred to contemporary events while summoning biblical themes for the spectators' enlightenment.

In *La servante*, current events are evoked through allusions to AIDS-related deaths, widowerhood in homosexual couples, and the Balkan civil wars, all of which forced Py to take a political stand. The writer also returned to the question of colonization, once again the order of the day in France a decade after the production of *La servante*. Born in Algeria, he frequently rose up against the crime of the colonizers. "We white men, the sons of white men, we carry the shame of our fathers," says one of his characters (327), and the critic Bruno Tackels has noted the recurrent expression of both "anger" and "desire."[17] However, it is less a true state of the world that Py proposes than a state of his own sensibilities, a "looping" of his favorite themes, his obsessions, from sadomasochism to the cult of beauty. *La servante* says no more on these matters than a short, resolutely autobiographical play like *Théâtres*.[18] The main objective of the monumentality of the work was to produce a theatrical event and to engulf the spectators in the often lyrical, even incantatory writing.

17. Bruno Tackels, *A vues* (Paris: Christian Bourgois, 1997), 193.
18. Py, *Théâtres* (Besançon: Les Solitaires intempestifs, 1998).

The same year *La servante* was published and staged in its entirety, the triptych *Gibiers du temps*[19] by Didier-Georges Gabily appeared. In this major work by an author who passed away prematurely, figures lifted from Greek myths mingle with a "Hermes-Archangel" in a syncretic vision in which Gabily exposes the dying moments of Western society. Phaedra, Theseus, their sons Demophon and Acamas, the goddess Cypris, and Pythia take part in the agony of a world that has forgotten its origins. It is a world that has lost its sacred aura, in which Phaedra's amorous passion has become the maniacal sexual obsession of a predatory old woman, while Theseus breaks into a headlong sprint toward the end of time, which will liberate him from his tragic curse. From the prologue, which unfolds in a "dump" cluttered with "the corpses of angels," where "a vague wingstroke" stirs "a bit of ashen bone, rubbish, burned tablets of law, sacred wood, objects thought useless," the survivor Cypris confirms the deaths of the other gods while Hermes and Theseus have given themselves over to grotesque attempts at coupling or self-mutilation. The tone is set. In each of the "periods" that constitute the triptych—each "period" as long as a standard play—these exhausted representatives of a dying culture encounter the agents of all contemporary perversions: first, the sexual ones, from the most sordid family incest to the peepshow and prostitution trade, but also those of the economy and the social relationships of power.

"Theater represents the immense city" is a stage direction that echoes the famous introductory indication of *Soulier de satin:* "The stage of this play is the world." This evokes immensity, but an immensity that does not encourage a Claudelian perspective, for this city only displays the same acts of barbarity reiterated everywhere. The female descendants of the Amazons are criminals who know only the street and the violence of the outlying projects. In this urban jungle, the right-thinking speech of a sociologist can only ring false and the agitation of a film crew eager to record some shady transfer of power only conveys the widespread corruption of media society.

But the gaze cast on this impasse of civilization is all the more impressive in that it is expressed in a heterogeneous text in which language borrowed from Greek tragedy or from sixteenth-century French,

19. Didier-Georges Gabily, *Gibiers du temps* (Arles: Actes Sud – Papiers, 1995). First production in November 1995 at the Théâtre de Gennevilliers, directed by the author, after the successive performances of three "periods" of the play in Brest, Montluçon, and Rennes between June 1994 and November 1995.

that of Garnier's *Phèdre,* and all of the contemporary idioms of a disparate society are mixed: the language of the street, of society's rejects, of immigrants, of hoodlums, as well as the language of the masters of business and the university. Gabily, like Guénoun, mixes genres and styles, while inserting himself in the stage directions and scenes of confidence as he shows the workings of the imagination of an artist who looks for ways to speak of the world.

In these voluminous books and these performances expanded in time by writer-directors (Denis Guénoun, Olivier Py, and Didier-Georges Gabily have all directed their own texts, as has Valère Novarina), will excessiveness have a lasting impact? Not necessarily. In each case, these works are difficult to stage and the budgetary and material constraints can discourage those who wish to restage them. Perhaps they have a destiny as plays "to be read," like Restif's *Le drame de la vie,* Hugo's *Cromwell,* or Roussel's *La Seine,* and only the power of the writing will distinguish among them. Only the future will tell what readers will retain of the power of visual evocation—see, for example, the end of Guénoun's *Printemps,* when Jeanne la Folle embarks on a ship of fools during Carnival in Thuringe, or the judgments on ancient and present History. If Olivier Py's moral lessons, his incantations of joy, are not always convincing, Gabily who was disenchanted or even in despair, knew how to create an ethical as well as epic work, to cite Todorov's compliment of Guénoun. In any case, the totalizing ambition is accompanied by a quest for meaning that gives these theatrical "monsters" their value.

—Translated by Christy Wampole

ARIANE EISSEN

Myth in Contemporary French Theater: A Negotiable Legacy

In her preface to Patricia Vasseur-Legangneux's book on Greek tragedies on the modern stage, Florence Dupont avers that whenever "a
contemporary author writes a new play that tackles a 'Greek myth,' the
break with the tradition of the tragic aesthetic . . . is total."[1] All the
same, even if tragedy in the ancient world may legitimately be thought
of as a particular way of looking at myth,[2] and if therefore a clear distinction needs to be drawn between myth as narrative and tragedy as
theater, surely the rewriting of myths for the modern stage must continue to imply a relationship with ancient forms of dramatic writing,
including the writing of tragedy—ever the main vector of myth in the
world of the theater.

If this be granted (and I shall assume so in what follows), present-
day playwrights who make myth the basis of their work will be led not
only to stage what they remember of the mythological story but also to
expose what they have chosen to preserve or reject of those classical
modes of dramatic writing from which myth cannot be culturally sev-
ered.

On this hypothesis, any new presentation of a mythical past must
be associated with the revival or subversion or even destruction of old
dramatic conventions; more dynamically, it may involve the invention
of fresh ways of writing for the theater. I propose to examine these is-

---

1. Patricia Vasseur-Legangneux, *Les tragédies grecques sur la scène moderne. Une
utopie théâtrale* (Lille: Presses Universitaires du Septentrion, 2004), 10. All translations
in this article are the translator's.
2. This coupling of tragedy and myth is central to the thinking of the Hellenists of
the Paris school, as witness for example the titles of two well-known works by Jean-Pierre
Vernant and Pierre Vidal-Naquet respectively: *Mythe et tragédie en Grèce ancienne*
(1973) and *Mythe et tragédie deux* (1995).

YFS 112, *The Transparency of the Text*, ed. Donia Mounsef and Josette Féral,
© 2007 by Yale University.

39

sues with reference to dramatic production over the last quarter-century in France, with brief side-trips to French-speaking Belgium.

THE "END OF IDEOLOGY"
AND THE RETURN TO INTIMISM

To the extent that, as I have just suggested, any current rewriting of a myth for the theater means revealing what the author takes from a cultural heritage (and particularly from the kinds of questioning and symbolization of reality that it proposes)—to the extent, in other words, that any return to myth in the theater entails a backward glance at a tradition—it should hardly come as a surprise that a playwright's attitude is bound to be affected by reigning views of history in the broadest (as opposed to a narrowly cultural) sense.

It is indeed clear that myths in the theater are affected by powerful moments in history and the new readings to which those moments give rise. There is thus a distinct break between theatrical revivals of myths in the 1970s and those in more recent dramatic works. The 1980s and 1990s marked the eclipse of a theater that pitted characters representing rival political views against one another. From the aftermath of the Second World War to the close of the 1970s, it was possible to return to the Greek tragedies for their agonistic confrontations between such figures as Creon and Antigone. The temptation was strong in those years to reframe these characters' words while preserving their antagonisms—as Jean Anouilh and Bertolt Brecht did, for instance, in their versions of *Antigone* (1944 and 1948 respectively).

Beginning in the 1980s, Antigone barely ever crossed paths with Creon on the French stage, and when the two did meet, they no longer engaged in ideological debate. In *Les voyageurs et les ombres* (1994),[3] Richard Demarcy pictures Antigone in exile with Oedipus. The characters' pasts are preserved solely in their memories—unless, perhaps, it is in ours, for Demarcy's play melds the wandering of Antigone and Creon with the rehearsals of a troupe of actors on their way to the Avignon Festival, where they are due to put on a production of the *Antigone* of Sophocles. The work orchestrates two forms of musing on the myth: that of the characters remembering their past lives, and that of the actors, revisiting Sophocles through the memory of the Holocaust (sharpened by the desecration of the Jewish cemetery at Carpentras in

---

3. *L'avant-scène théâtre* 943 (1 February 1994).

1990). Thus Demarcy's Antigone refuses to provide a new burial place for the dead whose tombs have been profaned so as to ensure that the horrific deed shall be known to all. Her attitude reaffirms the fact—though without putting it into words—that honoring the dead is the foundation of a civilized community.

Monique Castaignède's *Antigone ou le passage de l'Erèbe* (2006)[4] is even more intimist in tone, for it presents an exchange between Hecate and Antigone entombed alive in their cave: there, in the ultimate and ineluctable solitude in which one measures oneself against death, Antigone chooses suicide.

Even when a particular political context serves as the starting-point for a re-envisioning of Antigone, the attention paid to the inner workings of consciousness continues to be given pride of place. A case in point is *La jeune première* (2001),[5] by the Belgian playwright Jean-Michel Dopagne, which addresses the issue of communal tensions in the secondary schools of French-speaking Belgium and the degradation of the educational system in a consumer society. Against this backdrop Antigone comes to stand for rebellious youth, yet the story is told from the standpoint of a young schoolmistress who performs the feat of teaching her pupils about Sophocles, taking them to the theater and giving them the chance to identify with the heroine. The play is indeed a sort of log spoken aloud. Similarly, Cara's *L'autre Antigone* (1996)[6] is a response to the riots that broke out in the early 1990s in several communes in the Brussels area (Saint-Gilles, Forest, Anderlecht, Molenbeek). The work seems to hew fast to the structure of Greek tragedy (complete with prologue and stasimon), and Antigone does in this instance encounter Creon. But ideological struggle remains strictly off the agenda: Creon appears as a mild-mannered uncle with whom one converses over the family dinner table, himself beaten down by the stresses of life and even somewhat excluded from social life, having married above his class. The Labdacides are no longer open to the city, nor to the world of ideas; rather, the choices of each family member are above all individual survival strategies.

The case of Antigone is of course exemplary here, considering how frequently Sophocles' play was taken as a model for the political the-

---

4. Monique Castaignède, *Antigone ou le passage de l'Erèbe* (Saint Alban: Éditions n&b, 2006).

5. Jean-Pierre Dopagne, *La jeune première* (Carnières: Lansman, 2001).

6. Cara [Carmelina Carracillo], *L'autre Antigone* (Mons: Éditions du Cerisier, 1996).

ater of the 1970s. As George Steiner noted in his *Antigones* (without confining his observation to the French-speaking stage), "1943–44, 1978 and 1979 were . . . years of 'Antigone-fever.'"[7] The dates Steiner mentions are interesting, for what these two historical periods have in common is a sharply polarized world situation: in the first case, a World War dividing the globe into two camps, and in the second the Cold War, with its rival socioeconomic systems. In 1989, when the fall of the Berlin Wall became the tangible sign of the definitive collapse of ideological illusions, dramatic writing responded accordingly by refusing henceforward to make myth the locus of any cut and dried lessons.[8]

Of course, such dates are in no sense absolute: they are simply useful points of reference. The more attentive observers described the axiological and discursive crisis of the postmodern moment well before the fall of the Wall. It should be borne in mind, too, that while an intimist approach to playwriting was surely a sign of the times, it was also a matter of personal taste and point of view. Consider the Belgian Michèle Fabien, who seeks in her work to foreground female figures usually confined to supporting roles: in the monologue of the title character in her *Jocaste* (1981), as in *Cassandre* (1995), her stage adaptation of a Christa Wolf novel, or in *Déjanire* (1995),[9] Fabien gives women freedom to speak on the eve of their death, and thus to attain a kind of symbolic fulfillment, for to have given voice to one's being is in a sense to have existed fully. The connection with Christa Wolf's novel clearly indicates that Fabien's feminist perspective[10] reinterprets the classical texts and cultural memory.[11] In her *Cassandra* (1983), as in her *Medea* (1996), the German writer strove to identify the roots of the Western world's violence and concluded that they lay in a patriarchal system founded on the exclusion of female values. In this sense Wolf belonged to the tradition of Adorno's critique of rational domination.

Manifestly, several of the works cited above return to myths as a

7. George Steiner, *Antigones* (New York and Oxford: O.U.P., 1984), 108.

8. On this issue, see Didier Plassard, "De l'effondrement des récits à l'explosion des figures: les présences paradoxales du mythe dans l'écriture théâtrale contemporaine," in Ariane Eissen and Jean-Paul Engélibert, eds., *La dimension mythique de la littérature contemporaine* (Poitiers: La Licorne, 2000), 41–56.

9. These three plays have been collected into a single volume (Brussels: Didascalies, 1995).

10. For further discussion, see *Alternatives théâtrales* 63 (1999), a special issue devoted to Michèle Fabien.

11. This novel has also been adapted for the stage by Malika Bey Durif: *Tombeau de Cassandre* (Creil: Dumerchez, 1997).

way of weighing tradition in the balance: rewriting a myth means ask- ing oneself what it has helped make of us, so that we can decide whether to accept or reject what it bequeaths. The self-reflective side of a Richard Demarcy or a Christa Wolf can by no means therefore be taxed with some kind of postmodern dilettantishness, because to the con- trary it attests to the fact that reprising a myth is an opportunity to make a critical assessment of it.

Some authors take an even more radical approach by extending such an assessment to dramatic conventions themselves.

THE SUBVERSION OF THE LANGUAGE OF TRAGEDY

The end of ideology did not mean the end of political thinking. One might even venture to say that it facilitated a more acute and more des- perate meditation on the violence inherent in the Western social model, which ideological struggles had tended to obscure by focusing solely on the antagonism between capitalism and Communism.

Be that as it may, in Eugène Durif's *Meurtres hors champ* (1999), as in Didier-Georges Gabily's *Gibiers du temps* (1995), the representation of everyday barbarism exposes language itself as complicit in the world's brutality, in peace just as in war.

Durif turns the myth of Orestes into a sort of road movie, in which Orestes and Pylades, back from an unnamed war, passing through "a neighborhood of smoking ruins, of demolished buildings,"[12] prepare to commit matricide. They are haunted, as is their guide or corypheus, by images of "removed and discarded clothes [and] piles of hair and shoes" (10): this allusion to the Shoah is mixed up with references to wars more scrupulous in their apparent respect for the person ("Bodies sewn back together and laid out in orderly rows bearing little chains with identity tags around their ankles" [10]). All these images, however, are also weapons: the heaped-up clothing, shoes, and hair symbols of extreme violence; as for the corpses whose identification and care have thus been submitted to scientific rationality, they inevitably partake of the medical metaphor of "clean, surgically accurate operations" (36)—a metaphor in terms of which, scandalously, we are invited to conceive of (for example) the Gulf War.

For Durif, images and words may become the allies of murderous

12. Eugène Durif, *Meurtres hors champ* (Arles: Actes Sud, 1999), 27.

power. The massacre of human beings commandeers the way those human beings are represented, whence a macabre play on the word *vers* ("verse" and/or "worms") which conflates poetry and the decomposing body: "Viennent des vers anciens mourir dans ta bouche" (May ancient verses/worms come to die in your mouth)" (16). A related idea is expressed a few pages later: "A nonsense proposed by an earthworm/ At least it is spoken aloud" (20).

In these circumstances, the consciousness of the writer can only be an unhappy one, for his or her only weapon, namely words, is hostage to the enemy. The only recourse remaining is to use writing itself to show how far the old ways of representing violence, among them tragedy, are henceforward quite unable to arrest or channel that violence itself. In the case of *Meurtres hors champ,* the retention of the framework of the tragedies of Sophocles and Aeschylus for a play that depicts the circularity of action[13] and the immobilization of the characters[14] is instructive in this regard. What remain from the original tragedy are the oracle (speaking now, however, from an empty heaven), Orestes' reunion with his sister, and the commentary on the murder *"hors champ"* (i.e., off-stage). But these elements are kept merely to underline the disappearance of the most powerful moments of the ancients' tragic spectacle: the moment when Orestes becomes aware that he is at once—and inseparably—a dispenser of justice and a guilty suppliant; and the moment when the crisis precipitated by the setting up of the first trial (in the *Eumenides*), which introduces violence into the great ritualized system of the just and the unjust, is resolved. For classical tragedy's capacity to effect catharsis, for society as for the individual, was clearly bound up with force as ritual (judicial ritual, in this instance), a connection that has been well pointed up by René Girard in his book *La violence et le sacré.*[15]

A like subversion of the values of tragedy is found in Gabily's *Gibiers du temps,* which reverses the plot of Euripides' *Hippolytus.* In Euripides, the vengeance of Cypris, scorned by Hippolytus, leads to Phaedra's transgression of the rules of decency and sincerity and Theseus's flouting of the duty to be clear-sighted and protective; a correc-

13. At the end of the play, Pylades finds himself alone at the bus stop where he had been waiting with Orestes in the opening scene.
14. In Durif's version, the quest of Orestes has an Oedipal dimension: he meets a girl, who is at once Electra and the Sphynx, and at the close leaves to rejoin her in a closed family environment that embodies his inability to open up a future for himself.
15. René Girard, *La violence et le sacré* (Paris: Grasset, 1972).

tion, however, is supplied by the final intervention of Artemis, who reinstates the truth and removes the onus of guilt from the young Theseus by instituting a rite in his honor (lines 1423–30). In Gabily's play, by contrast, ritual comes first—and violence first and last. The action takes place on the anniversary of Hippolytus: a Phaedra now grown old demands of her children that they find her a lover, who is to be put to death after his union with her. Her sons Acamas and Demophon bring her Theseus, though without recognizing him. Thus the return of the Father does not restore order in this retrogressive universe, where the father succeeds his dead son. Indeed violence tears apart the entire primal horde descended from Phaedra, as brothers and sisters kill one another in a pitiless war of the sexes. As in Durif,[16] the archaic mythical past supplies a roundabout way to evoke the brutality of capitalism, under whose sway bodies become exchangeable commodities: Séguier, who brings the succession of humiliations, murders, acts of incest, and emasculations to an end by eliminating all the survivors, is the manager of a sordid peepshow. The de facto alliance between Cypris and Demophon (one of the personifications of capitalism in the play) redounds to the detriment of the goddess, who disappears in the closing pages, to become "part of the opacity of dead things. She will speak no more—no doubt of that."[17]

Greek tragedy is thus brought in by these authors solely in order to demonstrate the inability of our modern societies to rid themselves of their intrinsic violence. It survives, or traces of it survive, as an incomplete (Durif) or deviant (Gabily) version of its dramatic structure, as citations of varying intelligibility, and notably in the reference to the *me phunai*[18] of the Greeks—a formula that summed up the despair of the ancients in face of evil and misfortune. But tragedy is revived only in burlesque form—clear evidence of the loss of the sacred: if the rep-

16. For the intellectual friendship between Eugène Durif and Didier-Georges Gabily, see the interview with Eugène Durif in Eissen and Engélibert, *Dimension mythique*, 57–68.

17. Didier-Georges Gabily, *Gibiers du temps* (Arles: Actes Sud, 1995), 165. In *Quoi l'amour* (Paris: Éditions théâtrales, 1999), Roland Fichet proposes a Tiresias who despite his experience is unable to enlighten any of the beings in search of love whom he encounters.

18. The *me phunai* ("better never to have been born") is referred to in the Durif play on pages 15, 18, 20, 24, 41, and 42. In addition, there is a reference on page 44 to Clytemnestra's dream from Aeschylus. As for Gabily, he quotes (albeit in truncated form) the first lines of Euripides' *Hippolytus* (137).

resentation of tragic hubris is comical,[19] it is because no ethical question now attends it; what is more, the gods, guarantors of values in tragedy, are now all dead or dying. Another respect in which these plays differ from Greek tragedy is that they portray our own world, not a counter-society like those which ancient mythical kingdoms could stand for in the eyes of a democratic Athens. For us, the spectacle of transgression in every form (murder, incest, matricide, and so on) is no longer a horrific vision of an archaic anti-world from whose violence ritual has made it possible to escape; rather, it holds up a faithful mirror of our own universe, where force bows only to superior force.

Why return, though, to an obsolete aesthetic form only to deconstruct it? Perhaps, after all, because these "ancient words ground into our language"[20] may help in the struggle against the superficial and lethal discourse of politics and consensus. Somewhere between tragedy and buffoonery, the theater of Gabily and Durif gives us a clearer image of our barbarism than that offered by the television news.

THE DREAM OF ANOTHER THEATER

The works of Laurent Gaudé and Olivier Py have not a little to say about violence. In Gaudé's case, one need only mention *Cris* (2001), a novel of ordinary French soldiers, or *poilus*, during the Great War, and *Sacrifiées* (2004), a dramatic trilogy on the Algerian War and its present-day sequelae. As for Py, he is the author of *Requiem pour Srebrenica* (1999), which he himself directed on the stage. Both these writers, however, have preferred to use myth as a way of re-enchanting the world and proposing a theatrical utopia.

In Gaudé's *Onysos le furieux* (2000), a humanized Dionysos recounts his wandering life, which has led him from the Zagros Mountains to Troy, via Babylon, Egypt, and Galilee. In contrast to the gods of Gabily, who are slowly fading away, Gaudé's Onysos gets progressively younger as he recounts his story to a stranger on a New York subway platform. What is he reviving in himself of his youth in a long-ago Baby-

19. Durif speaks of the "illusion" (*leurre*) of tragedy (*Meurtres*, 41) and Gabily of "heroico-tragic folderol" and "tragicomic masquerade" (*Gibiers*, 78 and 168). In his *Saintes familles* (Paris: Éditions théâtrales, 2002), Michel Azama rewrites the Oedipus myth as pure comedy (see the central portion of this triptych, "Saint Amour").

20. Durif, *Meurtres*, 30. See also the interview with Durif, "Comment j'ai commencé à écrire pour le théâtre," in Joseph Danan and Jean-Pierre Ryngaert, eds., *Écritures dramatiques contemporaines (1980–2000). L'avenir d'une crise* (*Études théâtrales* 24–25 [Louvain-la-Neuve: Centre d'Études Théâtrales, 2002]), 171–85.

lon that New York reminds him of? The answer is no doubt the principle of disorder that has always characterized him. He is a Life Force, representing an ultimately monstrous desire, who seduces women and has conquered the world with an army of paupers. He brings a disorder that dismantles the distinctions upon which society is founded: good/evil, men/women. Yet the destruction here would appear to presage a new, utopian society: a theater that would address everyone, and conceive of death as a shared horizon. Gaudé's play may indeed be read as an account of the birth of the theater: "The Trojans discovered the theater. / On the eve of their demise, I played the fall of Troy and the fiery massacre of the Achaeans. / Everyone was weeping. / . . . and everyone who wept wept for his wife, his father or his brother. / . . . it was as though death were tamed and for the last time it was possible to share the sweet quietude of being together."[21]

A similar faith in the powers of language and a similar theatrical utopianism is to be found in Olivier Py's *Le visage d'Orphée* (1997). At the border between drama and poetry, Py's language is flamboyant, Claudel-like at times, and rich in literary echoes—especially echoes of Rimbaud. The dramatic discourse is centered on a promise with religious overtones, for Orpheus is the prophet of a religion without dogma that is summed up in the life-celebrating formula "Son of the earth and the starry sky."[22] Gradually gathering around him all the characters of the play, initially presented in distinct scenes or situations, Orpheus makes them into "faithful players" (64) who repeat the ancestral message. This is even communicated to the public, like a eucharist of words, by way of "a little slip of paper" (65) bearing the formula. Once again, then, rite is called upon to stem all violence: Orpheus founds a community, but he requires that every member completely embrace his or her own singularity, so that mimetic violence may come to an end ("And Cain, the sedentary Cain, would not have slain Abel had he sensed that they were not comparable" [66]). Another rampart against violence is evoked: "Fear no more, for fear makes for evil"; and, a little further on, "It is by pushing death away that you make death cruel" (103).

Now, at the end of this discussion, it should be apparent that contemporary French theater's return to myth amounts to the taking up of a critical perspective toward it.

21. Laurent Gaudé, *Onysos le furieux* (Arles: Actes Sud, 2000), 42.
22. Olivier Py, *Le visage d'Orphée* (Arles: Actes Sud, 1997), 65.

On the one hand, a myth will be reshaped by the features of the period that reutilizes it. In this regard it is striking to see how strongly these works emphasize the endemic violence of modern societies, and this applies not only to the works of Eugène Durif and Didier-Georges Gabily but also to those of Richard Demarcy, Cara, or Jean-Michel Dopagne.

On the other, and more significantly, the rewriting of myths is a look back in time, a look that appraises the ability of the ancient dramatic conventions to address reality, and challenges their ways of assigning meaning. A reading of contemporary French playwrights suggests that nothing is now capable of checking violence; it becomes clear *a contrario* just how inseparable Greek tragedy was from an ethical discourse, even if that tragedy proceeded by means of doubt and questioning. The contrast is all the sharper when it is drawn by reference to the *Oresteia* or to the *Hippolytus* of Euripides, both of which are peculiar in that they seek to stay the release of murderous impulses by ritual means.

That the theater in particular is the site of this largely despairing assessment should not surprise us, for the collective aspect of dramatic action and spectacle predispose theater to serve as a means for society to reflect upon itself. There are two specific issues, however, that explain the mission theater feels obliged to assume in the present circumstance: as the works we have been considering underscore, the violence of capitalist society rests in the first place on the obliteration of death and secondly on contempt for the body. There is a clear continuity linking the recurrent evocation of the last moments of Antigone, Jocasta, or Cassandra, Eugène Durif's reflections on war, or Didier-Georges Gabily's on the brutality of market relationships, and the return of the mythical figures of the descent into Hell—of Orpheus and Dionysus—in the work of Olivier Py and Laurent Gaudé. The Pythia, in *Gibiers du temps*, and Onysos in Gaudé's play, seem to express identical sentiments in their respective closing lines, where each assumes the role of witness to death and bearer of memory. Here is the Pythia: "For I say the names of all who were founders and of all who disappeared. I say the names. . . . For it is my task to read the names."[23] And thus Onysos: "I shall lean toward him [the Pariah] before he dies, I shall utter his name in low tones and tell him that Onysos is there, who knows him, and witnesses his leave-taking."[24] In a world that refuses

23. Gabily, *Gibiers*, 175.
24. Gaudé, *Onysos*, 47.

to face up to the physical horror of war, to the marks of power relationships inscribed on human flesh, in a world where the relationship
to reality is perverted by the adulterated language of television, the theater, as a living and transient spectacle, may thus be said to bring the
fragility of speaking and feeling bodies back into the light.

—Translated by Donald Nicholson-Smith

JOSETTE FÉRAL

Moving Across Languages

"What we cannot speak of, that is what must be spoken"
—Valère Novarina, *Le théâtre des paroles*[1]

Current theater texts, which are "rhapsodic" according to Jean-Pierre Sarrazac,[2] are no longer what they used to be. Of course, the format of the text has changed over the centuries, but more importantly, its status on stage has been radically transformed since the 1960s. In what way does this "new" status differ from that occupied by the text in the past? What new relations does this create on the stage between director and actor? How do the forms it endows transform stage aesthetics? Due to the diversity of contemporary writing and the multiplicity of stage aesthetics, answering these questions may not be an easy task. The richness of theatrical practice today is due precisely to this diversity and openness and to the conviction shared by all—authors, artists, researchers, and spectators—that anything is possible in this meeting of two arts: the dramatic and the scenic. Nevertheless, the analysis of one cannot minimize its reflection on the other. The dramatic cannot be considered in isolation from the scenic, and the scenic cannot be examined in the absence of the dramatic, because this intersecting reflection—from the director onto the text and from the author onto the

1. "Ce dont on ne peut parler, c'est cela qu'il faut dire." Valère Novarina (*Le théâtre des paroles*, Paris: P.O.L., 1989, 169). This collection of essays on theater assembles texts as important as the *Lettre aux acteurs* and *Le théâtre des oreilles*.
2. In *L'avenir du drame* (Paris: Circé/Poche, 1999), Sarrazac refers to contemporary dramatic texts as a form of "rhapsodic" writing, mixing genres and registers, and speaking in various modes: the tragic, comic, and lyrical.

YFS 112, *The Transparency of the Text*, ed. Donia Mounsef and Josette Féral,
© 2007 by Yale University.

50

theatrical performance—is the source of, on the one hand, performance style, and on the other, writing style.

A few examples will demonstrate this intersecting relation. The first is a director's perspective on the theatrical text: Claude Régy's theory of writing proper, which determines the very characteristic style of his staging. The second is the vision and technique a writer such as Valère Novarina brings to the stage, and more broadly, the confrontation that his texts elicit between the speech act and the actor interpreting the text. By generating a dialogue between these two creators, we will attempt to show how their reflections on writing connect not only the fundamental questions of current theatrical staging, but also to essential questions surrounding the notion of voice, in its various expressions: whether silenced or amplified, whispered or screamed. Both artists seek to articulate a position that transcends words. On the one hand, Régy is exposed as a true writer who creates the very conditions that make writing possible. Novarina, in turn, is revealed as a true director of actors who seeks out the conditions that allow genuine voice between body and breath to emerge. From this intentionally paradoxical comparison a powerful vision emerges of two creators animated by the same quest: to find, on the stage or in writing, something that precedes voice, and to travel back to the limits of the tangible, the quantifiable, and the performable. This is a difficult process that requires rigorous work on the part of the actor, who becomes a medium paradoxically compelled to make silences speak.

"THE SPECTACLE OF THE ACTOR AT WORK"[3]

"I have never been anything but an actor, not the author but the actor of my texts, the one who breathes them in silence, who speaks them without a word" (Le théâtre des paroles, 85), Novarina declares to anyone who seeks to understand his textual work. Not unlike for Régy, for Novarina, the stage is more than an extension of writing, it is writing itself. The journey from text to stage is already present on the written page. Conversely, the stage is both a form of verbal writing and the corporal writing of the actor who mediates between the page and the stage. It is simultaneously in the density of the material and the eruption of breath within the flux of words that the entirety of Novarina's theater

---

3. I am borrowing the title of this section from a stage direction in one of Novarina's plays, Le drame de la vie (Paris: P.O.L., 1999), 135.

resides; as such, speech is a form of "movement across languages" (*Le drame de la vie*, 135).[4]

It is without a doubt difficult to measure the density of such propositions. More than an aesthetic questioning, Novarina's quest—like Régy's—attempts to reach the origin of things and probes the physical origins of speech, its organic relationship to matter, to breath, and to the body. "To remove all meaning so that *what lies beneath* speaks . . . , to make the dead speak, the *hôm* buried within the man" (*Le théâtre des paroles*, 35) as Novarina states, as if echoing Régy's proposal when he asserts in *L'ordre des morts*: "From its origin, western theater, is . . . the order of the dead . . . , so is theater, if one can speak of the order of disorder, if only because of its inalienable link to the world of the dead."[5] The actor is located at the center of this process of speaking a dual language: the author's words move across the body of the actor, even as the author claims to write like an actor while clearly thinking like a director.

The speech in question, found throughout Novarina's work and at the nexus of his aesthetic, whether written on the page or spoken into space, is first and foremost a body of writing. In effect, for Novarina, writing is only a modality of performance, conceivable solely in relation to its stage potential; its unique meaning is in relation to performance and to the body of the actor that serves as its medium. Thus, writing is not addressed to an eventual reader, nor destined for a specific actor; it lies above these considerations and calls to the actor not as the medium for an action on stage, but as the medium for voice and words. The different texts that Novarina uses to accompany his work are aimed at this metamorphosis of the actor into the performer of the impossible. These texts, which are theoretical works to be read in conjunction with dramatic writings, seem to constitute an instruction manual, as if the writer's wish were not only to instruct the actors as to how they should speak the texts, but also, more specifically, how they should physically portray the relationship to words, and beyond it, the relationship to writing. In other words, Novarina's method is more than a simple lesson in "reading" his work or in performance. It touches on the mystery of speech itself, a speech for which the actor is an indispensable and unavoidable, if shockingly imperfect, medium.

4. "Traveling across the procession of languages . . . and . . . reinventing the fetters of flesh with speech," as Novarina states in *L'opérette imnaginaire* (Paris: P.O.L., 1998), 135.

5. Claude Régy, *L'ordre des morts* (Besançon: Les Solitaires Intempestifs, 1999), 60.

If it is evident that Novarina truly writes *as an actor,* it is less clear that the guidance he offers to the actor originates in the practical perspective of a director and requires, as in Régy's case, a genuine vision of the relationship that can exist between body, space, and speech on the stage. Novarina's theater puts a vision into play that not only embraces the performance of the actor, but further reassesses the entire phenomenon of representation, from the role of characters to their relationship to representation, story, and gesture. Although the rudiments of Novarina's reflections on theater touch on the status of speech and on the art of speaking, this art can only be understood if one grasps the unique place occupied by writing in Novarina's cosmology. For Novarina, writing is at the origin of things, it is voice, breath, and resonance (in space and in the body before it reaches the ear). Moreover, it is what allows "l'hôm" to be spoken outside of any performance and any meaning, to approach the yawning gulf of the unspoken, to touch silence and the void. This is a strange affirmation considering the extent to which speech has an operative virtue for Novarina, and also in light of the degree to which its proliferation and flux saturates and sutures everything, and fills the empty spaces both on the aural level as well as in the performance. This is the paradox of Novarina's vision of writing, and also the locus of its strength.

From this perspective, writing is the power of speech, proliferation, breath, rhythm, strength, and speed. The entirety of Novarina's thought is impregnated with this deep conviction. The proliferation of speech is related to a genuine instinct for survival. Novarina likes to provoke that indispensable investment of energy, made up of speed and acceleration, which strains the limits of actors' bodies, transforming the performer into a warrior, fighting the impossible. Consequently the proliferation of speech becomes almost animalistic. "Much of the text must be expressed in one breath, without drawing fresh breath, by using every trace of air. Expending it completely. Not holding back the slightest reserve, not being afraid to be breathless. It seems that this is how one finds the rhythm, the different breaths, by throwing oneself into a freefall" (*Le théâtre des paroles,* 10).[6] To exceed one's limits, to move beyond the frontiers of the possible, to invent another meaning. "Breathe, work your lungs!" Novarina demands from his actors,

---

6. Writing is also breath; without it no movement can take place. "Because the author's breath provokes physical, organic, and cerebral phenomena in the body of the actor, which awaken emotions, bewilderment, unsuspected manifestations," states Claude Buchvald, who directed Novarina's works, in "Une voix de plein air," *Europe,* Spécial Novarina 880–881 (2002): 79–86.

"working your lungs does not mean moving air, bawling, and inflating yourself, on the contrary, to have a real respiratory economy, to use all the air you take in, to expend it all before replenishing it, to go to the very end of breath, to the point of the constriction of final asphyxiation, to the period of the sentence, to the last reserves" (*Le théâtre des paroles*, 9).

If one extends the body so that it escapes the boundaries of representation, so that it simply *is*, and that it performs the speech, one is in the domain of the absolute performativity of language that empties the body by filling it. There is clearly an intentional juxtaposition of contraries in Novarina's work. Novarinian actors are subsumed in the body to body contact of text and actor, by this permanent challenge of breath that constrains actors to push their physical and verbal limits ever further;[7] they are consumed by this necessity of bending to the rhythms, the torrents of words that tumble, slide, drag, and drift, multiplying the paths of meaning, ultimately leaving them drained. All is excess, situations and performances extended to their furthest limits. In addition, working with a Novarinian text—full of neologisms, acoustic challenges, enumerations, infinite lists that are equally tests of physical, rhythmic, and respiratory bravura—implies that the actor has a certain taste for risk, for moving beyond the limits, for virtuosity, but also for generosity and physical and mental openness.[8] In other words, the actor breathes the text and makes the text breathe, becoming a pneumatic actor, like the author.[9] Writing becomes oral, visceral, a bodily function. It is a continual flux of sounds inviting a drifting in meaning and thought. "Speech is nothing more than the acoustic modulation of an empty center, nothing more than the dance of a tube of air sung" (*Le*

7. Including the limits of their memory. Actors are frozen by the fear of not being able to continue to the end of the text, by the simultaneous fear and the desire to go beyond their respiratory limits.

8. Buchvald writes: "It is very physical work to breathe a text, like swimming without taking air or descending into the depths completely blind. When one speaks a text with such respiratory energy . . . , one enters upon an action that abuses the body but that also carries and exalts it" (82). She also observes, as one who has undertaken *L'opérette*: "In order to speak, the body must be open, at the mouth, at the ears, at all orifices, otherwise the breath that moves through it is blocked. Moreover, the body must be open to space, although space itself tears the body" (80).

9. "I write with my ears" (*Le théâtre des paroles*, 9), Novarina affirms, or rather: an actor "must inspire and expire in order to know, burn things with contrary words . . . speak his drama. He must be one who thinks like he breathes" (*Le théâtre des paroles*, 160).

théâtre des paroles, 129). Hence his verdict: "actors do not execute, they self-execute, do not interpret, they self-examine, do not reason, but make their bodies resonate. . . . It is not the construction of a character, it is the deconstruction of the person, the deconstruction of man that takes place on the boards" (*Le théâtre des paroles*, 24).[10] All of this requires a performance without emotional states, without psychology, without character. In the words of Novarina, not characters, but "rhythmic characters" or "rhythmic postures." As Sarrazac stated about current dramaturgy, it is not made up of characters, but of figures, figures who speak.[11] Thus, nothing is told, nothing is represented: "Not to cut everything up, not to carve everything up into intelligent slices, intelligible slices—as today's current French diction demands, where the work of the actor consists of carving the text into salami slices, of underlining certain words, of loading these words with intentions" (10). For this, actors must divest themselves of their own bodies, their own thoughts; they must renounce the imitation of man, representation, and reproduction, as Novarina declares in an interview.

> Trop de reproduction de l'homme partout! Au théâtre l'homme doit être à nouveau incompréhensible, incohérent et ouvert: un fugitif. L'homme n'est pas l'homme, l'homme ne doit plus être vu: interdiction de le représenter. . . . Le théâtre tend toujours vers le visage humain défait; c'est un lieu où défaire l'homme et s'insoumettre à l'image humaine, où dereprésenter . . . Le théâtre est un lieu de retrait. Devant nos

10. This work on the performance, the challenge, the movement beyond self is also found in author/director Olivier Py. Memory, the body, breath, the articulation of poetic language, and the persistence of the body are also pushed beyond their limits. Py, a specialist in flowing pieces of theater, long performances, continuous performances, lasting hours and even entire days (*La servante*, 24 hours; *L'apocalypse joyeuse*, 10 hours), demands a profusion of energy and an uncommon physical and spiritual investment from actors. If he writes epics, it is to lead his actors to the heart of the voyage, the crossing: that of a language that has already been worked in order to be heard or read as a poem. This is also an extended, unusual space-time: it encompasses excessive durations, at uncustomary hours in theater (the middle of the night, at dawn). Finally, he does this for a journey across perception, because the codes he puts in place conflict with theater's traditional and accepted codes.

11. The rhythms of Novarina's characters are generated by their entrances and exits, by their words, their enumerations, but also by their breath, bodies, and the voice of the actor. In their way, they represent what Sarrazac describes as: "a human figure disassembled . . . mouth or anus, 'any given part' . . . occasionally crossed by access of language" (*L'avenir du drame*, 86). These characters contain nothing, they content themselves with showing the text as writing, as material. They are without evolution, grandeur, or falls. See Christian Biet and Christophe Triau on the subject, in *Qu'est-ce que le théâtre?* (Paris: Gallimard, 2005), 803.

yeux, s'ouvre un intérieur vide. Déchiré-déchirant. On va au théâtre
pour assister à la défaite humaine.[12]

> Everywhere there is too much representation of man! In the theater,
> man must be once again incomprehensible, incoherent, and open: a
> fugitive. Man is not man, man must no longer be visible: representation
> is forbidden. . . . The theater always tends toward the human face re-
> duced to its components; it is a place where one can disassemble man
> and defy the human image, a place to de-represent. . . . The theater is a
> place of sequestration. Before our eyes, a vacant interior opens. Both
> torn and tearing. We go to the theater to witness human undoing.

How can one avoid the representation of man? How can one avoid
recognition? Novarina recommends allowing sound, rhythm, and the
flux of speech to operate while inviting actors to address themselves directly to meaning, as is the case with the perforated text of *L'opérette
imaginaire.* The first part of the second act ends in a delirium of sound
and blood. The living word is taken in its most extreme sense here
while all representation is absence and death. This view does not differ perceptibly from the suggestions the 1960s helped to popularize: "It
addresses itself to something other than the common levels of the
brain, it puts hemispheres to work other than the two currently recognized, a chemistry experiment, a chemical experience" (*Le théâtre des
paroles,* 77).[13] On a deeper level, Novarina calls into question the function of speech itself as an act of communication. He further explains:
"Animals also communicate well: they do this perfectly without
speaking. Speech is something other than having to mutually transmit
feelings or share ideas . . . speaking is breathing and play. Speaking
negates words. Speaking is drama" (*Le théâtre des paroles,* 163).

How can one portray the drama of speech on the stage? How can one
ensure that only genuine speech is heard? According to Novarina, we
must rise above words, and in order to do so, actors must dissociate
from their psyche and dispossess themselves, emptying themselves in
order to become speech. Such a process of negation will allow them to
move beyond their own identities and forget themselves, ceding the

---

12. Interview with Valère Novarina, *Brochure de présentation de L'origine rouge,*
Yannick Mercoyrol and Franz Johansson (National Theater of Strasbourg, Strasbourg,
12–20 Dec. 2000), 12.
13. Novarina remains skeptical: "Those who believe that one can translate something from one body to another and that a head can command a body to action, are on the
side of the misunderstanding of the body, on the side of the repression of the body" (*Le
théâtre des paroles,* 23).

self to breath and speech. Despite appearances, this endeavor is neither Artaudian nor mystical, although it necessitates a true asceticism on the part of the actor since it entails an attempt "to make one's self transparent, to allow oneself to dissolve into the speech at the moment it is spoken, to allow oneself to die with each exhalation." Furthermore, Novarina adds: "it is the absence of the actor that is striking. . . . The actor who enters the scene overcomes his body and his presence, he is subsumed. The actor advances, nameless" (*Le théâtre des paroles,* 121–22).[14]

For Novarina, the function of theater is more profound than to simply "reproduce," "represent," or "imitate." Theater must show what cannot be seen or said, "what is unspoken," and what cannot be. This is the grandeur of theater's true destiny, hence Novarina's somewhat sibylline comment: "C'est intéressant le théâtre que quand on voit le corps normal de qui (en tension, en station, en garde) se défaire et l'autre corps sortir joueur méchant voulant jouer à quoi." (*Le théâtre des paroles,* 24). ["Theater is only interesting when one sees the normal body of who (tensed, stationary, at attention) undo itself and the other body emerge as a cruel performer wanting to perform the what."] Many directors—Régy included—readily accept the necessity of emptiness in the actor. The void in question is necessary to the performer, and is a dispossession that implies a certain destruction of self. As a writer, Novarina is also subject to this state of dispossession. He describes his writing style as a process of writing outside himself.

> In the downfall of a system of reproduction, in the downfall of a system of action, I write in the absence of myself, like a dance without dancing, I write forsaken, undone. Undone from my language, unmoored from my thoughts. Devoid of thought, words, memories, opinion, without seeing or hearing. I write by ear, I write backwards. I hear everything. (*Le théâtre des paroles,* 72)

This dispossession, this "undoing," is an indispensable step in escaping representation and allowing the actor to simply *be* in order to better transmit speech (*Le théâtre des paroles,* 125). Like the dead actor,

14. This is also what Claude Régy believes and he directs his actors accordingly. Valérie Dréville, who has worked with Régy on occasion, notes that the actor is not called upon to perform, but to be on stage as a person. She observes: "We cannot consider ourselves as actors on the stage; little by little we discover that we are people first." See the film by Élisabeth Coronel and Arnaud de Mezamat, *Claude Régy, le passeur* (France, Abacaris Films, SEPT-ARTE, 1997).

one of the characters of *L'opérette imaginaire*, "the actor who truly performs, performs with depth, performs from the depths in himself . . .
bears on his face . . . his own death mask, white, undone, empty . . . he
shows his face, white, bearing his own death, disfigured" (*Le théâtre
des paroles*, 24–25). We are no more in the universe of the perceptible
than in that of the edification of poetics. Novarina's quest aims at
higher realms than the being and seeming of actors. It calls for, if not
the void, at least an actor who can portray the void. In effect, what Novarina ceaselessly searches for in actors is the ability to let go and accept their undoing (in the sense of being *defeated*). To put it another
way, actors must consent to things being said through them, almost in
spite of them, despite the force within them that controls, orders, and
centralizes. They must avoid centrality, the centralization of meaning,
and the centralization of ideas. Novarina's work stresses the fact that
a concordance exists between the centrality of rhythm (of breathing)
and that of thought, which generates his desire to break "the emission
of the deep rhythm" of breathing (*Le théâtre des paroles*, 123).

It is difficult to successfully remain in a state of "dispossession" regarding objects, words, and speech. Inaction can assist the actor (*Le
théâtre des paroles*, 135) by allowing the performer to soar above meaning, *to do nothing*, or as little as possible, to unlearn. Like Régy, Novarina attempts to impel actors in their retrenching. He seeks to lead
them from their usual paths, to make them renounce what they have
previously learned, to empty them, so that the text, the speech, can fill
them anew and that gesture can emerge in the right way, namely, in accord with speech, sprung from the same interior space, the same flesh.
In this way, the actor can surpass the text to rejoin the sonic writing
and beyond this, can "make the dead speak" so that it is "from the deepest depths that he speaks" (*Le théâtre des paroles*, 35).

According to Novarina (and, as we will soon observe, to Régy), this
abnegation of the pre-existing, of the pre-constructed, is the sole way
in which one can approach the impossible, the inaccessible, what the
ordinary and the day-to-day have banished from our bodies and our spir-
its.[15] This explains, in part, why Novarinian writing is full of holes (in
the same way that Régy's writing is one of divergence). These holes

15. In such a method, actors become aware of their own codes, their own representation, and begin to transform them or even to shed them. "Toppling dead idols, burning
fetishes we have ourselves made, we can do this . . . all that we have petrified—and which
has become an object in thought—can be travelled across anew," Novarina claims (Interview, *Brochure de présentation de L'origine rouge*, 11).

deepen the distance from representation in order to attain the unspeakable. Both authors insist that orality is the foundation of the dramatic text, and that the actor's body, breath, and voice are the only means to transmit this speech: "Let the actor come and fill my porous text, and dance within it" (*Le théâtre des paroles*, 19).[16] There are two important images here: the dance and the hole. As Novarina continually insists, actors are dancers. They dance, they put words in motion. Yet movement can only be read in the present act of motion and adapts itself to the presence of the dancer in motion. "All good thoughts are danced, all true thoughts must be danceable. Because the world's foundation is rhythmic" (*Le théâtre des paroles*, 138). Novarina's writing itself has to do with dance, finding the dance in the spoken, but also in the written. It is this dance that must revive, restore, and rediscover the actor, for the word and the spoken have their source in the same depths of being. As the author states, it is a question of "finding the muscular and respiratory postures in which it was written. . . . It is not . . . the body of the author that must be rediscovered, but . . . the existence of something that wants to dance, and that is not the human body that we believe we have, that must be reclaimed" (*Le théâtre des paroles*, 21). "Something that wants to dance" as if, from the depths, as voice is heard, the voice of the "dead," "the hôm buried within the man" (*Le théâtre des paroles*, 35). More than poetics, Novarina's method touches on the very sources of creation.

The second image, that of the hole, is a metaphor that Régy and Novarina share. Régy, for example, tells his actors to "make words fall like stones in a well, listen to the echo to gauge the depth of the hole, the gap, the abyss in which the man and the actor are." To investigate holes, to fall into them, to lose one's self, to die and be reborn, to rediscover something in ourselves in the fall. This is, paradoxically, also the function of silence, a very important element in both Régy's staging and Novarina's texts. Curiously, Novarinian writing is nourished by the unspoken and in this respect is closer to Régy's vision than it may appear at first glance. As in music, Novarinian rhythms are always fed by the pauses, the punctuating silences and the unspoken. The author makes this the principle of performance as well as the principle of language:

16. For his part, Régy observes in *L'ordre des morts* that "the act of writing appears less as an arrangement of the real, than as its discovery. It is a process by which we place ourselves between objects and the names of objects, a way to stand guard in this interval of silence, to make objects visible—as if for the first time—and to possess their names" (121).

"if you do not want to speak mechanically, you must always keep something of yourself in your speech" (*Le théâtre des paroles*, 164) he observes to the actor, echoing Régy's concept of dissociation.[17]

Novarinian drama inscribes itself in the question of "where does our power of speech come from?" posed by Adam in the play *Le drame de la vie*. As an act and an action, speech is the only method and tool to speak of the human condition. It is perhaps in this single respect that it makes sense.[18] Speech is inexhaustible, yet remains insufficient. Hence this recognition of failure:

> Chute de la représentation, effondrement théâtral. Fatigue de plus en plus à représenter, à dire quoi que ce soit par du [sic] langue. Fatigue de la présentation, fatigue à représenter de plus en plus grande et qui met dans un état de givrage complet, destruction des lieux, outrage public à la langue française, effondrée et dessous. C'est dessous la langue qu'on est maintenant, effondré. (*Le théâtre des paroles*, 47–48)

> The demise of representation, a theatrical crumbling. The growing fatigue of representing, of saying anything through language. The fatigue of presentation, the fatigue of representing on an increasingly larger scale, a fatigue that places the destruction of place, a public outrage to the French language, fallen and beneath, in a state of complete deep-freeze. We are now, collapsed, beneath language.

On the subject of contemporary drama, Sarrazac argues in *L'avenir du drame* that the "placing [of] the dominant language in crisis" (136) is intentional in order to undermine mechanics in favor of bringing out diversity and richness. He observes that authors like to intermingle styles and genres in a play composed of fragments, but they also seek to hybridize language, to fight against linguistic uniformity, to create tension between languages: those which dominate or are dominated, secret languages, other languages, such as patois, jargon, citations in foreign languages, specialized languages, and so on. Of course, in his

---

17. This is that all true speech must retain an aspect that is mysterious, hidden. This is why the silent "e" is one of the characters in *L'opérette imaginaire* and why he uses silent 'e's', the suspension of breathing, the silence of rhythm in his writing. In *Devant la parole*, an interview by Ivan Darrault-Harris (Paris: P.O.L., 1999), Novarina situates "four suddenly white lifeless sequences, in the middle, four prayers in white at an inopportune moment" (np.). Correspondingly, he writes of Jean-Paul Kaufmann's texts: "I oppose Jean-Paul Kaufmann's silences and his mute prayer of possession to the idol of communication" (Interview, 162).

18. "I write books that have speech for a plot," Novarina exclaims in the essay "Drame dans la langue française" (*Le théâtre des paroles*, 10).

own way Novarina participates in the tendency, begun in the 1960s, that philosophy, especially Derridian philosophy, has abundantly helped to disseminate. Novarina writes: "I describe the battle within *the language of one* and the pulverising effect of *the language of only one* that can negate everything, reducing the world to dust: deny that it speaks" (*Une voix de plein air*, 165). Yet to stop there would be to misunderstand Novarina or to limit the relevance of his writing. Certainly, fighting against learned language, true language, official language, the language of ideology, is at the heart of his work as a creator. He himself defines his writing method as the "reinvention of languages" and proposes to "recreate the entire path of learning one's mother/material tongue ("langue matièrenelle"), reapprenticing one's tongue. A slip, loosened, barbarism" (*Le théâtre des paroles*, 34). However, currently the greatest strength of his theater does not reside in this constant battle against the unity of signification. Instead it resides in the language gap that he attempts, in his own way, to institute at the heart of words, a gap that is found at the heart of man, at the heart of writing, and at the heart of the stage.

> Il y a quelque chose de présent, d'absent et de furtif en nous. Comme si nous portions la marque de l'inconnu. . . . Il y a un autre en moi, qui n'est pas vous, qui n'est personne. Quand nous parlons, il y a dans notre parole un exil, une séparation d'avec nous-mêmes. . . . Parler est une scission de soi, un don, un départ. La parole part du moi en ce sens qu'elle le quitte. Il y a en nous, très au fond, la conscience d'une présence autre, d'un autre que nous-même, accueilli et manquant, dont nous avons la garde secrète, dont nous gardons le manque et la marque.[19]

> There is something present, absent and furtive in us. As if we bore the mark of the unknown. . . . There is an other in me, that is not you, that is no one. When we speak, there is an exile, a separation from ourselves in our speech. . . . To speak is a self-fission, a gift, a beginning. Speech leaves the self in the sense that it breaks away from it. Deep within ourselves, there is an awareness of an other presence, of an other than ourselves, welcome and lacking, of which we have the task of secretly guarding, of which we keep the lack and the mark.

It is this gulf, this voice of shadows, this void that Novarina unremittingly pursues. It is here that we find the originality of his work, its

---

19. Novarina, *Théâtres du verbe* sous la direction d'Alain Berset (Paris: José Corti, 2001), 134–35.

grandeur and its misery. It is also at this precise point that Régy and Novarina's methods converge in such a stunning way.

OF SAYING AND DYING

If western theater, as Régy insisted, is an order of the dead,[20] the dead
in question here do not refer to any mourning or loss, but to an absent
life that Régy is convinced exists beyond words and images, a life pre-
ceding words that writers and artists seek to reconnect with, a life that
the order of words and images, of the spoken, is incapable of rendering,
of drawing out, of bringing to the surface. Consequently, for Régy, any
type of writing speaks of the *indeterminate*. It has to do with the act of
creation itself, not a creation of origins, but of the *uncreated*, of what
is not yet and of what attempts to be spoken but remains unspoken. "I
have tried to think," he says, "that the only thing that matters when
we create an image, write a text, or rewrite a text, is that what we see
or hear refers us back to the uncreated, makes us aware of it. What we
show has no interest. . . . In the doing the 'not doing' should manifest
itself, at the same time we should feel the impotence in the doing" (*L'ordre des morts*, 64). This is a powerful idea and calls to mind Novarina's
concept, highlighted in the epigraph of this article. Hence Régy's conviction that writing is a method chosen by authors to make death and
the dead speak, the dead that all authors try to bring to light, will allow
their birth though they remain within the indeterminate and the unspoken. Writing is therefore a writing of what is not, because, beyond
what is spoken, another voice from the void must be heard. This is the
objective of theater. In order to fully grasp the influence of Régy's concept, it must be considered in its context: at the center of a reflection
in which he attempts to revisit the origins of writing—as Novarina
does—and to take both the writing of the author and the writing of the
director into equal consideration. Far from opposing text and performance, for Régy not only is there no contradiction between the text and
its journey to the stage, but there is actually a convergence between the
speech of the performer and the spatial gestures that the actor executes:

20. Régy's idea is echoed by Novarina's reflection evoked earlier in the first part of
this article: "to make the dead speak, the *hôm* buried within the man." The work he has
accomplished in this sense over the years, with actors such as Valérie Dréville or di Fonzo
Bo is the indication of this reflection. See Coronel and de Mezamat's film, *Claude Régy,
le passeur*.

When one begins to walk within a space, it seems to me that one should not move or speak without first seeking to encounter the source of speech and gesture, and I thought that one could suppose that there is a single point with beings (a point whose location I cannot define) where speech is doubtless born, where writing is born, and where in all probability the awareness of gesture takes shape. In order to never move or speak without gesture and speech being initiated at their common point of origin and moving at the same time, one must slow down. (*L'ordre des morts*, 66)

Thus, there is a space within the human being that is the shared point of origin for gesture, speech, and writing: working with one (gesture) necessarily allows access to the other (speech). Régy wishes to have the actor rediscover the state of the author, the state of the writer before he lays pen to paper, before he even makes the gesture to write, and consequently, to have the actor rediscover the impulse to write as if a single breath animated the written and the spoken. Régy puts it another way: to perform is to reconnect with that "immaterial part of the body" (92), to seek a body that can carry thought (95). If in Novarina's case, speech is body, for Régy it seems to be the reverse: the body is thought. Régy is convinced that body, voice, and writing are all part of a whole and that it is inconceivable to separate them. Voice comes from the body, it becomes the moment when certain bodily effects—most notably the vibrations of the vocal cords—become speech. The idea itself is not new; what is new is that, for Régy, the performance is always present in the writing. The writing is therefore already performance and staging. Also, the writing is the first and foremost material the actor must work with. This is the basis for all that follows, but this is also the conclusion to which everything leads. On this subject, Régy is truly the heir of Blanchot and all the other authors who questioned the relationship of language to representation in the 1970s. For Régy, one must work with language for its own sake, without pausing over characters or their psychology, dramatic action, or its progression through the story. There is no need for actors to attempt to incarnate or imitate something or someone. No "representation" is necessary. As in Novarina's case, albeit in a different manner, actors must *show* the functioning of speech, take possession of it, and make the spoken the sole action in the play.

To achieve this, and again, much like in Novarina's concept, actors must forget themselves (no character must be incarnated) in the realm of speech. As their most important role is as mediums for language, a discourse from outside themselves, they must work the language in order to avoid cementing the meaning of words and phrases, and maintain the sense of openness to allow the circulation of meaning. Given that language is "full of approximates, ambiguities, misunderstandings, fluidity, ambivalences," it is the task of the actor to maintain this openness, the space between words and thought, for it is within this gap that "poetry lives" (*L'ordre des morts*, 67). The idea of a gap in language at the very heart of the stage is fundamental for anyone who wishes to understand Régy's aesthetic. Again, it connects with Novarina's concept of the hole. What Régy seeks to attain beyond words is "the sound that language makes," and on a deeper level, "the organization of the movement of words within language" (*L'ordre des morts*, 92), in order for language to touch the spectator in the same places that music reaches the listener. Régy's avowed aim is to make music out of language, to make it the only music on the stage, and to do it in such a way that it affects the spectator in the same bodily regions as actual music. For that, Régy opts for an extreme deceleration (one of the important modalities of his work on texts); this slowness allows us to return to the very sources of writing: "To make writing and what language reveals audible, it seems to me that one must not speak quickly . . . speed creates nothing but speed. . . . The true fullness of writing is heard during the pauses, if one has not occluded it from the beginning" (*L'ordre des morts*, 65). In addition, he recommends that actors seek "non-doing," even as he admits the impossibility of perfect success. During rehearsals, actors must work at slowing their gestures and their words, their breath and their movement. The slowness is the tempo of creation. In effect, the deceleration of gestures allows one to fight naturalism and representation. It "unrealizes" ("*déréalise*") movement and forces the actor to move beyond the everyday. The very fact of slowing down accentuates presence with regard to space, length, sound, and perception, putting the imagination of the actor and that of the spectator into collision. This deceleration carries with it a sense of immateriality, the immateriality of the body and the performance that characterizes Régy's shows so well. This state is neither ecstasy nor trance; it sharpens the presence of the actor, who thus becomes the written and spoken word. Actors become permeable in all dimensions and thus fill the empty platform with their transparency.

Slowness of gesture goes hand in hand with slowness of utterance, an utterance that is also made of silence. Régy observes that silence is associated with slowed movement; it increases strength and energy exchanges, and it provokes a state of concentration in actors, a complete devotion to the moment. The actor must learn to listen to silence, to carry silence. Silence is present to control ambient agitation. It allows one to observe the details of gestures, enlarges space, which is the origin of speech and gesture, and highlights theater's collective appeal. Silence is scenic action: "The true fullness of writing is heard during the pauses, if one has not occluded it from the beginning" (*L'ordre des morts*, 65); it brings the actors "little by little, to be closer to themselves and to emit sounds from this closeness, hoping to touch the others—the spectators—as closely as possible and thus displace the peripheral noise in which we move" (*L'ordre des morts*, 15). These spaces of silence help to create the gap at the heart of words that was discussed earlier. The actor takes the form of a medium, a medium for silence.

It is often said that silence is one of the recurrent qualities of contemporary theater. All those who work on current theater recognize the extreme pregnancy of the texts. It goes without saying that in Régy's work, the silence in question has nothing to do with a lack, an incommunicability, an impossibility of speaking, or the desire to hold one's tongue. It is not related to the circumstances or the psychology of individuals. It is a silence that is infinitely richer and brings renewal, an almost existential silence that allows one to travel backward on the *paths of the uncreated*. In "creating silence" actors develop hearing: their own hearing and that of others. They can then open themselves "to the stage, the universe, all dimensions" in order to make "the gulf of speech" heard. It is by instituting silence at the heart of the stage that words can escape the representation that plagues them. Ultimately, words achieve density. Far from being static, such a silence is a medium for fullness on the stage. It permits the strength of speech as well as the amplification of the actor's presence and hearing, not to mention that of the spectator.

According to Régy, this silence and decelerated rhythm facilitate the circulation of the text among the actors. The actors on the boards are consequently open to forces of collective attraction. The dialogues fuse into a single voice and a single discourse, transforming the multiple speeches into an *ensemble*. They become *ONE*: "reproducing a monologue does not mean speaking the discourse of a single person, but speaking a single discourse" (*L'ordre des morts*, 68). The speech is no longer that of an individual, but that of a collective, much like that of the chorus that spoke in the name of the city in ancient tragedies. In this circulation of words that exceeds the individual to become a collective, the viewer has the impression that the actors do not speak in their own name, but in that of the group. This assemblage returns unity, poetry, and transcendence to the stage. It simultaneously gives writing, drama, and staging their strength back.

It is evident in the texts of the plays that Régy stages (Jon Fosse's *Quelqu'un va venir*, David Harrower's *Des couteaux dans les poules*, Sarah Kane's *4.48 psychose*, or Maurice Maeterlinck's *La mort de Tintagiles*, to cite only a few), and in the very simple sentences he makes his actors articulate, sentences that he renders simultaneously fragile and dense, that Régy is attempting to apply these principles. We are all familiar with the extreme slowness of Régy's performances, but bringing the reasons that explain his aesthetic choices to light illuminates the director's method for the public and allows them to grasp how this aesthetic is not only directly linked to a particular vision of writing, but that it emanates from and is even determined by it. It is because Régy searches for what is beyond writing, the place where writing is born—in his words, the place "from which it speaks"—that his staging displays the particular aesthetic that characterizes them. For, beyond the plays, stories, and dialogues themselves, Régy carries the true vision of an author within himself. Writing for the stage and writing a play arise from the same necessity and exploit the same resources. This is because Régy envisages writing between speech and breath, between body and spirit, between order and disorder, between density and spirituality, between immateriality and the unconscious that he adopts a performance method that is unique to him, founded on silence and slowness, which sometimes irritates spectators, but that is soon understood in its deeper meaning. This quest is fed by the almost existential perspective he brings not only to the dramatic texts he chooses to stage, but moreover to writing itself. It is also clear that Régy's method, far from being purely aesthetic, is ontological in nature and reflects an artist's ethic and a life ethic. His method is, paradoxically, that of moving across language, a language that he seeks to simultaneously render in all its density and fragility. Through this voyage across texts and language, Régy wishes to bring the actor to a self-crossing, a crossing in the course of which actors may succeed in getting to the heart of things, bringing the spectator with them.

It is interesting to note that Régy's work on contemporary dramatic texts (by Marguerite Duras, Jon Fosse, Peter Handke, David Harrower, Leos Janacek, Sarah Kane, Gregory Motton, Tom Stoppard, Botho Straus) is also applied to more classical texts chosen for staging such as plays by Maurice Maeterlinck, Anton Chekhov, and Jean-Paul Sartre, as well as to texts he has borrowed from non-theatrical forms (certain biblical texts from Ecclesiastes translated by Henri Meschonnic and poems by Charles Reznikoff). In other words, such a perspective is not unique to contemporary writing—which tends to privilege a fragmented dramaturgy, a dramaturgy of silence, of diorama, far from the linear, where language inscribes itself as a fractured sign—but it finds in it a privileged space.

*   *   *   *   *

For Novarina as for Régy, the relationship to representation, in the philosophical sense of the term, is very profoundly put into question. Their theater can no longer represent the world. It has become distant, not only from mimesis, but from theater itself. In this respect, both are the heirs of the 1970s. Of course, their method is not new, either in theater or in literature. Numerous poets and writers have joined this shift in the past, most notably Mallarmé and Artaud. There are also numerous literary movements that have placed this relationship to language at the core of their preoccupations. What is new, in contrast, for both Régy and Novarina, is the power accorded to speech mediated through a body that the actor attempts to empty of all its scoria. For Novarina, "it is in the transition between body and speech" (30) that the essential work of the text is located. Régy might say the same, but on a deeper level, he tends to orient the actor's efforts more toward the work of rendering the density and fragility of language. Régy's work does not take part in the banal task of simply staging a text; it touches the foundations of writing and the sources of speech, and in doing so, reaches the mysteries of the subject. Both are attempting to institute a course of action, that if not spiritual, is at least existential. Similarly, each attempts to reach the sources of the uncreated, of what is you, of what is not yet and most likely will never be. Both pose a fundamentally shared question that cements the whole of their work and their method: where does our power of speech come from?

The parallels between Régy and Novarina stop here. If Novarina seeks to reestablish the primary link between speech and body, a body of speech and body-speech, Régy attempts to go further. Performance after performance, he attempts to create a symbiosis between thought, body, space, text, and voice. Yet, in both cases, one can clearly observe an absolute quest for the word and its link to the spoken: creating a gap at the heart of words, making the gulf at the heart of things audible and beyond what is heard on the stage, making another stage audible. The task is almost impossible for one and the other. In this seizure of speech, in this courageous act of speech where actors forget themselves, spectators and actors are invited to make a journey across languages and pass beyond them.

—Translated by Leslie Wickes

II. (Under)writing the Stage

DAVID BRADBY

Michel Vinaver and *A la renverse:* Between Writing and Staging

Michel Vinaver's first play was staged by Roger Planchon in 1956. His
career as a playwright over the ensuing half century coincided with the
period when directors established themselves as the most powerful
force in French theater. Dismayed at the direction taken by the evolution of "directors' theater," Vinaver gradually formulated his own theories about the difficulties it posed for new writing, and about the best
method for staging his plays. However, it was not until 2006 that he
moved from theory to practice, taking full responsibility for a professional production of one of his plays. By tracing the relationship between Vinaver's development as a playwright and the rise of "directors'
theater," we can better understand the nature of the conflicts that have
opposed writers and directors in France, and measure the distance separating "writers' theater" from "directors' theater."

DIRECTORS' THEATER

The rise of the director in the twentieth century is a complex phenomenon and this is not the place to attempt a summary.[1] But if we are
to follow the development of Vinaver's thought over the period since
1956, we need to rehearse the fundamental attributes of directors' theater. In the first place, it depends on developing its own special idiom
through which stage performance communicates with spectators, an
idiom that combines a wide range of signifying practices including
movement, gesture, sound, light, color, costume, and mask. This idiom
is predominantly visual rather than verbal: from the experiments of
Meyerhold through those of Artaud or Grotowski to Robert Wilson, di-

1. For a detailed recent discussion, see the collection of articles in Jean-Claude Lal-
lias, ed., "L'ère de la mise en scène," *Théâtre aujourd'hui* 10 (2005).

YFS 112, *The Transparency of the Text,* ed. Donia Mounsef and Josette Féral,
© 2007 by Yale University.

rectors have developed a new approach to staging, starting not from the words of a playwright's text, but, rather, from the expressive possibilities of this stage idiom that they, themselves, are in the process of shaping.

In France in the 1950s and 1960s the director who took the lead in developing an aesthetic of directors' theater was Roger Planchon. Planchon is famous for having coined the term "écriture scénique" or "stage writing" to designate the expressive idiom elaborated by the director, putting it on an equal footing with the writing of the play's text. In fact he went further, celebrating the theater's independence from the playwright's text: "I was one of the first to sense the coming of stage writing. As early as 1955 I saw that theater would establish its independence from the text. . . . Robert Wilson came, I welcomed him, dazzled."[2] Now, this same Roger Planchon was also the director to whom Vinaver entrusted his first full-length play *Les Coréens* (staged in Lyon in 1956) and his masterpiece *Par-dessus bord* (staged in Villeurbanne in 1973). In the period separating these two productions, Vinaver's evolving aesthetic was moving in a very different direction from that of Planchon, and this helps to explain the hostile attitude that Vinaver was to develop toward directors' theater.

A second underlying principle of directors' theater is that, where it does not choose to dispense with the playwright's text, it creates the expectation of a novel interpretation of that text. Thus the majority of directors who are in charge of theaters in France today have established their reputations through new productions of classic plays whose claim to distinction lies in bringing inventive or challenging new interpretations to well-known texts. Again, Planchon has been at the forefront of this movement.

VINAVER'S DRAMATURGY

This privileging of directorial interpretation in any new production ran counter to Vinaver's own dramaturgical method, which sought to privilege multiplicity of viewpoint rather than providing any one, dominant interpretation of the events depicted on stage. In fact, Vinaver had begun his writing career as a novelist, and moved to theater precisely because he valued the opportunity to compose without the necessity

2. Quoted in Michel Bataillon. *Un défi en province: 1972–1986, Planchon* (Paris: Marval, 2005): 16.

of an authorial viewpoint: "Writing for theater gave me permission to do without a point of view. Points of view are expressed, but by means of voices that are not mine, that are those of the characters."[3] As a young aspiring writer, Vinaver had been much influenced by T. S. Eliot (he translated *The Waste Land* into French in 1947). He borrowed from Eliot a juxtapositional method of composition in which the most important thing is not the material itself but what he called "mises en relation" (bringing into relationship or contact) at the level of language: "They [*les mises en relation*] are *material* in nature—that is to say that they take place at the level of the linguistic material—rhythmic effects, collisions of sounds, shifts of meaning from one sentence to another, collisions setting off what one might call mini-phenomena of explosive irony."[4]

Vinaver enjoys comparing his compositional methods to those of painters or musicians. At the head of his play *Iphigénie Hotel,* he set a quotation by Georges Braque, in which Braque emphasized that what he painted was not so much the objects depicted on the canvas as the space in between, and Vinaver stresses the importance of the "in-between" for his writing. The earlier citation regarding points of view continues with these words: "and these points of view are not so much interesting in themselves, for what they are, but through the friction that occurs among them." From musical form, he adopted the method of superimposing different voices simultaneously. On stage it is not possible to have several people talking over one another, or all the audience hears is a babble; but Vinaver aims for a similar effect to that of, say, the string quartet, in which four instruments play separate melodic lines, by juxtaposing and intermingling two or more conversations, so that different discourses overlap and the reader of his plays is frequently uncertain as to whom a given remark is addressed.

The result of this compositional method is a series of complex, fragmented dramatic structures that superimpose different voices, situations, stories, presenting the world in an unexpected light and opening up cracks in what is perceived as the established order. Microcosm is juxtaposed with macrocosm—for example, an intimate conversation between two individuals about their private lives is set in counterpoint to a discussion about investments between two business leaders, whose decisions may turn out to affect the private lives of the two in-

3. Michel Vinaver, *Écrits sur le théâtre 2* (Paris: L'Arche, 1998): 93.
4. Vinaver, *Écrits sur le théâtre 1* (Paris: L'Arche, 1998): 129.

dividuals. Or a character who finds that she is attempting to face up to a problem in her private life uses the language and the mental structures learned in her workaday environment. In any one of Vinaver's plays, several different stories and situations are juxtaposed, with the result that it becomes impossible to identify a linear plot leading to a recognizable climax in the classical manner, or even to distinguish between main plot and subplots. Instead, one finds an interweaving of events, characters, and situations. In order to identify his method, Vinaver establishes a distinction between "les pièces-machines," i.e. those modelled on the rules of classical dramaturgy, and his own plays, which he terms "pièces-paysages," explaining that a "paysage" (landscape) can be mapped in a wide variety of ways. It can be a place in which to be lost as well as a place in which one can discover oneself, but no one way of entering it can be said to be better than any other.[5] Michel Corvin recently summed up the originality of Vinaver's method by saying that he short-circuits at one and the same time concepts of focus, of sequential chronology, of differential spatiality, in favor of a whole that can only be grasped by the reader's imagination.[6]

This dramaturgical method poses severe problems for the would-be director, since it is impossible to stage a performance without making choices about its setting. The stage direction at the head of *A la renverse* is not at all unusual in the Vinaver canon:

> Simultaneously an office space (including corridors and meeting rooms), the workshops of the Bronzex factory, the managing director's suite of the Sideral Corporation of Cincinnati, the drawing room of the Princess Bourbon-Beaugency, the arrivals hall of the Charles de Gaulle airport and, during the strike, the factory floor as well as a room to which the management has withdrawn.[7]

As Corvin pointed out, this stage direction short-circuits normal (that is, realistic) methods of differentiating spaces and times. If the play is to be realized on stage, and witnessed by an audience, rather than just brought to life in the reader's imagination, then a sophisticated approach to space and time is required. Director, designer, actors, and the whole production team need to adopt an approach that relies on the po-

5. Ibid.: 99–100.
6. Michel Corvin. "Jusqu'où un auteur dramatique peut-il être intelligent?" *Europe* 924 (2006): 13.
7. Vinaver, *Théâtre complet 4* (Paris: L'Arche, 2002): 92.

etics of the imagination more than on imposing stage sets. The approach recalls that of Peter Brook, who favors a performance space emptied of its conventional associations in order to maximize the appeal to the audience's imagination. Of Peter Brook's stage at the Bouffes du Nord, Vinaver wrote that he had managed to resolve "the problem of a space at once bare and alive, a space that will tolerate no stage sets, a space that can accommodate any and every performance, thanks to its own poetic force-field."[8]

LA MISE EN TROP

Unhappily for Vinaver's developing career as an author, Brook's work in Paris in the 1970s and 1980s went very much against the grain of most directors' theater, which was, at that time, developing a fabulously rich idiom of visual spectacle. In 1982 Vinaver published an article entitled "On the Pathological Relationship between Author and Director" in which he identified a situation of open conflict, a power struggle taking place between writers and directors.[9] With the rise of "mise en scène" as a creative force, he saw a new form of theater emerging, one that privileged the eye to the detriment of the ear. In this new form of theater, he argued, meaning was not conveyed principally through words, but through "a sequence of visual events." Words were reduced to the same rank as lighting effects, settings, noises, and movements on stage. Six years later, he coined the term "la mise en trop" to express what he saw as the inevitable drift of directors' theater.[10] In this article, Vinaver began by praising two professional productions of his plays that had taken place outside the main centers of directors' theater in France: one was the production by Sam Walters at the Orange Tree Theater in Richmond, London, of *Les travaux et les jours* (in 1987) and the other was the production by Charles Joris at the Théâtre Populaire Romand in La Chaux-de-fonds, Switzerland, of *Par-dessus bord* (in 1983). In addition he mentioned some school productions of his plays in France. What all these had in common, he argued, was that they were performed in the round, with minimal sets and props, and relied on the actors' ability to establish a direct relationship with their audience, and

8. Vinaver, *Écrits sur le théâtre 2:* 173.
9. Vinaver, "Sur la pathologie de la relation auteur metteur en scène" *L'annuel du théâtre 1981–1982* (1982): 131–33.
10. Vinaver, "La mise en trop," *Théâtre/Public* 82–83 (1988); reprinted in *Écrits sur le Théâtre 2:* 137–46.

depending principally on the interplay of dialogues in these texts rather than on visual spectacle.

He went on to argue that the new importance of "mise en scène" had resulted in a situation where the writer had been replaced by the director as the principal "auteur" of the performance, and so the text was treated as an element to be manipulated in just the same way as light, movement, costume, and so on. Indeed he maintained that the logic of this development meant that the director "cannot but do more than needed." Vinaver's argument was based on an investigation into the state of the playwright in the early 1980s that he had conducted for the Centre National des Lettres. His report concluded that a number of factors, including a crisis in the publishing of play texts, had led to the situation in which very few writers saw the theater as being a genre available to them: the writing of plays had come to be seen as a specialist's job, comparable to script-writing for the film industry.[11] Against this, Vinaver insisted on his dual vision of a play as both a literary work in its own right, complete and with its own integrity, and the pretext for a production that will seek to realize it in performance. He valued the comment of Antoine Vitez who said to him: "What interests me in your texts is that they are insoluble."[12]

Vitez only produced one of Vinaver's plays, but it was one of the few French productions with which the author felt basically satisfied: *Iphigénie Hôtel* at the Centre Georges Pompidou (the production then moved to the Théâtre des Quartiers d'Ivry) in 1977. The play was performed in traverse, on a long narrow stage, with banks of seating for the audience on both sides. On this space a number of locations could co-exist and the interlacing of dialogues between different characters in different situations was embodied in an interweaving of movements by the actors. The general effect was summed up by the critic Gilles Sandier: "A bare space and in it the ballet of bodies. [. . .] But each body has its dream, and this polyphony of bodies and dreams constitutes the work achieved by Vitez."[13]

With these words, Sandier captured the conditions that make for a successful realization of a play by Vinaver. But the vast majority of the directors who were in the ascendant at this time, even those who staged Vinaver's plays (principally Jacques Lassalle and Alain Françon), were

11. Vinaver, *Le compte rendu d'Avignon* (Arles: Actes Sud, 1987).
12. Quoted in Vinaver, *Ecrits sur le théâtre 2:* 173.
13. Gilles Sandier, *Théâtre en crise* (Paris: La Pensée Sauvage, 1982): 67.

not interested by experiments with theater in the round or in traverse: the illusionist proscenium arch suited them very well as it enabled them to develop sophisticated design and lighting effects. Even Ariane Mnouchkine's Théâtre du Soleil, which had experimented with various forms of promenade production in the 1970s, reverted to fixed seating and end-staging from the 1970s onwards.

Vinaver never denied the attraction and the excitement of "mises en scène" in which the visual element took precedence. He readily conceded that, in the case of classic texts, they could achieve new insights. A text by Molière or by Shakespeare is sufficiently established in its own right to survive even the most iconoclastic reinterpretation. In the case of a new play, however, he pleaded for an approach that would be much more discreet and that would aim for "neutrality and simplicity," allowing the text to develop its own characteristic idiom, free from additional "commentary" by the director.

A POETICS OF SPACE

Gaston Bachelard has shown how space is always experienced through its imaginative as well as its physical dimensions: an attic space at the top of a house, for example, may be experienced as a refuge or hideaway, but it may just as well be seen as a place of dreams offering escape into another dimension.[14] This kind of insight lay behind many of the most powerful directorial interpretations of the period. An outstanding example is Planchon's 1986 production of Molière's L'avare (The Miser). For this production, Ezio Frigerio designed a vast, gloomy warehouse room, with thick walls and gable windows set high up, representing the fortress-like space, filled with massive cupboards and coffers, in which Harpagon accumulates his wealth. This room was the location for the action, right up until the final dénouement, when Harpagon's carefully laid plans all collapse. The ruin of Harpagon's hopes was marked by a startling transformation: the apparently solid back wall split in two, leaving a gaping hole, through which a surrealist blue sky was revealed. This spectacular setting was thus used to underline the play's account of how the space inhabited by the family was entirely controlled by Harpagon until the end, when his power was finally shattered.

An approach of this kind can work well when applied to L'avare, a

14. Gaston Bachelard, The Poetics of Space, trans. M. Jolas (Boston: Beacon Press, 1994).

play that attempts to chart one man's obsession with absolute control, and its final undoing. Although critics may take issue with a staging that is presented from Harpagon's point of view, the internal dynamic of the play justifies such an approach since it centers on the figure of the miser. Vinaver, on the other hand, aims to devise a dramatic action in which it is literally impossible to present all the events from one character's point of view. Every action, every statement by a given character is likely to be seen in a different light or subject to an alternative interpretation by another. Even spaces are experienced this way: in *Les voisins* (*The Neighbors*) the setting represents a shared terrace linking two semi-detached houses. This terrace is sometimes experienced as a friendly space of shared conviviality, sometimes as a secret space (it is beneath one of the floor slabs that a character hides his savings in the form of gold bars), sometimes as a space of disaster (when burglars wreck it, in search of the gold), sometimes as the site of conflict, as the two families accuse one another and even come to blows.

Vinaver has frequently commented on the fact that, when he is writing a play, he never envisages a concrete space or location for the action. For Vinaver, as for Henri Lefebvre, space is socially produced: while it is a key factor in the way we experience the world, it is not stable but constantly changing under the impact of events and of the competing perspectives brought to it by the others who also inhabit it.[15] Productions such as Planchon's *L'avare* fit well into the traditional "scène à l'italienne," or proscenium arch stage, of most French theater buildings, but Vinaver's work sits uneasily within them. The reason is that this traditional form of stage is based on laws of perspective that privilege one central point of view (originally that of the monarch). In opposition to this, Vinaver has declared his preference for theater in the round, or any form of arrangement that creates an open dynamic between stage and audience. Since his plays depict a world in which no single viewpoint is sufficient to make sense of an event or a situation, theater in the round has the advantage of placing the audience in a position where a single viewpoint is literally impossible: instead, every member of the audience is aware that every other member of the audience has a different viewpoint, and this sets up the perfect dynamic for dramatic actions in which no single privileged viewpoint can ever be found. In France, Vinaver has found no professional directors who share

15. See Henri Lefebvre, *The Production of Space*, trans. Donald Nicholson-Smith (Oxford: Blackwell, 1991).

his enthusiasm for theater in the round. Despite some notable successes (one could cite Françon's 1986 production of *Les voisins* at Théâtre Ouvert, or the same director's *King* at the Théâtre National de la Colline in 1999), no major French director has followed the lead given by Charles Joris in Switzerland and by Sam Walters in London.[16]

Despite his profoundly held convictions, Vinaver has always been unwilling to make pronouncements about how his plays should be directed, choosing to respect the professional skills of the directors with whom he has worked. In 1973, he was even willing to give Planchon the benefit of the doubt, allowing him to cut and reshuffle the text of *Par-dessus bord*. The result was that this protean epic was reduced to a traditional succession of scenes, eliminating the fragmentary and interlaced quality that gave the play its originality. Since that experience, Vinaver has always insisted that directors respect his written text. On occasions he has attended the initial read-through of his plays in order to explore the rhythmic dynamics of the text, he has elaborated a special set of symbols with which he marks up each page, showing where there should be pauses or where two lines should run on without a break, where there should be special emphasis or intensity, and where other poetic effects of language such as rhyme or assonance should occur. After this initial stage, he withdraws, leaving the director and the cast to develop the production as seems best to them.[17]

VINAVER'S FIRST PRODUCTION: *A LA RENVERSE* (2006)

In 2004 Catherine Anne, herself a playwright and a passionate advocate of the rights of playwrights to direct their own plays, prevailed upon Vinaver, initially reluctant, to direct with her assistance a three-week workshop at her theater, the Théâtre de l'Est Parisien. This workshop was to experiment on one of his plays and Vinaver chose *A la renverse*, a play he had written 24 years earlier and which had received one previous staging at the Théâtre National de Chaillot in 1980, directed by Jacques Lassalle. The workshop was set up (using unemployed professional actors) in order to test out whether this large-scale play for 29 characters ranging across all social classes, and dealing with the major

16. It should be noted that both Joris and Walters have continued to explore the repertoire of plays by Vinaver with further productions staged in the round.

17. For a recent account of this process at work, see Jim Carmody, "A Certain Music. Françon Revives Vinaver's *Les voisins*," *TheaterForum* 22 (2003).

subject of the globalization of commerce and industry, could be staged using minimal means. The experiment was sufficiently successful to persuade him to go further and accept the invitation by the directors of the Théâtre Artistic Athévains, another Parisian theater, to mount a full professional production the following season. The opening night was on April 4, 2006, and the play ran for two months to full houses.

The architecture of the building that houses the Théâtre Artistic Athévains proved quite a challenge to Vinaver, since it has a traditional rectangular shape with an end stage faced by a single block of tiered seating. In order to approach as closely as possible his ideal theater in the round, Vinaver asked for tiers of sets to be erected at the back of the stage so as to have the audience on two sides. He also added a single row of seats along both sides of this performance space, so that the action was encircled by seats. The props and settings were minimal, recalling those used for the productions of several of Vinaver's plays by Sam Walters at the Orange Tree theater in the round. For example, the Orange Tree production of *Portrait of a Woman* in 1995 (the world premier), solved the problem of an action that switches between bedroom, courtroom, café, living room, art gallery, street, etc., by placing a large raised box-like structure at the center, which could serve as a bed, a courtroom table, and so on, as required. In the case of *A la renverse*, Vinaver limited the décor to one square table at the center of the flat performance space and to three identical small-size rectangular platforms, each with a bench, radiating out from the central table, like solar beams.

The play tells the story of a small French cosmetics business bought up by an American giant. Under instructions from Cincinnati, the French business invests heavily in the production of a popular suntan lotion, but sales are hit by an unexpected media phenomenon: the young and beautiful Princess Bénédicte, who is dying of skin cancer (contracted through excessive sun-bathing) agrees to be interviewed every week on television during her last weeks of life. Suddenly a tan is no longer fashionable, which ruins the company's carefully planned marketing campaign for a new sun-tan product. The firm's shares plummet and it is put up for sale; the workforce groups together to buy it back and attempts to run it as a workers' co-operative with everyone drawing the SMIC (minimum legal wage). At first all goes well, but the business only just covers its costs. Meanwhile the American parent company has collapsed, but its managing director has bounced back, investing in the production of solar energy. He returns to Europe on the look-out for small businesses he can buy up and add to his multinational portfolio of companies.

The play makes no attempt to judge the process of growth, collapse, and regrowth of global businesses; rather, it concentrates on assembling an accurate, detailed portrait of the workings of liberal capitalism and of the way in which individuals are sucked in, then spat out, unable to comprehend the economic processes at work, whose upheavals and regressions determine their fate in unforeseen ways. Having spent much of his working life as a manager in a multinational company, Vinaver understands the business world, its strange tribal rituals, its mania for hierarchies, its power struggles, and its seductive attractions. Above all, he has listened with a poet's ear to its special idioms and deformations of language that lead its servants (workers, sales force, and managers alike) to invest a simple advertising slogan with the force of a religious belief. The whole play is informed by a lightness of touch and an ironic vision that gives the audience the impression of standing back from the whole, complicated network of events and observing it with a detached humor, without precluding a certain human warmth for those caught up in its unpredictable mechanisms.

The first notable quality about Vinaver's own production was its pace: without any sense of undue hurry, the action moved forward with a tremendous energy and the various story lines emerged with great clarity. The impression of events and conversations taking place simultaneously was enhanced by using the whole space: while a meeting was taking place between some of the managers at the central table, for example, voices would come from all around the stage space, juxtaposing a different line of the action. Above all, the rhythms achieved through verbal collisions, the echoes of particular themes from one conversation to another, what Vinaver calls the "frictions of language" were deftly brought out, not calling undue attention to themselves, but building up a series of powerful poetic effects.

These linguistic effects were enhanced by the use of movement, a kind of "ballet" (to use Sandier's term) in which the different groups and individuals were constantly criss-crossing the same space, suggesting now an office, now the corridors, now the production line, now an international airport, now a television studio. In his program note, Vinaver wrote that he had aimed for "proximity"—wherever you are seated you are close to the action, and an element of chance is at work: if you were seated in a different place, you would see different things. He went on:

> Above all, the action is entirely in the text, embodied in the voices,
> faces, postures, gestures of the actors; in the in-between of faces and
> bodies; in the geometry of the figures traced by their movements in re-
> lation to one another. And no distractions.

These aims were well achieved in the performances of the 20 actors.
The sense of proximity was increased by the fact that, when not on
stage, they were on seats in the front row of the audience, and some of
their lines were spoken from these seats. The patterns of movement
mentioned by Vinaver varied greatly from scene to scene and were used
to provide an added emotional tension or relaxation, according to the
demands of the overall rhythm. The sense of cyclical movement, in
which what goes up must come down, and *vice versa,* was created by
having repeated actions move round, from one bench to another, recalling the hands of a clock moving round the dial. So, for example, the
televised interviews with the Princess took place first on one bench,
then on the next one around the space, and so on. And these interviews
had a distant echo in another set of repeated scenes, also taking place
on these benches, in which two female production line workers discussed their lives as they carried out their repetitive tasks.

The chorus passages of the play were particularly successful, also
moving at a great pace, and giving a vivid sense of how any business
seeks to subsume the individual ambitions of its workforce into a
"team spirit." In the scenes where the sales force is given its instructions, Vinaver was not afraid to tip the action toward grotesque carica-
ture, and this paid off in the scenes after the workforce has bought the
factory, when very similar scenes were enacted. The one difference was
that, as a workers' co-operative, they now believed in the importance
of "pulling together" in a way they had not before. The sincerity, or lack
thereof, of the workers' attitude is also shown to have relatively little
effect on the way the business develops or goes to pieces. The various
power struggles played out, now at the center, now on the periphery,
once again stress the necessary but arbitrary link between the attitudes
and interests of the Cincinnati business executives and the fortunes of
their small French outpost. The scene of the occupation of the factory
was performed in such a way as to capture with great accuracy the
utopian excitement of the mid-1970s, when several French businesses
were taken over by workers' co-operatives, notably the Lip watch factory in Besançon. And the audience's awareness that all of these experiments ultimately failed helped to provide both an ironic and a historical perspective to this episode.

The reviews all commented on the relevance of the play to questions about the globalization of industrial concerns in the twenty-first century. But Vinaver did nothing to emphasize contemporary relevance. He simply presented his action as precisely and as wittily as possible. In *Le monde*, Fabienne Darge described the result as secreting "a powerful sense of truth," continuing as follows: "And this is what allows the reflections opened up by the play to enter the consciousness of the audience, who find their own situation as 'economic man' challenged."[18]

CONCLUSION

Vinaver followed this production with a second, less fully developed production of *Iphigénie Hôtel* at the Théâtre des Amandiers, Nanterre, in June. Here too he followed the principle of a staging in the round, and felt that the result proved that this arrangement could be as successful in France as in London or Switzerland.[19] In some ways it seems extraordinary that no French director about to tackle one of his plays has been tempted to direct it according to his methods, or at least to invite him to direct himself. But perhaps we should not be surprised: as Vinaver himself has shown, the internal logic of developments in directors' theater during the last half of the twentieth century made it almost impossible for this to happen. Now, however, changes are in the air: since the establishment of the first major French theater run by writers (the Théâtre du Rond Point) five years ago, there is far greater awareness among professional theater circles in France of the need to redress the balance of power in favor of the writer. No doubt lessons will be learned from Vinaver's demonstration of how much can be gained by respecting the author's ideas, even if he may not always be the best director of his own work. Moreover, with other playwright-directors, such as Catherine Anne and Oliver Py, in charge of major theaters, there may be a greater awareness of how all theater must pay at least as much attention to the verbal as to the visual dimension in any production.

18. Fabienne Darge. "L''Homo economicus' selon Vinaver," *Le monde* (May 15, 2006).
19. Telephone conversation with the author, July 2006.

DONIA MOUNSEF

The Desire for Language, the Language of Desire in the Theater of Bernard-Marie Koltès

O take me away
From the thorns and the fire
And let me recline
On the Throne of Desire

—Leonard Cohen, "The Throne of Desire"

"THE FAULT OF *OEDIPUS REX*"

The text in modern theater is recalcitrant, refractory, and disobedient. The more we seek to disavow it, the more it returns with a vengeance to claim its place within the larger nonliterary and dramaturgical activities that constitute performance. It is undeniable that modern French theater, despite its numerous attempts at disowning the text, has been obsessed with its meaning making within performance. Even Artaud, who lead the attack in the first half of the twentieth century against the slavish devotion to the dramatic text, had to acknowledge that his contemporary theater needs to speak to its audience: "masterpieces of the past are good for the past," he wrote in 1936, and "if a contemporary public does not understand *Oedipus Rex* . . . it is the fault of *Oedipus Rex* and not of the public."[1] The merit of Artaud's condemnation is in de-centering the primacy of the text, announcing the advent of the theater director as the foremost regulator of signification on the stage during the second half of the twentieth century. Post-dra-

---

1. All translations are mine unless otherwise noted. Antonin Artaud, *Le théâtre et son double* (Paris: Gallimard, 1964), 67.

YFS 112, *The Transparency of the Text*, ed. Donia Mounsef and Josette Féral,
© 2007 by Yale University.

matic theater, as it has become known since Schechner,[2] and subsequently since the German theater critic Hans-Thies Lehmann popularized the term, re-opened the debate on the function of textuality in performance. After nearly half a century of debating the various implications of anti-textual biases in performance, it is now commonly accepted that the notion of "post-dramatic" does not refute the text unreservedly, or claim that plays will no longer be written, but focuses on shifting the attention from literary elements to dramaturgical and technical elements such as physicality, scenography, visuality, and acoustics. This, however, does not explain most writers' response to such a shift. While playwrights since the 1960s, in France in particular, sought to address in their writing the conditions of possibility of performance, they produced a sophisticated response to the vehement anti-textual bias. In contrast to the undermining suspicion with which Beckett or Sarraute treated language, the playwrights of the last twenty years responded to the repudiation of the text not by minimizing its influence, but by multiplying its heterogeneous elements. From Duras to Azama, from Koltès to Reza, from Vinaver to Lagarce, from Gatti to Py, the text returns, unapologetic, demonstrating an eminent desire to express the playfulness and subversion inherent in language and it ability to express the polysemous nature of stage textuality.

There is in contemporary drama an unruly desire for language, a desire to tell a story, to speak, to show, to encounter the other. The fundamental mechanisms of theatrical discourse inform and deepen our understanding of performative desire. Theatrical textuality is an already contested performative space, where meanings are produced, debated, and often occluded. However, like desire, the theatrical text is always in a state of displacement, always at play with what is said and what is done. Even after it is written and performed, the text continues to be rewritten in performance: an actor pauses or uses an ellipsis, creating a vacuum that funnels scriptural and spectatorial desire toward the speaker; an audience gasps or laughs at unintended moments, rewriting those parts of the text with audible markers of their pleasure or anguish; a director makes a choice to change a certain blocking of a movement on the second night of the performance—all simple ges-

---

2. Richard Schechner, *Performance Theory* (New York and London: Routledge, 1988), 21. Schechner popularized the term in describing happenings and other performances in the 1970s. See also Hans-Thies Lehmann's *Postdramatisches Theater* (Frankfurt am Main: Verlag der Autoren, 1999).

tures but each endowed with the power of desire to displace the determinate linearity of writing.

As such, theatrical writing brings back to the forefront fraught questions of desire, the body, and representation. Critics differed significantly however about the function of desire in stage writing. Derrida's reading of Artaud in "La parole soufflée" in *L'écriture et la différence* highlighted Artaud's desire for a purity of speech in theater that will exceed the system of representation without being reincorporated into it as negation. Artaud's dream is an impossible one according to Derrida, for, by advocating "not the absence, but the radical irresponsibility of speech, irresponsibility as the power and the origin of speech,"[3] Artaud found himself at an impasse: a pure speech is an impossible project in theater, because, as soon as I speak, as Derrida noted, "the words I have found. . . no longer belong to me" (177). Theatrical language eludes ownership; not unlike Artaud's vision, it is always ghosted by other words, breaths (*souffles*), stolen by an "always already" (*"toujours déjà"*), purloined by a pre-existing language, what Marvin Carlson called the "haunted text."[4]

As haunted as the text is by other texts, desire in theater is haunted by the body, which is often subverted under the rhetoric of amorous discourse, what Barthes called the philosophical solitude of the lover, which arises from the fact that no modern system can account for *Eros*. Barthes writes: "Today, however, no system of love exists. . . . Christian discourse, if it still exists, exhorts [the lover] to repress and to sublimate. Psychoanalytical discourse . . . constrains him to mourn the loss of his [beloved]. As for Marxist discourse, it has nothing to say."[5] The absence of a system to account for *Eros* is in turn linked to the problem of pleasure. Perhaps because, "we are a civilization," as Foucault declared, "where the problem of desire became much more important than the problem of pleasure . . . , we recognize ourselves as subjects of desire not agents of pleasure."[6] Such a statement can be most evident

3. Jacques Derrida, *Writing and Difference*, trans. Barbara Johnson (Chicago: University of Chicago Press, 1978), 176.

4. Carlson writes: "Although recent writings on intertextuality have called our attention to the fact that all literary texts are involved in the process of recycling and memory, weaving together elements of preexisting and previously read other texts, the dramatic text seems particularly self-conscious of this process, particularly haunted by its predecessors." *The Haunted Stage: The Theater as Memory Machine* (Ann Arbor: University of Michigan Press, 2003), 8.

5. Roland Barthes, *Fragments d'un discours amoureux* (Paris: Seuil, 1977), 250.

6. In "An ethics of Pleasure," a 1983 Radio interview reprinted in *Foucault Live: Interviews (1961–1984)* (Cambridge, Mass.: MIT Press, 1996), 371.

in the theater where the nature of the exchange between performer and audience highlights the moment of recognition of one another as subjects of desire, while denying each other the material conditions necessary to assure a transfer of pleasure.

From Derrida's *"toujours déjà"* of other texts to Foucault's endless imbedding of desire in the subterranean machination of power, the two major orientations in theorizing desire in the modern period are linked to the dichotomy between desire as a pursuit of pleasure and desire as a need for knowledge, or the Freudian and Hegelian positions.[7] Whereas the Faustian ideal of desire for knowledge leads to damnation, the desire for libidinal satisfaction leads inevitably to a labyrinthine and endless pursuit. Not surprisingly, theater is located at the intersection of these two postulations: it is at the same time a site of pleasure and a quest for knowledge, the meeting point of *Eros* and language. Desire enters the spectacular domain of the theater by displacing the need for fulfillment while repressing it. However, sublimation is itself a paradox: theatrical desire transcends the usual limits of eroticism, thus asserting its distinction from carnal desire by being a representation rather than a presentation. The moment we move to presentation we enter the realm of the pornographic (live erotic performances, peep shows, snuff, and so on). As Susan Sontag's groundbreaking distinction between art and pornography established, "[p]ornography has a 'content,' and is designed to make us connect (with disgust, desire) with that content. It is a substitute for life. But art does not excite; or, if it does, the excitation is appeased, within the terms of the aesthetic experience."[8] Similarly, theater does not excite, it rather sublimates the excitation within the realm of the theatrical and aesthetic experience.

Not only is theater *about* desire, in its relationship to the stage, it is structured *like* desire, since it gives spectators the experience of objects, bodies, space, movement through representation, while denying them the possibility of touching, possessing, or making a definitive material record like a book or a film.[9] Theater's ephemeral nature engages the reader/spectator in the dynamic movement of the text on stage. It

7. For an in depth discussion of the opposition between desire as a pursuit of pleasure and desire as a quest for knowledge, see Hugh J. Silverman, introduction to *Philosophy and Desire,* ed. Silverman (New York & London: Routledge, 2000), 1–13.

8. Susan Sontag, "On Style," in *Against Interpretation and other Essays* (New York: Farrar, Straus and Giroux, 1966), 26–27.

9. Although one could argue that theater can be filmed or the play script reproduced, the nature of the live event prohibits total capture of all the elements of spectacle itself with its sound, space, liveness, and audience-performer transactions during a particular performance.

is the dialectical aspect of this movement that I will analyze in what follows in two major plays by Bernard-Marie Koltès (1948–1989). The discussion will be characterized by two lines of argument: first, the search for a language capable of translating desire through the search for an absent body, as in the play *Combat de nègre et de chiens* (1979); second, the articulation of a desire for language through the elaboration of a complex rhetorical structure that disrupts desire and functions beyond and sometimes against the field of signification, as in the play *Dans la solitude des champs de coton* (1987). What will become clear in the unfolding of this double helix is the way theatrical language is at the same time an expression of desire and its prohibition, an interdiction that taunts the speaking subject with the coveted object's availability.

THE LANGUAGE OF DESIRE

Koltès's oeuvre from *La nuit juste avant les forêts* (1976) to *Roberto Zucco*, the last play before his death in 1989, deals with desire and the status of the body as a "desiring machine" structured by social forces and subjected to cultural and moral regimes of restraint. Koltès's theater is always "ghosted" by desire; a mediation between a violent individuation of pleasure and the demands for its articulation through collective consciousness. His plays are elaborate systems and structures of argumentation that stage the tension between the availability of speech and the paucity of landscape. Protagonists first enter the space of representation to assert their supremacy in the verbal realm, as Patrice Pavis noted:

> Koltès's protagonists are not characters in the conventional sense, concrete beings engaged in dramatic situations; they are logical abstractions, marking the progression of an argument, they are the actors of an abstract drama of philosophical dialogue, the orators in a quasi-theological debate, theoreticians of communication and even of meta-communication.[10]

Furthermore, characters are in constant conflict between their verbal language and their physical language, between their bodies and utterance, between telling and living. Every character reaches a paroxystic moment where conflict can only be resolved through physical violence, deferred for the duration of the spectacle but constantly placing him or

10. Patrice Pavis, *Le théâtre au croisement des cultures* (Paris: José Corti, 1990), 100.

her at the edge of a menacing and ominous incident, such as in the play *Combat de nègre et de chiens.*

Written in 1979 during a trip to Guatemala, *Combat de nègre et de chiens* was initially recorded for radio France-Culture by Gabriel Monnet in 1980, then performed the same year in New York, directed by Françoise Kourilsky at the experimental theater la Mamma. It was subsequently produced in France in 1983 at the Amandiers-Nanterre theater, directed by Patrice Chéreau. Since the author's death the play has become the most widely produced of his oeuvre. Its popularity is due in part to its poetic lyricism, its universal theme, and its tragic undertone. The action takes place in an unidentified "place in the world," in a west African country, somewhere between Senegal and Nigeria, where a black laborer is killed on a work site of a foreign company's public construction project. Alboury, the main character, has mysteriously slipped into the site to reclaim the body of his murdered brother. No one on the work site, neither Cal, the white engineer who killed the worker in a fit of rage, nor Horn, the French foreman—a man in his sixties, attempting to cover up the murder—is prepared for this intrusion. Alboury will soon find out that his brother's body may never be found, since Cal disposed of it in the sewer. While this realization has serious consequences for the shift in racial relations between a mythical Africa and an exploitative European enterprise, a surprising twist takes place when Alboury is seduced by Léone (the woman brought over from France as a bride for Horn). Inevitably, a battle ensues, fueled not only by differences of race, but also class and gender, cleaving the characters between the need for vengeance and the encounter with *Eros.*

From his arrival on the work site, Alboury makes clear his intent to recover his brother's body: "I'm Alboury, sir; I've come to reclaim the body; his mother went out in the field to lay branches on the body, sir, to no avail, she was not able to find anything; and his mother wandered all night in the village, screaming, if the body is not given back to her . . ."[11] The desire for this absent body, coupled with the accompanying elliptical threat of violence, is the modus operandi of the whole play. Unlike absurdist theater, such as Beckett's *Happy Days*—which parodies the idea of a desiring body as the primary evidence of the impossibility of communication—Koltès's theater transforms the desiring body into spectacle, using language to both address and disown repre-

11. Bernard-Marie Koltès, *Combat de nègre et de chiens* (Paris: Minuit, 1989), 9.

sentation. However, this desire is not a typical one; it is a desire for a
dead body, a cadaver unlike any other. For, after killing him, Cal could
not bury the body; he tried to drown it in the lake, then threw it over
the truck dump, and finally pitched it into the sewers.

The opening scene between Alboury and Horn is indicative of the
opposing systems of signification between the west and the colonized
global south. Alboury, hidden behind the bougainvillea[12] shrub, is
called out by Horn, who is concerned that the intruder was sent by the
police. Between them is instituted a sort of *pas de deux* where words
and intentions are woven around each other, with an imminent danger
lurking in the background:

> Horn. — Is it the police or the village that sent you, sir?
> Alboury. — My name is Alboury, I'm here to take back my brother's
> body, sir.
> Horn. — Oh yes, a terrible accident; an unfortunate fall, an ill-fated
> truck charging at high speed; the driver will be punished. The workers
> are not careful, despite the strict directives given to them. . . . Well, your
> command of French is impressive; no doubt you're equally at ease in En-
> glish and in other languages too; you have a real talent for languages in
> this part of the world. . . . You probably know a lot more than you let
> on. In the end, all of this must sound like too many compliments. . . .
> Alboury. — As for me, I've only come for the body and I will leave as
> soon as I have it. (9–11)

Despite Horn's flattery, Alboury does not lose sight of his mission; he
repeats incessantly, "I am here to claim the body." This bodiless crime
transforms, like Strindberg's *Ghost Sonata* or Genet's *Les paravents*,
the dead into specters. The absent ritualistic body that Alboury is here
to reclaim is the primary signifying matrix against which all others are
posited. The body's absence transforms the theater of murder into a theater of evidence: without the body, the crime may never be uncovered
nor justice served. But unlike the legal definition of evidence, which
confers justification and rationalization on a situation where access to
truth is problematic, the desire of the body in theater confers a sort of
reverse *habeas corpus* where signification is inferred through absence
rather than presence. While the empirical status of evidence in legal
terms is linked to the forensic value of objects, classified and analyzed
based on their material and circumstantial value, in theater evidence
plays a mediating role.

12. The "bougainvillea" plant was named after Louis Antoine de Bougainville, the
first French navigator to cross the Pacific.

Even after multiple attempts, Cal could not hide the evidence; the dead body wouldn't disappear, it became the emblem of a resistance, a kind of a figure deceptively near, yet infinitely distant. Banishing the body may only reduce the possibility of resurrection of the flesh, but the body as a signifying apparatus remains stubbornly recalcitrant. Here the dead challenge the assumption that they must leave the world of the living in order to rest in peace. The corpse is there, but not there, occupying a Soja-esque "third space,"[13] a space between subject and object, narrative and memory, articulated in language, both material and symbolic. Alboury, like his absent brother, is configured in migratory and horizontal terms, moving in space, in contrast to the insipid colonial social order translated by the verticality of the "enterprise" with its kitchen sink realism and commonplace melodrama. The text is in fact constructed to reflect this paradigmatic opposition: while Alboury (and by extension Léone midway through the play) masters the language of space in this semi-lit jungle, frequently referring to movement and locations, Cal and Horn live out their sentence in time and memory, frequently referring to their past in France, invoking nostalgic memories of an origin fantasized as pure.

In the absence of a body for the African nation to lay to rest, Alboury finds a proxy, a replacement in this space of arrest and brutality. Léone's seduction of Alboury is a counter to the stubborn absence of the dead brother's body. Koltès explores by this parallel the instability between a profound material inherence present in Léone's body and a corresponding emblematic absence of the brother's body, who is fetishized, approaching its vanishing point while precluding a complete disappearance. Conversely, the menace increases when gender intersects with race. Léone's desire for Alboury becomes the new threat that endangers the enterprise. It is not only the world of the jungle and the reality of colonial exploitation that puts the enterprise in peril, it is the fact that the woman who was imported from France to provide the pleasures of companionship for Horn has turned her attention toward the other, the outsider (to colonial order). Through desire, Léone's oppression as a woman connects to the oppression of Alboury; this position of double-marginalization allows for an alliance of racial and gender op-

13. Following Henri Lefevbre, Edward Soja proposed a "third space" as the "third existential dimension," along with the history dimension (as story or narration) and the social dimension (as characters and their relationship to one another). *Thirdspace* (Oxford: Blackwell, 1996).

pression that challenges the overworked typical formula of one trumping the other. Such an alliance opens up a space of coalitional politics, possible through a discovery of an erotically charged common language that transcends cultural and racial differences. This is the meaning of the multilingual exchanges that happen between Léone and Alboury in scenes six, nine, and eleven. In scene six, approaching Alboury, Léone speaks German and French while he answers in Wolof.

> Léone. — I'm looking for water. Wasser, bitte. . . . Do you understand German? . . . When I saw the flowers I recognized everything; I recognized these flowers though I don't know their name; but they were hanging from the branches like that in my mind and all the colors I already had them in mind. (42)

As Léone recognized the African exotic flowers before having seen them, similarly, without looking at Alboury, she recognized her desire for him (a didascalia indicates that "*she touches him without looking at him*"). Eventually, in scene nine, they will succeed at understanding each other although they both "speak foreign": "Léone—I speak foreign and you too, so we'll soon be on the same wavelength. . . . Oh of course the grammar takes time . . . but even with mistakes . . . what counts is a little vocabulary; not even that, it's the tone of voice that's important. In fact you don't even need that, all we need to do is to look at each other, without speaking. . . . We'll be silent when we understand one another" (58–59). The final exchange between them in scene eleven achieves a complete conversion; from being able to understand each other through words they move to a kind of corporeal symbiosis confounding any distinction between the linguistic and the embodied, between the said and the lived:

> Léone. — you have wonderful hair. . . .
> Alboury. — they say our hair is wiry and black because the father of all blacks, abandoned by God and then by humanity, found himself alone with the devil, who had also been abandoned, the devil caresses his head as a sign of friendship, and that is how our hair was burnt. . . . (69)
> Léone. — I love the stories about the devil, I love the way you tell them. . . . I was looking for someone to be faithful to, I found you. . . . I think there's a devil in my heart, Alboury; I don't know how he got in, but he's there, I can feel him. He's caressing my soul so that I'm burning, all black on the inside. (69–70)

Regardless of the flux of languages, words, foreign utterances, Alboury and Léone will not be able to escape their flesh. No matter how much they elaborate a linguistic web around their material existence—how much they debate, embroider, and weave—they remain trapped in the flesh they inhabit. Léone's final gesture is symbolic in this sense: she tattoos herself in the same hieroglyphic inscriptions found on Alboury's body, vampirically translating her desire for the forbidden other. Written on the body, Léone's mimetic desire for Alboury's bodily inscription enacts a compulsive repetition of an imagery drawn from the realm of the senses that prevails over the intractability of language.

THE DESIRE FOR LANGUAGE

If the body in *Combat de nègre et de chiens* serves to excavate the language of desire, *Dans la solitude des champs de coton* (1987) frames a desire for language that places the character at the opposite pole of the speech and gesture dialectic. The search for a language that can translate desire haunts *La solitude*, since no amount of telling can adequately express the meaning of the bodily desire or exorcise it in the materiality of the flesh. Written in 1987 and produced the same year at the Amandiers-Nanterre theater by Patrice Chéreau, *La solitude* has become a classic of contemporary theater, the play that sums up Koltès's entire aesthetic.

It is "a simple and obscure story,"[14] of two characters, anonymously identified as the "dealer" and the "client," who accost each other at night, in a clandestine urban space where shady business is usually conducted. However, when typically the players involved in illicit deals hastily conclude their business and leave for fear of being apprehended by the authorities, these two players are in no hurry to end their transaction. Neither the dealer nor the client is prepared to divulge what he desires of the other. The dealer tracks the client in a circuitous movement, while inviting him to express what he has come here seeking. While the client stubbornly withholds his desire, he in turn attempts to elicit the dealer's interest by teasing him and making him decipher his intent. The entire play is based on a theorem stated by the dealer in the opening lines of the play: "If you're walking in this place and at this hour, it's because you desire something that you don't have, and that I can provide for you."[15] The exchange of rhetoric between them con-

14. Anne Ubersfeld, *Bernard-Marie Koltès* (Paris: Actes Sud, 1999), 57.
15. Koltès, *Dans la solitude des champs de coton* (Paris: Minuit, 1986), 9.

tinues throughout the play, creating a kind of philosophical dialogue where the performance of thinking patterns becomes more important than the object of the exchange. As such, each intervention is at the same time an answer to the logical problem posed previously by the other, appended with an additional logical twist, upping the stakes. That's how the client's response to the first conditional statement of the dealer comes a few pages later: "I'm not walking here and now in particular, I'm just walking" (13). The blocks of monologues perform a sort of interlocutive topology, as proposed by Francis Jacques in his study on dialogism. For Jacques the two dialogic registers are generally characterized by utterance (*énoncé*) and enunciation (*énonciation*) related to the allocutive and the delocutive registers.[16] While the utterance modalities are "related to truth, falsehood, doubt or certainty" of propositions, the enunciative modalities are a function of the confrontation of the propositional attitudes between interlocutors, while "mutually influencing them in terms of questions, declarations, responses, objections, etc." (Jacques, 28).

The epigraph of *La solitude* is a definition of the word "Deal": "*Deal*: transaction commerciale portant sur des valeurs prohibées ou strictement contrôlées" (7) [*A Deal*: a commercial transaction based on illegal or strictly controlled goods]. Setting up an entry point to the text, the use of the English word however produces a process of estrangement in the reader, for no French equivalent exists for the word "deal"; even French words such as "trafic," "affaire," "commerce," "marché," and "négoce" do not convey the clandestine nature of the deal. But even in English, the word carries ambiguous meanings. In addition to its old English root (etymologically, the word means "a part," or "share"), a second root from the Germanic "*dala*" or "*dell*" means "valley" or "low point." This is perhaps why the dealer queries the client on the reasons that brought him down from his high and well-lit place to the subterranean sinking hole on this shady street corner where they find themselves. If they met, it was by virtue of having to cross this sullied gulley to get from one high point to another, as the client observes: "There's no way for someone to get from one height to another with-

16. Although discourse analysis exceeds the scope of this article, it is important to define the relevant terms: the "allocutives" are generally terms that address other people and are predominated by the pronoun "you"; "elocutives" refer to the person speaking, or the predominance of "I," and "delocutives" refer to the person or thing spoken about or the predominance of "it." Francis Jacques, *Dialogiques I. Recherches logiques sur le dialogue.* (Paris: Presses Universitaires de France, 1979), 158.

out coming down in order to go up again" (13). Aside from the apparent reference to the withdrawal that separates two highs in drug use, this reference also hints to a third meaning of "deal," derived from the Arabic "Zholl," meaning *shade,* and that explains the obsessive recurrence of textual references to shade, darkness, dimness, and shadows.

The three semantic axes of the word "deal" (the transaction, the valley, and the shade) conspire to illuminate the relationship between clandestine business, shadiness, and dejection. As much as the epigraphic definition thrives to be a metalinguistic device meant to narrow down the possible semantic fields, it risks achieving the opposite by opening up multiple sites of meaning not contained within the realm of the singular and binary rapport of signifier to signified. In the face of such a radical openness, the protagonists become obsessed with the question as to whether there can ever be desire within the logic of the deal. The client articulates this impossibility when he says: "If it is true that we are, you the dealer and I the buyer, in possession of goods so mysterious . . . Why then do you still keep your goods under wraps?" (26). As for the dealer: "What all men and beasts dread . . . is not suffering itself, . . . it is the unfamiliarity of suffering and having to endure a strange suffering" (29–30).

The desire for language does not facilitate the relation between the dealer and the client; words fall like lashes of a whip, they injure and wound. The root of the verb "to speak" in Arabic, *Kallama,* is also to wound, because, as the client says, "My desire, if I have one, if I reveal to you, would burn your face, would make you pull back your hand, screaming, and you would run away in the dark like a dog running so fast that you don't even see its tail" (15). The flood of the long dialogic tirades is opposed to the scarcity of space, deeply experienced by the characters as a condition of their encounter, sharpened by the illicit nature of the deal with which they are constrained. The confrontation between them marks the simultaneous rigidity and fluidity of the isolation of "solitude" and the consolation and comfort of cotton (as the title of the play suggests). The friction between these two references and their corresponding inhabiting bodies opens the space for the potential of violence, deferred as long as the characters desire each other and have something to say to one another.

Desire in *La solitude* is thus a radical project, offering a counterpart to the sinister rapport of want to the capitalist machine. In this paradigm, there is no merchandise to trade hands, no deal to conclude; no transaction will ever take place. The dealer is as fictional as the mer-

chandise hidden and the client's presence is as elusive as his unnam-
able desire. No culminating exchange will take place, except the turn-
ing of rhetoric itself into commodity. Does the deal allow for the
exchange of any meaningful affection that escapes the fetishism of
commodity? Desire, like commerce, is a circulation of values. In the
same way as Georg Lukács's "reification of commodity" is an obstacle
to class consciousness, or Guy Debord's "spectacle" an obstacle to true
inter-relational dialogue, so the commercialization of human relations
is an obstacle to desire. The dealer and the client have different responses to this obstacle: while the dealer declares that what he was selling was not merchandise but waiting, anticipation, patience, the hope
and the promise of selling, the client is instead "looking for one thing
when he wants something else" (59), playing the perverse game of the
buyer who draws pleasure from being able to refuse what is offered to
him. The impasse reached by this double game inexorably culminates
in violence. Violence promises to succeed where dialogue failed because neither the tender menace of the dealer, nor the passionate aver-
sion of the client succeeds at concluding the deal. They realize in the
end that the impossible game must end in a battle:

> The dealer. — Is there anything you said you wanted from me that I
> didn't hear?
> The client. — I didn't say anything, and you? Is there anything, . . .
> you've offered that I haven't figured out?
> The dealer. — Nothing
> The client. — So what weapon? (58–60)

The choice of weapon to replace language announces the imminent
battle at the end, transforming *La solitude* into more than a play in the
traditional sense. The quasi-monologic dialogues become rehearsals
(in the French sense of "répétitions") of incantatory songs of war
preparing for combat. It is significant that the cadence of the monologic
blocks accelerates as the play progresses leading up to a very fast stac-
cato of short elliptical answers at the end enunciating more impersonal
maxims such as: "a man can't let his clothing be insulted. Clothing is
the self that doesn't suffer, the balancing point between justice and in-
justice"; "there are no rules; there are only means, there are only
weapons"; "there is no love"; "a man dies first, then looks for his death
and finally meets his, by chance, on a dangerous journey from one light
to another, and he says, 'So, that's it'" (60).

Each actor in this rhetorical dance relates not to his interlocutor but to language itself. The momentous oratorio continues until speech is exhausted, at which point the two protagonists must choose: either leave each other without having gained or lost anything, or resort to physical violence to restore a semblance of order. As such, the two actors are engaged in a dance of death where the stakes are placed not on objects of exchange or on spatial victory, but on the conquest of words. Their relationship to language triangulates, performing a kind of Girardian desire. For René Girard, desire is always in a triangular relationship. In his now classic study *Mensonge romantique, vérité romanesque*,[17] we desire something or someone based on a model of desire whereby the other desires the same and it triggers in us a "mimetic desire," thus making the relationship between subject and object always mediated indirectly by the model. Through their relation of triangulation, the client and the dealer are not in fact drawn to each other but to the model itself. Girard writes: "the attraction toward the object is in fact an attraction toward the mediator" (24). Although Girard was dealing with a different genre (namely, the novels of Stendhal, Flaubert, and Proust) and did not specifically address theatrical writing, his analysis of mimetic rivalry is relevant here. In *La violence et le sacré*,[18] a kind of sequel to *Mensonge romantique*, Girard explains that "mimetic rivalry" ensues when the two poles desiring the same object fail to resolve their need for satisfaction and inevitably end up wanting to destroy the model on which their desiring attention lies. The consequence of mimetic desire is thus the inescapable menace of violence.

Evidently, unresolved and unsatisfied desire in *La solitude* leads to the destruction of language, which becomes the shared fatality sacrificially immolated between the client and the dealer. Theater reenacts violence as linguistic repetition, until death (*Thanatos*) triumphs over *Eros*. The coup de grâce is delivered when the protagonists realize that their desire to verbalize the language of desire, though rehearsing its various articulations, is in the end an error of judgment. This is the meaning of the long tirade recited by the dealer that explains in theatrical terms the title of the play:

> The dealer. — So please don't refuse to tell me what you want, the object of your feverish desire, the reason for looking at me. . . . If you're worried about wounding your dignity, say it as if you are talking to a

---

17. René Girard, *Mensonge romantique, vérité romanesque* (Paris: Hachette, 1961).
18. Girard, *La violence et le sacré* (Paris: Grasset, 1972).

tree, or in front of a prison wall, or in the solitude of a cotton field, where one can wander naked at night. . . . Because the only true cruelty of the dusk where we both find ourselves is not that one man might hurt the other, mutilate him, torture him, or tear his limbs apart, or even make him cry. The true and terrible cruelty is when man or beast makes the other forever incomplete, interrupted like an ellipsis in the middle of a sentence, turns away from him after exchanging glances, making beast or man an error of judgment, an error, like a letter that one begins and abruptly crumples, just after writing the date. [31]

Like Theseus retracing Ariadne's thread in the labyrinth, the maze of desire is thus woven in language, which in turn is made to produce a complete breakdown of language. The need to express this impasse, however, haunts the text, simultaneously celebrating and disavowing language. As violent as the result may be, the articulation through language of the desire for the other cannot cease or remain in a state of quiescence, for that would be merely a short circuit, a false death, not the true nature of desire, which persistently returns the subject to a state of theatricality, because, as the client concluded "if blood is spilled, it would be on both sides" [61].

*   *   *   *   *

In theater, the text operates as such within the materiality of the body, where representation highlights the perverse aspect of the dialectic relationship of language and desire. As engaged as the characters of these plays are in the madhouse of language, contestants in the arena of the symbolic order that makes reference possible, they remain subjected to the semiotic, what Julia Kristeva called "the bodily drive," the desire that generates rhythms, tones, and movement that allow the identification and differentiation necessary for signification. Desire is possible because of the awareness of this materiality made obvious by theatrical representation that exploits the gap between body and speech, between metaphysical purity and carnal corruption. Like reading, the theatrical text involves what Barthes called a "passion du sens," where "sens" is to be understood as both meaning and sensing. The two meanings are, like the dealer and the client, in a dialectical relationship whereby the two terms are completely and mutually dependent, each presupposing the other. The theatrical text is thus located at the conjunction of eroticism and writing.

CLARE FINBURGH

Voix/Voie/Vie: The Voice in Contemporary French Theater*

> At my birth I was locked up inside a
> few words. Something must fall.
> Afterwards, everything is free.
> —Valère Novarina, *Le théâtre des paroles*

"In theater, in the world, in physics, in the universe, in theology and in history, in politics language is the actor. Elusive, active, language is *actual matter*. Active empty matter."[1] In a recently published theoretical text, "Attraction," Valère Novarina seems to imply that language is an agent that determines human action and dictates human speech. He describes linguistic features as actors that possess their own expressive powers: "Words act like grammatical actors, vocal characters, syntactical actors" (164). Here, he reiterates thoughts articulated twenty years earlier in "Entrée dans le théâtre des oreilles ("Entry into the Theater of the Ears"): "He saw language all alone, he saw the world without man."[2] His use of the third person adds to the sense that language dispossesses and excludes the speaking subject. In *Devant la parole* (*In Front of Speech*), Novarina clarifies the title of this volume of theoretical essays, stating that humans are located behind, outside, or

*I thank the actor Christophe Brault for his invaluable insights into the use of voice in contemporary French theater. I dedicate this piece to Daniel Znyk, whose premature death has deprived the French stage of one of its great voices.

1. Valère Novarina, "Attraction," in *La bouche théâtrale: Études de l'œuvre de Valère Novarina*, ed. Nicolas Tremblay (Montréal: XYZ, 2005), 163. Unless otherwise indicated, all translations are my own.
   2. Novarina, "Entrée dans le théâtre des oreilles," in *Le théâtre des paroles* (Paris: P.O.L., 1989), 70.

YFS 112, *The Transparency of the Text*, ed. Donia Mounsef and Josette Féral, © 2007 by Yale University.

in front of language, but not within it.[3] In this essay, I consult Novarina's theories, play-texts, and productions, notably his August 2003 staging of *La scène* (*The Scene*) at the Avignon Festival and his 2005 production of *L'espace furieux* (*The Furious Space*) at the Comédie Française.[4] In *La scène*, characters admit that they find their language hermetic. One admits, "I do not understand a single [*traître*] word of what I say."[5] Another grieves, "My life is the story of a puppet shaken by things that are already all said" (32). They describe the words that fall from their mouths as pebbles, stones, rocks—recurring motifs in Novarina's works, who writes in "Attraction" "this is the theater where language is a missile: blind blocks are rolled, carted along, pebbles catapulted, objects resonate against words. Language is anthropogenic and bounces off the walls" (162). Words appear to be as unyielding, impenetrable, and obdurate as granite. The massive permanence of language that precedes thoughts and emotions, fixes and crystallizes those thoughts and emotions; language prescribes the parameters of its own expressive possibility. It is "anthropogenic," namely it produces humans, instead of their producing it.

Novarina appears here to claim that humans are subjected to verbal victimization. He is consequently often described by critics as antihumanist or nihilist. For Guy Cloutier, the Novarinian subject is not a subject; it constitutes an empty vessel into which pebbles are lobbed and which has no control over its contents.[6] For Pierre Jourde, too, the Novarinian subject is objectified by language: "Speech does not represent a reappropriation of the individual by her/himself, self-control, self-reflexive domination of the self, but a disappropriation."[7]

I suggest that Novarina proposes a far more affirmative, even euphoric and utopian relationship between humans and language. I argue that for Novarina, subjectivity is able to leave traces on language. In Brechtian terms, humans are a function of the linguistic environment into which they are born, but this environment is equally a function of humans.[8] In this post-modern era where the abolition of the subject,

---

3. Novarina, *Devant la parole* (Paris: P.O.L., 1999).

4. This production transferred to Paris's Théâtre National de la Colline in November 2003. A DVD recording is available: *La scène* (Paris: P.O.L./La Dernière bande, 2003).

5. Novarina, *La scène* (Paris: P.O.L., 2003), 18.

6. Guy Cloutier, "Le déverseur de rémission," in *La bouche théâtrale*, 139–43.

7. Pierre Jourde, "La pantalonnade de Novarina," *Europe*, Novarina special issue 880–881 (Aug-Sept. 2002), 22.

8. Bertolt Brecht, *Brecht on Theater*, trans. John Willett (London, Methuen, 2001), 97.

the Othering of the Self, the death of the author, can impose a wan and mechanical automatism both upon the living subject and upon the literary critic, Novarina's ludic and ecstatic subversion of verbal language, most notably via the introduction of the voice's musicality, provides revitalizing potential. I elaborate in detail the ways in which Novarina foregrounds the voice in theater. I show how Novarina establishes a dynamic tension between linguistic determination, and the means of transcending it; between automated speech, and "authentic" expression. I demonstrate how Novarina creates this liberated language by means of vocal sonority. And I ask, does he dismantle the hegemony of the rationalist linguistic text in order to attain an essentialist affirmation of the body's vitality, an essential plenitude of being?

In Novarina's *La scène*, characters adhere strictly to institutionalized formats of linguistic interaction that seem beyond their control to alter. La Sibylle (The Sibyl) recites an extensive genealogy of her descendants that appears to emblematize the inescapable influence of inherited discourses that traps her: "Militude who begot My Action Teacher who begot My Blocks Teacher who begot My Management Teacher who begot my Wedding Teacher . . ." (21–22). In the 2003 production, Laurence Vielle, who played La Sibylle, recited her unpunctuated monologue in a frantic and seemingly unstoppable tirade that gave the impression that the lineage of teachers who dictate her education is inescapable. I think Novarina's description of language as alienation is social and political rather than metaphysical. The play contains numerous references to mass media and the press where, in today's society, language has become instrumentalized, repetitive, and bland. It exposes the common clichés of political public rhetoric, one character exclaiming, "Vote for Marcel Billandeau: the future is his" (126). The main character in the play, La Machine à Dire la Suite (The Machine for Saying What's Next), seems capable of speaking only in the predetermined linguistic styles and registers of news-reading and television presenting: "One hour later, after the weather that will give us news about the weather, our colleagues and colleaguesses from the Canadian program *Mustn't Push*, joining Mirelli Mirella in link-up for her program *The Overflowed Vase* . . ." (102). He is joined by La Machine à Dire Beaucoup (The Machine for Saying a Lot) and La Machine sans Savoir Pourquoi (The Machine without Knowing Why), whose names underscore the verbose, yet vapid nature of "mechanized" media discourse. In Novarina's 2003 production, these three characters wore large square tables around their waists, calling to mind a typical television newsreader whose upper body can be seen but whose legs are hidden. This costume accessory also gave the impression that the characters were literally stuck in, and unable to extract themselves from, their scripted language.

For Novarina, while it might appear that humans exploit language to utilitarian ends, the opposite occurs: language exploits humans, since it suppresses their creativity, imagination, subjectivity. Prosaic, descriptive, realist language "is affected in its activity of production, harmed in its reproductive activity," he writes in an early essay, "Le drame de la langue française" ("The Drama of the French Language").[9] In *La scène,* La Sibylle indicates this mechanization of the individual: "We humans, we have no other solution in the end but to think via the machines that are inside us" (120), while Le Pauvre (The Poor Man) laments, "Not life: the mechanical human!" (157). In the 2003 production, Diogène was played by a robotic mechanical puppet head that symbolized the programmed automation of human language. Diogène acknowledges the mental stagnation that results from the unimaginative use of language: "I struggle too every day against a mental thickening, a glue, that gets me here, all over the bottom of my brain" (157). The scenography designed by Philippe Marioge encapsulated this sense of confinement within language. Each of the three Avertisseurs carried a long metal car shape around his waist, his upper body protruding from the cockpit, and his legs running frantically around the stage. A refrigerator was then placed central stage, and characters were confined to three tiny open-fronted houses.[10] The characters' dialogues illustrate the banality of their domesticated existence, which, in this production, centered visually around cars, sitting rooms, and household appliances. One character claims, "We French, we have more and more canine dogs and more and more automoohbiles: we put the canine dogs in the autos, then we hoist the French flag above them" (14). Another says, "We Frenchiculturalists, . . . we have the world record for the taking of tranquillizers, for the rearing of domestic animals in the home, for crash accidents, and for the production of bedroom slipper ears" (17). Novarina says, in the epigraph to this essay, that people have been "locked up inside a few words." This linguistic incarceration is the consequence not of language in general, but of the systematized use by our civilization of information technology and network systems, of prefabricated,

9. Novarina, "Le drame dans la langue française," in *Le théâtre des paroles,* 62.
10. For photographs, see *La bouche théâtrale,* 154–56.

archetyped discourses, and devalued, crude, and debased everyday speech.

Novarina turns this recognition of the prosaic and predictable use of language into a motivation to transform and recreate language. La Machine à Dire la Suite reports that someone has tried to "violate the order of language" (10). And Novarina declares in both the content and the style of "Le drame dans la langue française," his determination to "form a fissure in the French language. Something we no longer tolerate in French. . . . Change all the endments of the radicles: the evacuation, the fallment, the speechment, the plummate, macabiate, the destructiam [l'évacuaison, le tombement, le parlement, le chutat, le macabiat, le saccabiam]" (33). He insists that he refuses to subscribe to "current dominant language," namely the faded and jaded language of the everyday (62). He protests most of all against realism—the descriptive style that dominates the press, media, and quotidian speech. Firstly, realist narrative constitutes a vain endeavor, since it can never represent reality fully: "Everything revolves around a scene that one cannot describe," says Novarina.[11]

Secondly, realist, descriptive representation discourages poetic creativity. In the 2003 production of La scène, the three-sided house structures literally framed the actors within them. In addition, the walls of the houses bore picture frames, through which the Tête de Rachel (Head of Rachel) and the Tête d'Isaïe (Head of Isaïe) stuck their heads. And when Diogène asked for a door or window at the end of the play, the stage hands brought on a huge empty picture frame, into which he walked. In the 2005 production of L'espace furieux, Jean Singulier carried a similar frame, through which he spoke. On the one hand, all these frames confined and enclosed their inhabitants and subjects, like the forms of language I have described. Concurrently, however, these frames, and the plinth on which Frégoli stood at the end of La scène, self-consciously indicated theater's artifice. This artifice means that the play is liberated from the constraints of naturalist reproduction, and is free to explore the near limitless fictional space of aesthetic creativity. Novarina writes in "Attraction," "We have come to see on stage the defeat of representation" (163). He excludes psychologism and naturalism from plot, characterization, dialogue, and scenography, in order to replace a trite copy of reality with an exploration of the aesthetic potential of visual imagery, acting style, and verbal language. In all his

11. Novarina, "Impératifs," in Le théâtre des paroles, 96.

plays, conventional psychological characters are replaced with poetic
voices that utter what in "Le drame dans la langue française" he calls
"slogans": a "language without a thread" that eludes the coherence of
traditional thematics or linear narrative, and is divided into linguistic
"sessions" instead of scenes: "Theatrical writing *with holes in,* where
the place is always missing, the link from one theme to another" (55,
56, 33). Novarina explains how he constantly cuts up his texts and re-
arranges them, precisely to preclude thematic coherence (41). Furthermore, he excludes from his theater the representation of supposedly
real-life characters, themes, stories, or time-space references. He announces in the same text an "End to the representation of man by
man!" (56). Novarina's insistence that language be spared from purely
instrumentalist use is manifested most obviously in his highly poeticized use of language, which demands an equally aestheticized use of
the actor's voice. Instead of eliminating language altogether from his
theater, Novarina, in Antonin Artaud's words, "multiplies its possibilities."[12]

If the aural density of dialogues is palpably evident both on the play-
text page and in the auditorium, then speech is no longer exploited
merely as a vehicle for empirical description. Back in 1975, Roland
Barthes's "The Rustle of Language" described a language of sonorous
sound rather than semantic sense—"value passed to the sumptuous
level of the signifier"—as euphoric and utopian.[13] Like Novarina, he
states that when language functions automatically, like a machine
with minimal human input, it poses "the most serious of threats: *loss
of the body*" (99). But when the sound of the linguistic machine comes
not from its mechanized use, but from the fine tuning of its musical
properties—"the convulsive movements," "the patina of consonants,
the sensuousness of vowels," "the breathiness, rattling, the fleshiness
of the lips" (88–89)—an industrialized whirring is replaced with a sen-
suous *rustle*. In the 1970s, Barthes gave the example in *Le plaisir du
texte* of Philippe Sollers's novels, but stated that as far as theater was
concerned, this musicalization was attained only in the Far-Eastern,
and not in Western contemporary theater.[14] It is true that from the

12. Antonin Artaud, "Lettres sur le langage: Deuxième lettre," in *Le théâtre et son double* (Paris: Gallimard, 1964), 172.
13. Roland Barthes, "Le bruissement de la langue," in *Le bruissement de la langue* (Paris: Seuil, 1984), 88–89.
14. Barthes, *Le plaisir du texte* (Paris: Seuil, 1973), 89. Barthes is right here. Many Asian theaters use a vocalization between song and speech that employs the whole

eighteenth century onward in Western Europe, the Enlightenment's emphasis on rationalism meant that the voice's musicality was effaced from theater and the voice became a transparent organ for the transmission of intellectual thought and psychological emotion.[15] Positivism and its corollary, mimetic realism, banished the excesses of sensual Dionysian poetry and song from theater. Musicality was removed, as song and drama were categorized as separate arts, except for in the "vulgar" forms of operetta, cabaret, and musicals. This remains much the case today, where cinema, television, and most commercial theater are dominated by naturalist acting technique, where the organic corporeality of the voice is silenced.[16]

A minority of directors and practitioners has emphasized the musicality of the human voice since the early twentieth century. In the first half of the century, theater-makers like Paul Claudel or Antonin Artaud began to incorporate the voice's sonority into theater, after having become acquainted with non-European traditions through their travels, or through international exhibitions held in Paris. Artaud's theories have had a profound impact on contemporary theater practice. Jacques Derrida writes that Artaud's theatrical aesthetic is "against technical reproduction, genetic or genealogical reproduction, it enjoins us to reaffirm the singularity of the moment."[17] Like Novarina, Artaud refuses to exploit theatrical language for realist representation or adhere to genealogically conventional grammatical norms. The actor's voice is appreciated for its immediate concrete materiality, not just for its ability to communicate semantic signification and teleological die-

---

phonatory apparatus: *jing xi* from China; *Nô* and *kabuki* from Japan; *hat tuông, hat chèo, hat cai luong* from Vietnam, *Ta'asié* from Iran, are just some examples (see Trân Quang Hai, "Techniques vocales dans les théâtres musicaux en Asie orientale," *Théâtre/Public*, special issue *Les chemins de la voix*, 142–43 (1998): 64–70. In Europe, the actor's voice had been central to ancient Greek and Roman tragedy, where speech and song formed a continuum. But in the eighteenth century, the voice's materiality lost importance, as I explain presently (see Florence Dupont, "La voix de l'acteur tragique à Rome," *Théâtre/Public*, special issue *Les chemins de la voix*, 59–63).

15. Novarina speaks of the "cleansing of the body" that takes place in today's society: "a toilet of the voice, filtering, tapes edited and carefully purified of all laughs, farts, hiccoughs, salivations, respirations, of all the slag that marks the animal, material nature of the feet and the TV, makeup applied to the skin of heads-of-state." Novarina, "Letter to the Actors" [1986], trans. Allen Weiss, *The Drama Review* 37/2 (Summer 1993): 100.

16. See Pierre Voltz, "La voix parlée," *Théâtre/Public*, special issue *Les chemins de la voix*.

17. Jacques Derrida, *Artaud le Moma* (Paris: Galilée, 2002), 18.

gesis. Derrida describes how for Artaud, the actor's voice is no longer an "organ"—an instrument at the service of the text's logical "organization"—but is an *organic,* physical presence, as much as set, costume, and lighting.[18] The voice was always central to the performance and directing of Louis Jouvet, for whom the actor must "pronounce the words, render them sonorous by exercising the lips, the throat and the larynx, the tongue's racket that whacks the words, thrash them out of their straitjacket stamped with the heat of sentiments."[19] In the second half of the twentieth century, oral sonority in theater was developed by directors like Jean-Louis Barrault, Antoine Vitez, Ariane Mnouchkine, and Peter Brook, who emphasizes what he calls the "sudden changes of pitch, the crescendos, the fortissimos, the piano-pianos, the pauses, the silence—the immediate vocal music" of the actor's voice.[20] For Barrault, actors require musical training in order to learn about the voice's potential intensity, pitch, and rhythm.[21] More recently, Claude Régy's 1997 production of Maurice Maeterlinck's *La mort de Tintagiles* deployed a range of vocal effects, including slowed diction, low and monotone melodic pitch, and very regular rhythm, with few pauses between sentences. The word *voice* derives from the Latin "vox," which denotes the physical organs that make speech. Novarina joins these directors and performers, for whom the voice is no longer a transparent means for transmitting clear messages, but becomes an opaque and concrete part of the actor's body. Novarina writes, in his "Letter to the Actor," of the experience of listening to what Barthes terms the *rustle* in theater:

> A blind spectator should be able to hear it crunched and swallowed, to ask himself what is being eaten over there, onstage. What are they eating? . . . Mastication, sucking, swallowing. Pieces of the text must be bitten off, viciously attacked by the female eaters (lips, teeth); other pieces must be quickly gulped down, swallowed, gobbled up, breathed in, guzzled. (95)

Words take on such sensuality that they can be savored. As Barthes states in "The Rustle of Language," pleasure can be derived not from

18. Derrida, "La parole soufflée," in *Writing and Difference,* trans. Alan Bass (London, New York: Routledge, 1978), 233–35 (Derrida's emphasis).
19. Louis Jouvet, *Le comédien désincarné,* quoted in Michel Bernardy, *Le jeu verbal* (Paris: L'aube, 2004), 30–31.
20. Peter Brook, *There Are No Secrets* (London: Methuen, 1993), 80.
21. Jean-Louis Barrault, *Mise en scène de Phèdre,* quoted in *Le jeu verbal,* 200.

"the succession of utterances," but from "uttering"—the prosody of the text (21). The physicality of the voice is thus foregrounded among this select minority of contemporary theater-makers. Novarina writes, in "Le drame dans la langue française": "Nobody has ever dared do it: treat language like a thing" (48). He is somewhat disingenuous here, since several other contemporary French playwrights write poetically acoustic theater, not least Michel Vinaver, Noëlle Renaude, Michel Azama, Olivier Cadiot, and Jean-Luc Lagarce. Novarina, however, more than any other contemporary French playwright, writes the Barthesian *rustle* or "*grain* of the voice" into the texts of his plays.

Novarina describes frequently how his writing is determined by sound rather than sense; with his ears and feet, rather than with his brain. Once again in "Le drame dans la langue française" he asserts that "everything by chomping, nothing by hand [tout à la mâche, rien à la main]" (45); and in "Entrée dans le théâtre des oreilles" he writes, "with my feet, by tapping, by speaking with the ground" (76). The use of breath, the mouth, tongue and teeth determines the elaboration of his dramatic texts, as he writes in the latter essay:

> Descend into the hole from the light of the tube of the column of air, experimental lesions, holes in memory, voids in meaning, languishing dizziness, languism, perpetual begetling, fall of the system of reproduction. . . . Undoing of my language, undoing of my thought. Without a thought, without an idea, without a word, without a memory, without an opinion, without seeing and without hearing. I write with ears. I write backwards. I hear everything. (72).

Novarina seeks to elude the imperatives of rationalism, semantism, thematics, narrative organization, and structured argument. Language is liberated from the limitations of realist representation, as he states in "Attraction": "This here is not at all a view of the universe, of the world, of man within, of history, but something that is suddenly revealed to us of grammar, syntax, apparition." (162). The everyday language of prosaism is replaced with "languism":[22] a vertiginous freefall into the soundscape of the signifier, where vowels, consonants, syllables, and pauses generate and perpetuate themselves according to their grammatical and melodic properties. This concept becomes the premise for Novarina's play *Le babil des classes dangereuses* (*The Babel of Dangerous Classes*), as the following example illustrates: "I one eve-

---

22. Novarina defines this term in "Le drame dans la langue française": "languism: language that itself produces itself, that reproduces itself" (44).

ning was illuminated and begot Ibe who begot Ipe who begot Ile who begot Ime."[23] Rhyme and homophony are pushed to the limits of cacophony, in this linguistic "furious space" where language is no longer bland communication; it becomes litany, incantation ("Le drame dans la langue française," 44).

The textual devices Novarina employs for producing incantatory prose are multiple and varied. Alongside the classic poetic devices of alliteration, assonance, rhyme, homophony, and lexical and grammatical repetition, Novarina also uses his hallmark seemingly interminable accumulative lists: 1,111 birds at the end of *Le discours aux animaux* (*Discourse to the Animals*);[24] two pages of plants in *L'espace furieux*;[25] three pages of characters' names in *Transfiguration*;[26] the successive stream of subordinate clauses in *La scène* (58); and the hyperbolic use of numbers, for example "23,968," in the same play (143). Novarina explains, in "Entrée dans le théâtre des oreilles," how he employs these lists, which he calls "a fugue, a flight, an accumulation, a massing, a heaping, a verbigeration, an avalanche" (75). These processes are employed purely for the purposes of rendering his texts more, or less dense, as he explains in "Le drame dans la langue française": "The need to aerate with numbers, with figures, with artists, with articles, with measures, with dates, with music-hall, with entertainers, with the measures of figures of kilometers covered. Asphyxia" (48). Similarly, Novarina uses words, expressions, and whole paragraphs from foreign or dead languages, especially Latin, or else from invented languages, for example "flvndvmnlslmnvmn" in *La scène* (71), to craft what he calls in "Le drame dans la langue française" a "lingual hubbub" that obtrudes common-sense interpretation (62).[27] And his technique of "auto-generation" can be noted most clearly in his accumulation of words according to their suffixes (-ion; -thrope; conjugations like -ons, -ont) or prefixes (anti-; trans-; antropo-). As Novarina states, he

---

23. Novarina, *Le babil des classes dangereuses* (Paris: P.O.L., 1989), 214.
24. Novarina, *Le discours aux animaux* (Paris: P.O.L., 1987), 321–26.
25. Novarina, *L'espace furieux* (Paris: P.O.L., 1997), 144–45.
26. Novarina, *Transfiguration,* in *Scherzo* 11, special issue on Novarina (Oct. 2000): 20–22.
27. Pierre Michon's narrator in *Vies minuscules* (Paris: Gallimard, 1988) describes beautifully the sonorous properties of Latin, as he alludes to the church services of a local priest: "the words suddenly streamed, ardent against the cool vaults, like copper marbles thrown into a lead basin; the incomprehensible Latin text was of a moving clearness; the syllables under his tongue multiplied infinitely, the words cracked like whips" (182–83).

"changes all the endments of the radicles." In an essay on glossolalia—
a flow of phonemically segmented linguistic utterances constituted almost entirely of neologisms—Michel de Certeau criticizes the fact that
analysts frequently try to reduce the "desire to say" of glossolalia to the
"desire to say something." Instead, de Certeau advises the reader/lis-
tener to appreciate "the serious and jubilatory game of saying."[28] The
linguistic devices Novarina uses to generate what, in an interview with
Noëlle Renaude, he calls "pure phonic gush" ensure a perpetual referential deferral of meaning, and consequently unfetter language from
the utilitarianism of communication, releasing it into an elocutionary
euphoria.[29]

Since Novarina's texts are structured predominantly according to
their acoustics rather than their semantics, the actors who perform
them require specific vocal skills. Veteran Novarinian actors Roséline
Goldstein and Daniel Znyk highlight the great challenge Novarina's
texts pose to the actor: "Playing Novarina is, for the actor, a terrible
challenge that requires courage. You must enjoy putting yourself in the
way of danger."[30] Novarina says in "Letter to the Actors" that the actor's approach to the text should be almost gustative, rather than intellectual: "You must not be clever, but rather put your abdomen, teeth,
and jaws to work" (95).[31] The actor must develop a sense of how her/
his mouth, breath, and body will move, to what rhythm they will beat,
to produce the text, as Novarina explains in "Letter to the Actors": "It's
by starting from letters, by stumbling over consonants, by breathing in
vowels, by chewing, by vigorously working it over, that we discover
how it breathes and how it is rhymed" (101). I have explained how Novarina's texts are segmented into "slogans" or "sessions" "without a
thread" at a semantic or thematic level. He insists in "Letter to the Ac-

28. Michel de Certeau, "Utolies vocales: Glossolalies," *Traverses*, special issue *La voix* 20 (November 1980): 30.

29. Novarina, "Le désir du vertige: entretien avec Noëlle Renaude," *Théâtre/Public* 72 (1986): 9.

30. See Roséline Goldstein, "L'acteur transparent," and Daniel Znyk, "L'orgueilleuse modestie de l'acteur," *Théâtre/Public* 101–102 (Sept.-Dec. 1991): 16.

31. Claude Régy provides an illuminating insight into his rehearsal techniques, echo-ing Novarina's request that actors recognize breath and sound around which the text is constructed: "I make the actors over-articulate. We realize that in the actual articulation there is an energy, there is meaning. . . . The enlargement of sounds with a magnifying glass immediately creates a different way of perceiving the text. . . . The sentence circu-lates like a ribbon and passes through everyone. In this way we are not just playing each scene, we are playing the total matter of the work" (Claude Régy, "Les sons et les sens," in *De la parole aux chants*, ed. Georges Banu [Arles: Actes-Sud, 1995], 90–91).

tors" that actors do not attempt to articulate his texts according to rational logic: "Don't cut everything up, don't cut everything into intelligent slices, into intelligible slices, as normal French diction would have us do today, since the actor's work consists of cutting up the text like a salami, underlining certain words, loading them up with intentions" (95). The segmentation of speech and the distribution of pauses must not take place according to a subject-verb-object logic, where words are stressed depending on their contextual semantic significance. Novarina provides coherence, however, at an auditory, rhythmic level, as he explains in "Attraction":

> In contrast to the style that is segmented, chopped, that paralyzes, prevents the deep wave, the stream of thought, use the greatest respiratory length like swimming breaststroke ever more expansively, lengthening breath, movement, understanding that thought is in the order not of apprehension but of respiratory renewal, understanding that it is set in motion at the same time as language and the body. (163)

Actors must construct what critic Richard Monod calls a "text-for-speaking"[32]: they must treat the text like a musical score, where the pronunciation of every vowel, consonant, and syllable, the location of each stress and pause, must be meticulously interpreted. In French, "l'accent tonique" (primary stress) generally falls on the last syllable of a word and "l'accent d'attaque" (secondary stress) falls on the penultimate syllable. The vowels of these syllables (all syllables are formed around a vowel phoneme) are therefore lengthened, and the intensity of breath utilized to pronounce them must be increased. In French, the length of any other syllables in a word is not specified, which accords actors considerable interpretative freedom, and the Novarinian actor must decide how to weight each syllable. Like with verse, actors must articulate and reveal the repetition of sounds and rhythms that create the acoustic armature of Novarina's texts. In the following example from *La scène*, which I leave in the original French in order for Novarina's linguistic craft to be seen clearly, he distributes primary stresses evenly, to divide the sentence into four "verses" with a meter of 3-3-5-3-5-3: "Moi Adam, / point vivant, / je n'ai que la terre / pour matière, / je n'ai que la mort / pour segment!" (54, my emphasis and segmentation). Novarina also enhances rhythmic regularity by enabling rhymes, for example between *Adam, vivant,* and *segment,* and *terre* and *ma-*

32. Quoted in Pierre Voltz, "La voix parlée," 76.

tière. The even distribution of stresses also systematizes the voice's intonation, or melodic line, since pitch rises on stressed syllables. In this example from *La scène,* which I also leave in French, an intonational pattern is repeated with each repetition of the phrase "qui engendre":

> Les Psaumistes du Repas de Terre *engendrent* les Sabriers Gendre et Ut,
> les Sabriers Urde et Urcet *engendrent* les Sapiants de Nurcie et Potrique
> *qui engendreront* les Savatiens et Savatitiens Urs et Manger *qui engendrent* les Spermidés *qui engendrent* les Splendeurs Plurielles. (18–
> 19, my emphasis)

Each time a phrase is repeated, the same intonation is likely to be used. The alliteration of /s/ highlighted here also augments the acoustic homogeneity. The actor must be able to recognize Novarina's intricate structuring of sound, in order to give formal coherence to the play-text. In addition, actors must master their use of breath—like a swimmer, he says—especially in order to manage the vast lists I have mentioned. In an interview with Noëlle Renaude, Novarina says "good actors don't let their breathing be heard, they inhale all the time, at the slightest opportunity; but in a way that is absolutely inaudible and invisible" (12).[33] Régy states that, like movement and gesture, speech is a physical act performed by the body, and thus requires physical training.[34] And in "Entrée dans le théâtre des oreilles," Novarina describes the intensive preparation required for the vocal organs in terms of a daily work-out: "He thought he had constructed a method for making his mouth say everything it wanted. He wanted to flex it, to work it, to submit it every day to breath training [*l'entraînement respiré*] to strengthen it, to soften it, to develop its muscles with perpetual exercise" (67).

Many contemporary theater directors complain that actors do not receive appropriate training in order to transpose a play-text into a "text-for-speaking." In many acting schools, training programs are dic-

33. Farid Paya, a theater-maker whose work revolves around the actor's use of voice, explains the physical training required. Like for singing, the actor must understand that the voice derives from all parts of the anatomy. S/he must learn how to position the soles of the feet squarely on the ground, stand upright, distribute body weight evenly, breathe from the diaphragm, and control the speed and intensity of air by regulating movement in the throat, glottis, and rib cage. Paya states, "we could not understand the voice without understanding the organicity of the body taken in its globality" (Paya, *Théâtre/Public* special issue *Les chemins de la voix*, 91).
34. Régy, "Les sons et les sens," in *De la parole aux chants*, 88.

tated by television's needs for psychological character acting.[35] In 2005, a play by Novarina was staged for the first time at the Comédie Française—*L'espace furieux*. In spite of the fact that Novarina himself directed the production, the rhythmic acousticity of the delivery was insufficiently foregrounded. Save the outstanding exception of veteran Novarinian performer Daniel Znyk (who played the Sosie), actors did not seem to interpret the text with their ears, breath, and beat, as Novarina recommends. Novarina's play-texts depend on the geometric configurations of repeated syllables, words, phrases, and rhythms that provide the play with coherence, seemingly lacking in this production. The actor of Novarina's texts needs to possess the full range of tones and rhythms located in the interstitial space between speech and song, text and voice.

Novarina appears at times to claim that his "languism" and its euphoric, harmonic utterance by the actor, not only transcend the humdrum, the routine of language found in the press, media, and everyday speech, but moreover, that they become pure matter, complete non-representational presence. In "Letter to the Actors" he states that "the actor is neither an instrument nor an interpreter, but rather the only place where it happens, and that's all" (102); "The actor does not execute but is executed, does not interpret but penetrates himself, does not reason but makes his entire body resonate" (103). Novarina wishes to affirm, with reason, that reality and art are not defined by, and must not be confined to the syntactics and semantics of common speech. But does the voice in his theater constitute sound as pure presence—presense? Novarina sometimes describes his language of sound in sacred terms, as in "Attraction": "To go far and deep into the underneath of language, into the unseen of language; until it is proven that it is matter. God-matter-itself" (167). Artaud's messianic exclamation "burn forms to reach life. It is to learn to stand up in the incessant movement of forms that one successively destroys," resonates with Novarina's desire to "fissure" language and attain pure unmediated "matter."[36] For Artaud, when the voice is no longer codified into linguistic signs, it be-

---

35. See, for example, the discussion between theater makers Claude Buchvald and Alain Astruc (Alain Astruc, *Or, Hors, Oreille* [Paris: La Guillotine, 2001], 164); and the complaints by Régy ("Les sons et les sens," 88). Few acting teachers, with the exception of Michel Bernardy, who worked at the Paris Conservatoire National Supérieur d'Art Dramatique during the 1970s and 1980s, provide dedicated courses on vocal training.

36. Artaud, "Messages révolutionnaires," *Œuvres complètes* vol. 8 (Paris: Gallimard: 1971), 202.

comes "pure forces," "natural forces."[37] He even suggests that precise sounds or breaths might evoke specific moods or emotions: "breath accompanies emotion and one can penetrate emotion through breath; on the condition of having been able to discern among the breaths the one that corresponds to the required emotion."[38] Is Novarina an Artaudian, who proposes an iconoclastic sacrifice of abstract textual forms that will lead to a unity of being between anatomy and expression? Does the voice for Novarina constitute an essential, non-representational plenitude, presence, matter?

I think Novarina has no pretensions toward the transcendence of representation. He enlists the poetic signifier and its realization through the actor's voice, in order to loosen language that has become stone-like and sclerosed by unproductive and sterile repetitive use. In this way, instead of being the servile mouthpieces of language; instead of repeating language like automatons, speakers can renew and recreate language like a sculptor can shape stone. But this language is still just that—language—and not unequivocal bodily expression, as Novarina makes clear in "Le drame dans la langue française":

> In contrast with those who serve tongues, him, he loosens it, undoes the centers and makes a hole, in the place where that tongue was most knotted. In contrast with those who clutch their tongue, use it in ter-

37. "En finir avec les chefs-d'œuvre," in *Le théâtre et son double*, 127, 128. To label Artaud an unequivocal essentialist would betray the fundamentally contradictory nature of his writing, since Artaud often refers to theater as "illusion," "virtual," "hieroglyphs." Moreover, since Artaud presents his poetics of corporeality on stage, the body and voice are automatically expropriated, virtualized, aestheticized. In "La parole soufflée," Derrida applies a deconstructionist exegesis to Artaud, stating that central to his oeuvre is an acute consciousness that all representation—*parole* or "speech"—is irreducibly *soufflée:* "prompted" by inherited discourses, and "spirited away" from any essential union with the body, once it is interpreted by others. For Derrida, at the heart of Artaud's exploration of the voice, is a conscious acceptance of the impossibility of this project to reconcile flesh and spirit. In "The Theater of Cruelty and the Closure of Representation," Derrida states: "Artaud knew that the theater of cruelty neither begins nor is completed within the purity of simple presence, but rather is already within representation" (*Writing and Difference*, 313). In his last study of Artaud, however, Derrida foregrounds primarily the essentialism of physicality in Artaud's works. He describes the letters and words inscribed on Artaud's pictures as literal matter beyond transposition and figuration (see *Artaud le Moma*). I feel it is essential to respect Artaud's irreconcilable and conflicting gestures toward both poststructuralism and essentialism, and also to respect his paradoxical tension between the total body, and total figuration of the body, for these unresolved ambiguities have ensured his enduring impact on contemporary theater.
38. Artaud, "Théâtre sacré," *Œuvres complètes* vol. 4 (Paris: Gallimard, 1964), 282.

ror, do not show their tongue in case anyone sees its tip and where it is pointing, him, he shows his tongue, its tip, so we can see and really say it's not he who is speaking. (61)

For Novarina to claim that his poeticized language of the voice was any more immediate or direct than more common discursive forms would be tantamount to liberating the voice from the confines of the text, only to incarcerate it within the localized anatomical zones of the voice. The voice as incantation in Novarina's theater does not precede all texts. He describes the actor's presence on stage as "very close," but "full of holes."[39] As he states, "it's not he who is speaking," since the voice as sound, when configured into verbal text, becomes no less representational, contingent, formalized, or artificial than any other form of textual language, with a void. This absence will then prevent any one discourse from imposing ideological dominance, since the universality of artifice guarantees the total relativity of all truths, realities, and values—including the materiality of the voice—and the transcendence of none.

Novarina, more than any other contemporary French playwright, enables the voice to become non-denotative, non-connotative acoustic matter. Language must, as he says in "Le drame dans la langue française," "produce. Produce and not represent" (29). But while sound in his theater evades representation at a micro-textual level, it is reincorporated into symbolization at a macro-textual level. He places the voice centerstage in theater, but reminds the spectator that it is still theater, play, aesthetics: "[the actor] lowers all his flesh for us deep down to the bottom in front of everyone down to the hole at the bottom through which light and voice pass. All this through playing himself. And through native nothingness. Through playing, through such great playing, that when he plays the actor has emptiness everywhere."[40] I feel, however, that this "playing" delivers a serious message. Novarina's celebratory use of the voice in theater poses as a metaphor for the refusal of complacency, passive acceptance, and the unquestioning habit of repetition. Alain Astruc, a theater practitioner who worked closely with one of Novarina's directors, Claude Buchvald, theorizes in *Or, Hors, Oreille* the utilization of the voice in ways invaluable to understanding Novarina. For Astruc, the *voix*—voice—constitutes a *voie*—a metaphorical way, or means of moving away from

39. Novarina, "Entrée perpétuelle," *Théâtre/Public* 66 (1985): 11.
40. "Entree perpétuelle," 11.

the stasis of theatrical naturalism and linguistic realism (169). In *Devant la parole*, Novarina employs this same metaphor of the *voie:*

> We all know very well, deep down, that within is a place that is not *mine*, not of the *me*, but of a passage, of an opening through which a foreign breath seizes us. Within us, in the deepest place within us, the way [*voie*] is wide open: we are, so to speak, *full of holes*. (14–15, Novarina's emphasis)

The hole, or absence of inherent meaning in all representation, constitutes an inexhaustible vacuity that can be filled and refilled with renewed forms. It therefore paves a "way [that] is wide open" toward new possibilities. "The future belongs to those who are not afraid of emptiness," declares Novarina in "Entrée dans le théâtre des oreilles" (80). Instead of using language simply as a reflection or a shadow of our present history of familiar faces and predictable events, we must use it to envisage renewed, reinvigorated lives, as Novarina recommends in the same essay: "Not reproduce everything one has in front but reproduce everything one has behind. See behind one's head. Everything that trembles behind one's head, not the fixed block in front. Reproduce the other space, the space in which man must live and die tomorrow" (74–75).[41] I believe that Novarina's exploration of a vast plurality of acoustically opaque rhythmic structures and his celebration of the voice's potential provide an example of the determination and capacity to pose a radical opposition to the solidity and inflexibility of established institutions. As Novarina himself states in this essay's epigraph, "Something must fall. Afterwards, everything is free."

41. He also writes in *Devant la parole*, "Speech is not commentary, a shadow of the real, the cashing of the world into words, but something come into the world as if to tear us out of it" (17).

MARY NOONAN

L'art de l'écrit s'incarnant: The Theater of Noëlle Renaude

In diminishing the mimetic function of theater—theater as representation of "reality"—a number of contemporary writers for the French
stage are following in the line of authors such as Samuel Beckett and
Marguerite Duras, for whom the stage was essentially a "de-realizing"
space, a place that denies the reality of everything that appears within
its frame. A form of theater that seeks to undermine mimetic representation is free to explore the equivocal nature of identity, and the relationship between identity and language. According to Patrice Pavis,
alterity is the subject of new French writing for the stage: "The over-
arching theme is that of the human being's struggle to make sense of a
world that has lost its center, a world without stable values. Has theater become focused then on the question of alterity?"[1] While I agree
that many of the writers for the contemporary French stage present a
de-centred universe (Koltès, Minyana, Novarina, Renaude), I would
have to disagree on the question of alterity. The strand of theater I will
be examining here—the plays of Noëlle Renaude framed mainly by
Valère Novarina's thoughts on the nature of theater—are not preoccupied with alterity, intersubjectivity, or questions of inter-relationality.
What this theater is concerned with is the promotion of theater as a
place of reading, that private and individual act. Here, the spectator is
engaged in a reading of the actor's body as it sounds the writer's tran-
scription of her origins in the in-between of body and word.

The theaters of Renaude and Novarina set out to dismantle the grids
we apply to knowledge within the representational frame of page or
stage: the dialectical opposition of subject and object, identity and dif-

---

1. All translations are my own. Patrice Pavis, *Le théâtre contemporain* (Paris: Armand Colin, 2004), 218.

YFS 112, *The Transparency of the Text,* ed. Donia Mounsef and Josette Féral,
© 2007 by Yale University.

ference, presence and absence on which specular systems of representation rely. Novarina, in his "Lettre aux acteurs," calls on the actor to abandon the grid of intelligent diction "where the actor's work consists of cutting his text up into slices of salami, underlining certain words, loading them with intention, breaking language up into segments, just like you learn to do in school."[2] This would seem to suggest that not only are plot and character abandoned, but meaning or sense at the level of the sentence are also evacuated, in favor of a "chute dans la parole," where "the spoken word is like a tube of air, a tube with sphincters, a column pressing air out at irregular intervals, in spasms, sluicing it out, letting it leak, stopping and starting the flow, pressurizing it." (*Le théâtre des paroles*, 10). The stage, according to Novarina's conception of it, is no longer a space of representation, of images, but what he calls "the boxing-ring of the spoken word, the enclosure of language, an arena of transfiguration and metamorphoses, a place of attractions, of transmutation"[3]—a space where actors and spectators come to be broken down in language. Participants in this theater are stunned, dazed, stripped of linguistic, cultural, and ideological defenses and brought to a place where they can be amazed by the simple collision of body and word in the voice, carried on the breath. Page, stage, and body are enmeshed in this theater, which stages above all the materiality of the word, written and spoken. Deprived of the usual hiding-places in logical thought, the body of the writer/reader/actor/spectator is built up again through language and breath. The form of theater proposed by Novarina is a theater that is an attempt to move participants away from the tyrannies of form, naming, and ideology, and toward an affair of muscle and breath:

> Le texte devient pour l'acteur une nourriture, un corps. Chercher la musculature de c'vieux cadavre imprimé, ses mouvements possibles, par où il veut bouger . . . C'est ça la vraie lecture, celle du corps, de l'acteur.

> The text becomes food for the actor, a body. He must find the muscles of this old printed cadaver, its potential for movement, find out where it wants to go . . . That's what reading really is, a reading of the body, of the actor. (*Le théâtre des paroles*, 20–21)

---

2. Valère Novarina, "Lettre aux acteurs" in *Le théâtre des paroles* (Paris: P.O.L., 1989), 10.
3. Novarina, "La parole opère l'espace," in *Lire* 400, (Juillet-août 2001): 100–01.

In this theater, then, the actor—and we must all become actors if we are to access these texts—is called upon to open up the body/text with voice and breath, to follow the text's breath patterns in order to find its rhythms, and not to force it into blocks of "meaning," which it will in any case resist. Pavis suggests that a similar method should be used by the reader of these texts, and that this new form of theater therefore calls into question the traditional definitions and separations between writer, reader, actor, and spectator (*Le théâtre contemporain*, 228). The distance between orality and textuality is not wide, according to Novarina: writing is a precipitate of the writer's body, the product of a "chute," a descent into language. The actor is called upon to re-visit the writer's original experience whereby the acting goes through a process of passivity, of laissez-faire, of letting go ("La parole opère l'espace," 101–104).

According to this view of writing for the stage, the writer must attempt to achieve an abnegation of the ocular-centric self, and enter an acute state of listening. Writer, reader, actor, spectator are all actors on the stage of the page, in the audio-vocal theater of writing. And yet, Noëlle Renaude achieves something more than this, for her theater is both a theater of the spoken word and a theater that attempts to stage the visual dimension of the printed page, and the reader's movement through it. My claim for her theater from the outset then is that it is perhaps the first theater to truly stage the *movement* of the self in the in-between of body and language, in the gap between the visual image (the body narrating) and the narrative text (the narrated body). Hers is a theater of the text in the true sense of the term, in that it stages the activities of writing and reading, and engages actor and spectator in these activities. It is also a theater that stages movement in space—the crossings and re-crossings of a page by a body or bodies.

Throughout the 1990s, Renaude experimented with theatrical form in a series of plays that take narrative representation to its limits. Her theater has evolved from one that stages a terrifying babel of voices emanating from the body of one actor to one where a small group of actors gives voice to the making of a world in words. This is not a theater of address in the conventional sense—it is not concerned with dialogue, or with intersubjectivity. Renaude is concerned only to evoke a world on the borders of self and world. She plunges actor and spectator into the roots of the French language, into an excavation of the language's stratified histories. Thus, the experience of acting or viewing one of these plays is that of wandering, without apparent direction, in the magma of a particular language and culture, an experience that exercises the auditory memory and imagination:

> La terre de vos ancêtres? Charmant comme paysage. Les miens étaient de Thionville pour une branche et de Sarreguemines pour l'autre. Vous connaissez Jean Prélat? Il a herité d'une baraque un peu comme la vôtre, dans une campagne sinistrée un peu comme ici. Du côté de Guéret?

> The land of your ancestors? Lovely spot. One branch of mine was from around Thionville, and the others were from Sarreguemines. Do you know Jean Prélat? He inherited a shack—something like yours—in a townland that was a bit of a disaster zone—a bit like this place. Over near Guéret?[4]

In her theater, page, stage, body, are surveyed, their measure taken by writing, but—what country, friends, is this?[5] This is the question that is often on the lips of spectators at Renaude's plays. For the director Frédéric Fisbach, who directed Renaude's *Les cendres et les lampions* in 1993, "it was the space of memory."[6] In this 'interior' space, there was no question of "exits" and "entrances" by the actors. Here, Renaude gives voice to 94 "apparitions," who represent between twenty and twenty-five centuries. In order to bring about the apparition, animation, and disappearance of these 94 "characters," these 25 centuries, Fisbach chose to work with five actors—four women and a man—and 94 chairs. The author uses the device "je suis né, je suis mort" (I was born, I died) as the starting-point for giving voice to a multitude of "figures" (in talking about character in Renaude's theater, nouns such as "figure," "apparition" or even "silhouette" seem more appropriate).[7] These figures are introduced by a narrator—the author?—who simply announces the name of the figure. And yet, the text requires the actor to create the entire drama of this family's history from his enunciation of the successive first names of "apparitions" summoned to the stage: "Baptiste . . . Amédée . . . Jules . . . Bertrand. . . ." What Fisbach has to say about the role of the narrator, is revelatory: "His task was to make these first names spring to life, so that one would be able to tell, from

4. Noëlle Renaude, *Ma Solange, comment t'écrire mon désastre, Alex Roux 1–3* (Paris: Éditions Théâtrales, 1996, 1997, 1998, new edition containing all three volumes, 2004), 15. I will refer to the 2004 edition throughout.

5. Shakespeare, *Twelfth Night*, Act I, scene ii.

6. Interview with Frédéric Fisbach, quoted in *Trois pièces contemporaines* (Paris: Gallimard, 2002), 132.

7. Jean-Pierre Ryngaert and Julie Sermon, *Le personnage théâtral contemporain: décomposition, recomposition* (Paris: Théâtrales, 2006), 70.

the sound of the way he said the name, ah yes, he knew that one, that one had a bad reputation, that one was the family idiot" (Interview with Fisbach, 135).

The first of the theatrical conventions to be undermined by Renaude therefore is that of character. And while the diminishment of the dramatic character is not new, Renaude takes it to new depths: "Can the name alone create the character, free of all other fictional detail?" she asks in relation to her play *La comédie de Sainte Etienne*.[8] In their recent book on the status of the character in contemporary French theater, Jean-Pierre Ryngaert and Julie Sermon note that a number of contemporary writers for the French stage (Vinaver, Koltès, Lagarce, Renaude, Minyana) have manipulated the naming of characters in order to counter any tendency toward representational versimilitude. Instead, these writers place their characters in an "ailleurs," an elsewhere, alienating both actor and spectator from the character, to make of him or her a creature of sound, of language: "The names—colorful, exotic—are almost too effective in evoking what they are meant to evoke: they are acoustic snapshots, eminently representative" (*Le personnage théâtral contemporain*, 74). These nominal vestiges of character are effective in pulling the play away from the real and into its own poetic space.

In addition to the nominal identity and figural or spectral nature of her characters, the devices of accumulation, excess, and proliferation are features of Renaud's theatrical universe. The story of the creation of *Ma Solange, comment t'écrire mon désastre, Alex Roux* is by now well known. Written for, and with, a single actor, Christophe Brault, between 1994 and 1998, it features at least two thousand figures or voices, and runs to 16 hours of theater if played in its entirety—which it has been, on many occasions. The eponymous Alex Roux is a constant, if intermittent figure throughout, a mediator for the proliferation of fleeting speakers that appear and disappear and seem to represent a wide range of types and spatial and temporal locations—a frenzied journey through the history of the types of people who might have inhabited, who still inhabit, a rural French townland. A small number of characters recur throughout the text—which runs to 351 pages in the 2004 *Théâtrales* edition—giving it a vestigial structure or scaffold.

8. Interview with Noëlle Renaude, "Entretien avec Noëlle Renaude conduit par Emmanuelle Borgeon, Joseph Danan et Julie Sermon," in *L'avenir d'une crise: Écritures dramatiques contemporaines (1980–2000). Études théâtrales* 24–25 (2002): 240.

During the period of writing, Renaude produced portions of text, piecemeal, which were performed by Brault in theaters around France. The play contains "le journal crypté d'une écriture en train de s'inventer," according to Renaude (Interview with Renaude, 238). The secret diary of the writing process, inscribed in the text, tells of "how writing comes into being, how it suffers, how it falls apart, how it recovers abandoned fragments, how it sets itself free from fiction" (Interview with Renaude, 238). The coming and going between the writing process, the work with the actor, re-writing and staging enabled a liberation from the codes and conventions of theatrical forms and institutions, and allowed her to produce writing that was based on the principle of sutained discontinuity and fragmentation. This process, which resulted in the successive invention of two thousand "figures" raised one key question: how to stage "this piling up of voices" (Interview with Renaude, 238), the seemingly impossible task for a single actor of incarnating such a multitude. According to Renaude, the body of the actor in this theater is, first and foremost, a 'corps vocal'—his physical body is not called upon directly by the text, but it gradually invents a choreography of bodily movement in space that mimics the movement of the writing itself: "a choreography of perpetual beginnings, one that re-creates the typography of the page, the movement of the writing (long, short, broken, punctuated, un-punctuated" (Interview with Renaude, 235).

Created according to a principle of discontinuity and breakdown between fragments, the play is a marker for where Renaude wanted to take her writing for the stage—to the limits of the genre. The challenge she set herself early in her career was that of resisting the generic boundaries—in order to see how they would hold—to work with impossibility, unrepresentability. In the course of 350 pages of writing, she summons two thousand figures through fragments of encounters, scraps of memories and anecdotes, sections of letters, lists. An array of forms is also traversed: story, theater, diary, letter, dialogue, monologue, eclogue, correctional tales for children ("LES JOLIES PETITES HISTOIRES de Tante Mick"). The dead are resuscitated and speak their own tongue; there are talking tomatoes, frogs and stones (dolmens), and a talking moon. And all of this is delivered by a single actor. Form in this theater amounts to the shape conferred on blocks of writing by the breathing body. The actor twists his body into the shape of the writing, its syntax. What counts above all in this kind of work on a text is its rhythm, Renaude's theatrical writing being closer to the form of poetry than to narrative fiction.

> Vivons et tentons d'y aller voir, aux replis des ces secrets noueux, ce qui
> nous agite et nous fait tant hurler.
> J'ai mal, Solange, de ne plus rien y voir.

> Let's live and try to discover, in the folds of these old secrets, the rea-
> sons for all our agitation, our howling.
> It hurts, Solange, no longer being able to see anything there. (*Ma So-
> lange*, 272)

This play, and Renaude's subsequent writing for the stage, presents a
world teeming with life, with bodies, with languages. Her theatrical
writing starts from a principle of excavation, followed by profusion and
expansion, multiplication to the point of excess—a world spilling over,
overflowing its frame or limits:

> Entendez-vous ce martèlement, ils montent des hors-fonds, des abîmes,
> des rives sombres . . . ils avancent, sous nos pas, nous rient la gueule
> béante de nous voir ici même à rectifier leurs danses.

> Do you hear that hammering, they're coming up from the depths, from
> the abyss, from the dark shores . . . they're advancing beneath our feet,
> howling with laughter at our attempts to correct their dances. (*Ma
> Solange*, 235)

In undermining syntax and punctuation, blurring the generic boundaries and confusing the distinctions between popular speech and discourse of the highest register, Renaude uses the stage to put both language and the actor's body under extreme pressure. The ultimate target
of this writing is the frame itself, that of the page or computer screen,
that of the stage. The writer's desire is to explore, and possibly explode,
the frame, the limit of what can and cannot enter the space:

> Tout texte est une carte à décrypter, avec ses itinéraires balisés, ses car-
> refours, ses plis. Au bord des cartes, le monde ne s'arrête pas. Il continue
> à exister. À son echelle à lui. Le texte, lui, comme la carte, soumis à de
> constantes variations d'échelle, s'occupe à occuper le monde.

> Every text is a map to be read, with its routes marked out, its crossroads,
> its folds. Beyond the edge of the map, the world doesn't stop, it contin-
> ues to exist, on its own scale. The text, like the map, subjected to con-
> stant variations in scale, gets on with the business of occupying the
> world.[9]

---

9. Renaude, *Par les routes* (Paris: Théâtre Ouvert/Enjeux, 2005), 110.

Here Renaude raises the question of occupying space—space of textual and human bodies. The space of the text is a function of the writing as it emerges from the writer's body, the weave of conscious and unconscious selves. The actor is called upon to inhabit the space of writing, to live inside it, to bend her/himself to its rhythms. It is clear that what Renaude is staging is the page of writing, with a body or bodies moving across it. And the question she poses for her writing project is that of the limits of that page, where it begins and ends, and the extent to which she can experiment with its apparent fixity, explode its borders.

A theater then of dispersal and displacement, of voices and fragments of writing untethered, adrift. This is writing that does not envisage a form. No formal provision is made at the outset by the writer. It is, after all, a theater of disaggregation, one that makes identification with the stage image difficult if not impossible. The image of the self projected by Renaude's theater is that of a displaced migrant wandering off the map, in unfamiliar landscapes, without signposts. A number of the more recent plays—*Promenades* (2003), *Ceux qui partent à l'aventure* (2005), *Par les routes* (2006)—use the trope of the wanderer. In *Ceux qui partent à l'aventure*, one of her latest plays to be published,[10] the story of the search for their missing son by the parents of a man who disappeared following his bankruptcy, is contained within a framing narrative, that of a group of walkers hiking in a landscape somewhere in France. The play opens with the exchanges of these hikers, who become increasingly intrigued by the story of the bankrupt young man who disappeared. Gradually, this anecdote in turn explodes into a series of other "stories" or fictional modules, recounting the efforts of various people (his best friend, his parents, his ex-partner) to make financial gain from the man's disappearance. His mother, in visiting the morgues of France in search of her son, begins to invent obituaries for the abandoned bodies she visits. Background and foreground are blurred as a plethora of fictions accumulates, and the writing moves back and forth between the initial story of the hikers, the second story of the missing man, and the multiple tertiary stories that spring from this. An added difficulty for the spectator/reader is that the fragments are not chronological, there is no spatial or temporary coherence. A possible thread uniting the fictions is the story of a country—France—traversed by a multiplicity of bodies, stories, and histories.

However, to add further to the confusion, Renaude has interspersed

10. Renaude, *Des tulipes/Ceux qui partent à l'aventure* (Paris: Théâtrales, 2006).

the text with pictograms, and plays freely with layout, fonts, and other typographical features. According to director Robert Cantarella, for whom the play was written, the text calls for, and engages, the full panoply of theatrical languages in ways that other pieces of writing for the stage do not. Her writing demands to be read, first and foremost, and yet, initial readings render little by way of understanding: "The text presents itself to be looked at and read. These two dimensions are equally important. The text is on the right of the page, so let's say it from the right of the stage."[11] Cantarella describes his process when working with actors on Renaude's plays as one driven by the imperative of delving into the writing, its rhythms, its physical disposition on the page. Speaking of his work on the 1998 production of *Fiction d'hiver* at the Théâtre Ouvert, Cantarella describes the actors' attempts to sketch the links and transitions in the text, to situate themselves in relation to the voices of the text. Gradually, they trace the map of the text, which is both a chart of the movement of writing across a page and the movement of a body in/through that writing. The result is, or should be, a performance that lets the framework or scaffolding of the writing and the actors' work on it, show through. Cantarella likens the pleasure of this type of performance—for both actor and spectator—to that of the pleasure given by the line drawing as art form, communicating the sense of a gesture that is reaching toward, but never reaching, completion or closure (*Par les routes,* 164–65).

The "chantier," a form of work in progress structure offered to artists by the Théâtre Ouvert in Paris[12] provides the right environment for this type of work on a text, and many of Renaude's plays have been performed there, including her most recent. *Par les routes*[13] was staged in January 2006, under the direction of Frédéric Maragnani. Described in the publicity as a "theatrical road movie" and by the author herself as a "dramatic poem," the play is written in short lines that mimic verse, where there is no attribution of character. Two actors sit in what appear to be car seats, facing the audience; behind them is draped a large white screen. As they begin to speak, a non-stop flow of words, phrases,

11. Robert Cantarella, "L'art de l'écrit s'incarnant" in Renaude, *Des tulipes/Ceux qui partent à l'aventure,* 7.
12. See David Bradby and Annie Sparks, *Mise en Scène: French Theater Now* (London: Methuen, 1997) for an overview of French theatrical institutions, and an interview with Micheline and Lucien Attoun, directors of Théâtre Ouvert in Paris, which has staged and promoted Renaude's writing since the mid-1980s.
13. Renaude, *Par les routes* (Paris: Théâtre Ouvert/Enjeux, 2005).

and pictograms streams across the screen—the road signs, place names, tourist information, and advertising material that is the stuff of any motorway journey. The two men are "on the road," traveling, it seems, from the Île de France region, though the center of France and on to the Italian Alps. In the course of their journey, they make stops and detours, encounter animals, traffic jams, and a range of strange characters, all of whom are played by the two actors. Both men have recently lost their mothers, and so, it seems, have many of the people they meet along the way: "It's crazy the way everyone's mother is dying at the moment" (*Par les routes*, 11). As they make their way across the map of France with difficulty, the writing creates the impression that they are not in fact advancing—the text itself comes full circle, the end re-joining the beginning. With elegance and humor—her signature "light touch"— Renaude brings us to the edge of representation, the horizon of language, where death resides: "The map is mute, and words open up a void, that of absence, of the death of Mothers."[14] From the pile-up of ordinary detail and banal memories, the circular, repetitive nature of loss emerges.

The challenge to the reader of the text is to distinguish the speech of the two men from the profusion of text emanating from the road signage. In the theater, the effect of this is that the spectator is placed from the outset in an interior world, where thoughts float freely: mesmerized by the hundreds of verbal messages wafting on the screen before her eyes, the spectator is both in the car as the road flies by, and in her own mind, with her thoughts. Thoughts that are stimulated by the words spoken on stage by the actors, as they lose their way, find it again, and generally enact the vagaries of their journey. According to Michel Corvin, what Renaude achieves here is nothing short of "writing the world": "What she proposes is not a theater in space, but a theater of space, in other words the *theatrum mundi*" ("L'esprit du lieu," 44). Hers is, therefore, first and foremost a spatial imagination. But this country is, in the end, the interior space of auditory memory and imagination. Ultimately, her theater charts the movement of words between interior, auditory space and the exterior visual field of the page/screen/stage. She engages us—reader, actor, spectator—in a staging of the everyday shiftings and flickerings of words in the subconscious; she

14. Michel Corvin, "L'esprit du lieu. D'Eschyle à Renaude" in *Théâtre/Public* 183/4 (2006): 36–44. This issue of the journal feataures a dossier "Autour de Noëlle Renaude," 25–47.

shows us our imbrication in language, how each word triggers a hinterland of historical, social, and cultural associations. And the hinterland, in this theater, is very much that of provincial France.

Renaude's theater "fait théâtre de la page" [makes a theater of the page] ("L'art de l'écrit s'incarnant," 8)—its writing does not aspire to a particular form or genre. Her focus is the movement of writing within the space of the page: "The author has few tools at her disposal: letters, words, grammar, her fingers, her keyboard, her pen, punctuation marks, a lot of blank space, the frame of the page and everything that can and cannot come within that frame" (*Par les routes*, 110). Interestingly, in her more recent plays, there is evidence of the effects of word processing on her writing—a text such as *Ceux qui partent à l'aventure*, for example, uses the full range of possibilities offered by the computer program, with the result that the writing metamorphoses into a myriad of different shapes—fonts, character effects, pictograms—and the layout on the page is dizzying in its capacity to explore every corner of the blank page, to inhabit the page as fully as possible. Such a text presents a number of challenges to actors and spectators attempting to "decode" it, but this is the desired effect: both reader and spectator are disorientated, deprived of their usual navigational tools and safety nets, and are cast adrift in the text. Technology, it would seem, has enabled Renaude to go further in her attempts to free her writing from theatrical norms and traditions.

The necessity of anchoring the theatrical text in a recognizable space has been abandoned. The theatrical space is henceforth "the place from where the text is spoken" (*Par les routes*, 109). The cartography engaged in by the writer, as she makes tracks across the space of the screen/page with words, is re-enacted in the imagination of the actor and spectator. Ultimately, actor and spectator are called upon to cross a field of landmines, and to allow themselves to be exploded by the text, to become disaggregated and dispersed across the page: "To read is to work the body . . . in response to the text's signs, to the languages that traverse it and give the words their shimmering depth."[15]

Renaude creates the conditions for a form of reading that will not deliver its meanings easily—the reader is in a position of lack, despite the profusion of words, voices, fragments. Ultimately, her theater is a true theater of the text, where the text demands first and foremost to

---

15. Roland Barthes, "Écrire la lecture" in *Oeuvres complètes III* (Paris: Seuil, nouvelle édition, 2002), 604.

be read, and read very closely. She draws the reader into an obsessive decoding that amounts to a form of map-reading. This focus on reading draws attention to the status of the word in her theater. According to the director Michel Cerda, "you need to have an almost pictorial appreciation of the shape of words, the shape of phrases, of written pages, of paragraphs."[16] This theater stages the sensuality of the form of words, of the form of the page, its borders, its margins, its blank spaces, the disposition of words in space. For Duras, the joy of theater was in "the extent of the precision in speaking the word, its measure, the perfection of that measure. . . . That is the incredible joy of theater."[17] They may seem like odd bed-fellows, yet the theaters of Duras and Renaude are both driven by a desire to represent the writing body, the body's struggle with words on a page—the body of the book, the book of the body. The possibility of graphic representation of writing's struggle with its limits, marked by the frame of the page, is one of theater's key attractions for writers seeking to stage the birth and death of the self in language.

For Valère Novarina, "there is nothing like the joy people get from coming to the theater to see the animal talking. We have come to see language. The action, in the theater, is that of seeing language, our flesh."[18] Novarina describes a form of theater that fuses the visible and the audible, textuality and orality. For him, the power of theater is that it can show that the material world is a world made of language: a place where it is possible to "to anchor language in the body again, make it resonate to the depths of matter" (Lire à trois cents yeux, 8). This seems to me to be a perfect description of Renaude's writing project for the stage. And although she claims the new technologies as a liberating force for her writing, what she is doing in the theater is re-affirming the bodily-sonorous nature of language, its resistance to mediatization, or even to interpretation. The word retains its quality of sign, and it is the relationship between bodies and signs in the hermetic space of the page that is played out on her stage. The challenge is that of finding one's way in the troubled terrain of writing by following a map made of voices coming from a multiplicity of different directions—which thread

16. Michel Cerda, preface to Renaude, À tous ceux Qui/La comédie de Saint Etienne/Le renard du Nord (Paris: Théâtrales, 2002), 8.

17. Filmed interview with Marguerite Duras by Michelle Porte, Savannah Bay, c'est toi (Paris: Institut National de l'Audiovisuel, 1983), broadcast on ARTE (19 March 1996).

18. Novarina, "Lire à trois cents yeux," in Théâtre: Le retour du texte?, Littérature 138 (June 2005): 7, 17.

should one follow, which voice should one focus on? The experience for the actor/spectator is ultimately one of wandering in a landscape peopled by voices that tell the troubled history of a body in language.

The theaters of Renaude and Novarina seek to develop a permeability to the qualities of sound: attentiveness; dynamic connection and exchange between body and world, body, and word; openness to indeterminacy, excess, inarticulacy, and traversal. Any theater that stimulates an intensity of auditory activity in its participants is attempting to make them vulnerable, to return them to the brink of identity, to open them to their origins in liquidity, in breath, in the fusion of the noises of the body with those of other bodies. These theaters seek to mine the disruptive and disintegrative qualities of sound and hearing, the auditory realm's potential to return us—writers, actors, spectators—to the equivocal nature of lives lived in the in-between of the material and the intelligible.

III. Disputed Textualities

JUDITH G. MILLER

Is There a Specifically Francophone African Stage Textuality?

We are the renters of the French language; we regularly pay our rent.
Even better, we contribute to improvements on the old house. That is,
we're embarking on the adventure of co-ownership.
—Sony Labou Tansi, 1989[1]

My culture isn't uniquely Ivoirian or French; it's also American from
all the films I've digested. . . . [I] try to find a kind of complexity in the
usual rapport with African identity, to force others to rethink
certitudes about the African soul.
—Koffi Kwahulé, 2002[2]

I cite above Sony Labou Tansi (1947–1995) and Koffi Kwahulé (b. 1956),
two of Francophone Africa's most potent playwrights, as a prelude to a
discussion of Francophone African stage textuality. To answer the
question about whether or not such a category legitimately exists, we
will need both to unpack the terms of the question and eventually to
ask what Labou Tansi means by "co-owning" the French language as
well as what Kwahulé suggests by refusing a fixed image of African
identity. Focusing on these authors as representative of contemporary
Francophone African theater situates the time frame encompassing my
discussion from the mid 1970s—and the end of the exhilarating phase
of the African independence period—to the present. While one can

1. Quoted in an invitation to an evening of Francophone theater at the Théâtre Paris-
Villette, April 2006, first appearing in an interview with Michèle Zalesski, "Locataires
de la même maison," Diagonales (9 janvier 1989): 4.
2. Quoted in Sylvie Chalaye, Afrique noire et dramaturgies contemporaines: Le
syndrôme Frankenstein (Paris: Editions théâtrales, 2004): 39.

YFS 112, The Transparency of the Text, ed. Donia Mounsef and Josette Féral,
© 2007 by Yale University.

trace the beginnings of Francophone African theater to 1933,[3] in the hands of Labou Tansi, African theater experienced a sea change that has oriented the production of African works ever since. No longer preoccupied primarily with celebrating historical subjects within Western theatrical conventions that foreground plot, character depiction, and the exploration of ideas, Labou Tansi, among others, introduced a performance mode and thematic concerns more apt by their immediate relevancy to engage African audiences.[4]

The move away from an effort to assimilate French cultural expression is one of the markers of what I call Francophone African literature—in this case, dramatic literature—which has a vexed relationship with both France and the French language, but which is still anchored in a self-conscious love of working with French as an expressive medium. In a typical Anglophone African jibe, Kenya writer Ngugi wa Thiong'o chides Francophone African writers for thinking that: "French is the linguistic ladder to Heaven."[5] Taking my cue from postcolonial theorist Achille Mbembe, I prefer to term the Franco-African literary connection troubled but "convivial."[6]

In Africa, this relationship with French spreads across the north

---

3. In 1933, under the tutelage of Professor Charles Béart at the William Ponty School (Senegal), an institution established to train Africans for service in the colonial government, students began writing classical dramas in French that were based on a Corneillian model, with African historical figures in the central role. For an excellent history and overall analysis of Francophone African theater, see John Conteh-Morgan, *Theatre and Drama in Francophone Africa* (Cambridge: Cambridge University Press, 1994). Other very useful works for the history of Francophone drama and for theoretical concerns include: John Conteh-Morgan and Tejumola Olaniyan, *African Drama and Performance* (Bloomington: Indiana University Press, 2004), Sylvie Chalaye, *L'Afrique noire et son théâtre au tournant du xxe siècle* (Rennes: Presses universitaires de Rennes, 2001), Anna Paola Mossetto, ed., *Théâtre et histoire: dramaturgies Francophones extraeuropéennes* (Paris: l'Harmattan, 2003).

4. While I concentrate on Sony Labou Tansi and Koffi Kwahulé, I believe it possible to include in my suggested model of Francophone African stage textuality, making allowances for the specificity of each, well-published writers such as Werewere Liking, Tchicaya U'Tamsi, Bernard Zadi Zaourou, Souleymane Koly, Caya Makhélé, Kossi Efoui, José Pliya, and Senouvo Agbota Zinzou.

5. Quoted in a rough cut version of Manthia Diawara's documentary film, "Who's Afraid of Ngugi?" on Ngugi Wa Thiong'o's return to Kenya after some twenty-five years of absence, viewed at The African Literature Association conference, Accra, Ghana, May 2006.

6. Dominic Thomas cites Achille Mbembe's nuanced musings about Franco-African relations from Mbembe's book *On the Postcolony* in his introduction to a rich study of African literatures and the process of constructing a nation: *Nation Building, Propaganda, and Literature in Francophone Africa* (Bloomington: Indiana University Press, 2002), 4.

through the western and central regions—the latter two once known as "French West Africa" and "French Equatorial Africa." West and central Francophone Africa, or "Black Africa," as Sylvie Chalaye, the most prolific and mobilized scholar of contemporary Francophone African theater would put it,[7] not only lived through a more centralized French colonization than the north, but also experienced a steadier growth of Francophone theatrical production. While it is, then, possible to address Black African theater as a coherent object, the situation in the north is more varied and ambiguous. It is for that reason that I do not include the Maghreb in my considerations of Francophone African stage textuality. I will, however, extend the problematic to include Black African playwrights, who because of political upheavals, personal histories, or work opportunities, live and write outside of Africa.[8]

Being located out of Africa raises rather starkly the issue of reception. We can rightly ask just how "African" is this theater when performed before a non-African audience—a question which itself occludes the obvious existence of several different kinds of African publics. We know, for example, that in general Francophone African theater is very physical, invested in signifying through dancing and drumming, the latter crucial for bonding the audience to the work and the performers. The impact of such theater would surely vary, depending on whether or not spectators had dancing and drumming as part of their own cultural practice.

The dearth of easily accessible studies of actual Francophone African performances before African audiences urges me to return to the more approachable definition of stage textuality—even though theater, or the meeting of two bodies across a divide and within a controlled time frame happens, only happens, during performance. Leaving aside, then, other languages of the stage, such as lighting, costumes, props, scenography, choreography, and sound, I will define stage textu-

---

7. Chalaye is widely published on African theater. In addition to titles cited elsewhere in these notes, see *Dramaturgies africaines d'aujourd'hui en dix parcours* (Brussels: Lansman, 2001), *Nouvelles dramaturgies d'Afrique noire francophone* (Rennes: Presses universitaires de Rennes, 2004), and her regular columns on Francophone African Theater in the French journal *Africultures: africultures.com.*

8. In addition to Koffi Kwahulé, we can mention Kangi Alemdjorodo, Valérie Goma, José Pliya, Marcel Zang, Koulsy Lamko, and Caya Makhélé among the better known Francophone African playwrights working outside of Africa. Chalaye also groups with these authors writers still working in Africa but whose thematics and style are comparable, notably Kouan Tawa of Cameroon and Idris Youssouf Elmi of Djibouti. See her interviews in *L'Afrique noire et son théâtre au tournant du xxe siècle.*

ality as how the dramatic text (dialogue and didascalia) functions to create a virtual on-stage world of meaning by conjuring living beings, actions, ambience, and location. Any analysis of stage textuality will of necessity include a sense of theater's three-dimensionality.

Certain common qualities in professional trajectory, form, and theme justify a comparative analysis of Sony Labou Tansi and Koffi Kwahulé and situate them as representative of Francophone theater artists. Each is from a country (respectively The Republic of the Congo and Côte d'Ivoire) with a rich Francophone literary community and quality educational system. Each has won the prestigious Radio France International (RFI) prize for best Francophone African play (Labou Tansi in 1973 for *Conscience du tracteur*, in 1977 for *Je soussigné cardiaque*, and in 1979 for *La parenthèse de sang* and Kwahulé in 1992 for *Cette vieille magie noire* and in 1994 for *La dame du café d'en face*). Both writers are self-aware hybrids—neither stuck in a notion of "pure Africanness"—but rather open to examining an Africa in progress.

Their theatrical production is resolutely allegorical and distinguished by a volatile lyricism and defiant sociopolitical denunciation.[9] In addition, each privileges in his writing certain components of what constitutes the experience of a dramatic text. These are: articulation (or the arrangement of the story); construction of space (or the spatial dimension); performativity (that is, both what mode the performance must take and how the characters take shape); and lexical and syntactical creativity. Examining each of these elements separately and seeing how they combine to create a structure of feeling will constitute my proposal for a contemporary Francophone African stage textuality. At the same time, I hope to signal the ways in which Kwahulé's deviations from the model indicate that Francophone African theater is taking its place in a postmodern, transnational theatrical world. Each one's best play, to my mind, which also happens to be the most frequently performed, will anchor my study: Labou Tansi's *La parenthèse de sang* (1981) and Kwahulé's *Bintou* (1997).[10] First, however, it will be useful

9. It is telling of their local stature that despite their critical stance they have been so little censored. Labou Tansi was jailed in Brazzaville only after he embarked on a political career with a major opposition party (1992) and Kwahulé has had one play (*Le Grand-Serpent*) closed in Abidjan during his student days in the early 1980s because his lambasting of the power structure apparently struck too close to home.

10. Dates given in the body of the paper for prizes and productions of plays may vary from their publication dates. I will cite from or mention the following published plays: Sony Labou Tansi, *Conscience de tracteur* (Abidjan/Paris: NEA-CLE, 1979); *La Parenthèse de sang*, suivi de *Je soussigné cardiaque* (Paris: Hatier, 1981); *Moi, veuve de l'empire* (Paris: l'Avant-scène théâtre 815, 1987); *Monologue d'or et noces d'argent* suivi de

to ground my analyses by looking briefly at the artistic profiles of both men and the "stories" embedded in each focal play.

As mentioned, Sony Labou Tansi represents for most critics and African theater people the breakthrough artist for a theater practice that can be considered "African," rather than a copy of a European model. He wrote some twenty-five plays, half still unpublished, with and for the fifty members of his Rocado Zulu, or "Tough and Sinuous Combat," Ensemble (1979–1995). Located in a popular neighborhood of Brazzaville, this company put into action what Labou Tansi always proclaimed about ethical action: "African wisdom tells us that we can't be right all by ourselves. One is always right with someone else";[11] his was the official company of the Brazzaville French Cultural Center from 1985 until 1991 and his work became the centerpiece and centrifugal force of the Limoges Festival of "Francophonies" in its earliest and most influential years (1985–1990).

Labou Tansi's theater can be characterized as grotesque farce—vulgar, physical, and rapid-paced, incorporating music and dance in pointed but metaphorical criticisms of presidents for life, one-party systems (whatever their ideological stripe), collusion between government bureaucrats and multinational neocolonialists, and the omnipresent brutality that blurs the boundaries between life-in-life and life-in-death. We can situate his theater's raging energy by repeating what he says of his central character, a teacher, in his 1981 play, *Je soussigné cardiaque:* his purpose is to "build a storm in [our] skulls" (83). Sharing traits with what has been termed the "theater of the absurd" (robot-like characters, repetitive actions, dreamscapes), his plays are nevertheless mired in militaristic horror, not unlike a holocaustal real to which only absurdity gives form.

La parenthèse de sang illustrates well Labou Tansi's dramatic *oeuvre*, although it is a more narratively coherent and less spectacularly overblown piece than some of his later works. *Une chouette petite vie*

Le trou (Brussels: Lansman, 1998); Qui a mangé Madame d'Avoine Bergota (Brussels: Lansman-Editions Promotions Théâtre, 1989); Une chouette petite vie bien osée (Brussels: Lansman, 1992) and Koffi Kwahulé, Big Shoot suivi de P'etite souillure (Paris: Editions théâtrales, 2000); Bintou (Brussels: Lansman, 1997); Cette vielle magie noire (Brussels: Lansman, 1993); Fama (Brussels: Lansman, 1998); Il nous faut l'Amérique (Paris: Acoria, 2000); La dame du café d'en face, suivi de Jaz (Paris: Editions théâtrales, 1998); Misterioso 119 suivi de Blue-S-Cat (Paris: Editions théâtrales, 2005); Village fou ou les déconnards (Paris: Acoria, 2000). All translations from these texts in this essay are my own.

11. Quoted in Dominic Thomas, *Nation Building, Propaganda, and Literature in Francophone Africa*, 56.

bien osée (1992), for example, while taking place in the usual Labou Tansian allegorical African country, banishes some 4,500 characters to a desert island where they are meant to be shown crucified on stage until an American journalist, named Coppola, helps reverse their situation by descending in a helicopter to reveal that their island is the archeological site of the original human couple. This is Labou Tansi's jokey take on the modern apocalypse: international scientific interest and gem-studded potsherds and celebrities reward flayed flesh and torture.

The crucifixion field in *Une chouette petite vie bien osée* is repeated in a variety of literal and metaphorical ways in all of Labou Tansi's plays. In *Parenthèse de sang*, it materializes stage center. During all of the second and fifth movements of this five-part play, members of the family and friends of Libertashio, the absent object of desire, are handcuffed to execution posts. In Labou Tansi's vision, life under dictatorship is a gallows experience that should be communicated through gallows imagery and humor. This is obvious from the outset of *Parenthèse de sang* when an announcer prefaces the first movement by a prologue that equates life in Africa with a "parenthesis of blood," or an "entertaining" (5) soccer match between two forms of violence in which all players are covered and the referee is insane. The announcer tells us, in a gesture that recalls Brecht, that the only possible partner to whom one might pass the ball is the audience.

It is in this spirit of bemused hopelessness that the army arrives to look for a Libertashio the soldiers must never find, for their job is to look. They end up imprisoning the entire family (wife, daughters, and nephew Martial) and the village-fool (the family historian and praise singer who watches over Libertashio's grave). Each sergeant who cedes to the temptation to believe that Libertashio has died will be shot by a new sergeant. During a parodic wedding ceremony meant to honor the last request of the youngest daughter, the ambient hysteria contaminates all the guests: the Doctor falls in love with the bride, the priest loses God and the Doctor's wife loses her grip. A messenger finally arrives to exclaim that the new provisional head of state has declared Libertashio a national hero. Refusing to kowtow to this shift in logic, the latest sergeant-in-charge guns down the messenger and the prisoners. Only the Doctor survives, screaming his objections to remaining within the bloody parenthesis.

Labou Tansi's claustrophobic and *grand-guignolesque* universe finds a less caustic, more angst-ridden echo in Koffi Kwahulé, who affectionately acknowledges Sony Labou Tansi as his mentor. Like Labou

Tansi, Kwahulé is a university-educated artist. He studied at both Abidjan's National Theater School and the Parisian conservatory on the Rue Blanche, and earned a doctorate in theater studies from the University of Paris III. Unlike Labou Tansi, Kwahulé works primarily outside of Africa, residing in Paris but produced throughout Europe and North America. He returns from time to time to work in Africa. With some twelve published plays to his name to date, he writes texts that are quirky, linguistically *jouissif,* and deliriously angry.

Most of his pieces are open-ended explorations of identities unmade or being pieced together. Many, such as *P'tite souillure* (2000) or *Il nous faut l'Amérique* (1997), satirize the Western gaze on immigrants or, conversely, the developing world's fascination with the West. All are rooted in the question of whether or not human beings are condemned to murder and rape, to flight, and to the refusal of fraternity. Kwahulé expresses this in the biblical refrain punctuating *Big Shoot* (2000): "Then the Lord said to Cain, 'Where is your brother?' 'I don't know,' he replied. 'Am I my brother's keeper?'" (9, 10, 18, 26, 44). Illusive, his plays read like tone poems, in part because of the music that infuses their writing.

Within his highly kinetic theatrical production, *Bintou* is the least abstract and most obviously socially engaged of Kwahulé's plays. An urban tragedy, replete with a chorus of "furies," the play follows the destiny of Bintou, a thirteen year-old second-generation African immigrant who lives in the projects outside a major city. With her multiethnic gang, the Lycaons or "Wild Beasts," composed of three boys— one Black (Blackout), one North African (Kelkhal), and one White (Manu)—she opposes African patriarchy and European manners. She loves only her gang, the belly dancing she practices (partially as a form of creative release), and the knife she wields as part of the treacherous phallic apparatus that helps position her as "bisexual" in the Cixousian psychic sense—and thus unbearable to most everybody else. Her family—with a brutal and lecherous uncle standing in for an absent father—has determined to bring her under its control by having her excised. They finally accomplish their goal in the last movement of this seven-part piece, thanks to the collaboration of a rival gang, the Pitbulls. Bintou bleeds to death, while the three-girl chorus threatens to haunt the uncle forever.

Although this recounting of what takes place in Bintou would seem to indicate a linear structure, the play in fact proceeds in fits and starts, organized, as are all Kwahulé's plays, as a montage, with somewhat conventional scenes of dialogue giving way to revealing flashbacks (the uncle molesting Bintou), to jazzy, interrupted monologues (such as Blackout's, Kelkhal's, and Manu's individual stories told to the double interrogator of spotlight and audience), to rap numbers (Bintou and the chorus scolding the Pitbull's heroine-addicted leader), or to dream sequences (Bintou's dying hallucination of a mystical marriage). This stylistic and rhythmic roller coaster communicates the nervous energy of the projects and the impossibility of grounding experience in anything approaching stability. The latter lesson is most obvious in the bar scene (movement six), in which P'tit Jean kidnaps Bintou: boom boxes battling (Bintou's oriental dance music versus gangsta rap), the Lycaons take on the Pitbulls. But when the dust settles, all that is left to hear are the saccharine notes of a French chanson from the 1930s: France has again vanquished Africa.

The foregoing account of Labou Tansi's *Parenthèse de sang* and Kwahulé's *Bintou* tells two stories that are obviously my own reconstructions. These texts are ripe for interpretation, both soliciting the active participation of readers or theater-going public and calling on music and choreography to help establish meaning. Despite this interpretive openness, it is safe to say that the articulation of both texts functions to set up a response pattern of edginess and uncertainty. Each, as should be clear from the synopsis of what happens, has an episodic structure, with individual tableaux being self-contained, even, in the case of Labou Tansi, resembling gory cartoons. Kwahulé's montage structure switches registers with tremendous speed, as if a process of "zapping" were taking us from a moment of sit-com pathos to a moment of MTV pastiche. This form of articulation, without building suspense, with leaps in time and space, makes it unlikely that the audience would identify with the psychological plight of individual characters.

As in the case of all of Labou Tansi's and Kwahulé's works, neither of these plays has an ending that serves as resolution. In *Parenthèse de sang*, the bloodiness and civil war continue but so does the hope given shape by the name of Libertashio. In *Bintou*, while Bintou dies, the problem of mutilated adolescents and the frustrating clash of cultures lives on. There is no catharsis to be had, but rather an insistent questioning of what might be done.[12] Articulation, then, channels mood and tone, shocking and agitating the sensibilities of the public.

---

12. In certain of his more recent plays, Kwahulé complicates the role of the audience

This destabilizing effect echoes and is likewise ballasted by the spatial dimensions of both plays. *Parenthèse de sang* and *Bintou*, by dint of the framing devices and the shifts in types of tableaux, move their publics out of a space of material reality. The announcer in *Parenthèse de sang*, as discussed earlier, repositions all that is to come as a crazy game. He informs the audience that it is in a land of limbo, like "the hole" in Labou Tansi's *Le trou* (1976), like the very parenthesis of the play's title—in an elsewhere where lines between psychic life, material concerns, and metaphysics are blurred. This is further reinforced thematically by growing confusion about whether the characters are "in life" or "in death." The realms interpenetrate and establish a sense of the thickness of being, of a borderlessness verging on insanity.

In *Bintou*, the introductory choral lines present a heroine who is not of this world, or who is rather located in a space of transformation and metamorphosis. Rather than proposing the story of adolescent revolt, Kwahulé exposes its mental landscape, with wrenching debates figured by musical as well as physical fighting, with fantasy projections borrowed from fairy tales and juxtaposed with nods to Hollywood films about the "hood," and with images of dysfunctional families only too aware of their dysfunctionality. It is Bintou herself who tells the flashback story that the scenic action brings to life, as though her mental world were projected on stage to be shared with her audience (members of the family and the theater public), in homage both to oral tradition and to cinematic devices from the 1940s.

Kwahulé's use of liminality, his creation of a hovering space only tentatively anchored in place and time and Labou Tansi's nether world embolden me, in a bow to Victor Turner, to conclude that both these works can be read paradoxically as ritual theater. I say "paradoxically" because for ritual to take place there must be a form of identification, which I have argued as not directly possible with the characters in either play. However, the distance suggested between audience and characters and created through patterns of articulation is abolished, or at least muddied, through the creation of a theatricalized storytelling space that reaches out to enfold the public in the mental universe of the tale being told.

Furthermore, both playwrights prioritize on-stage bodies as central conduits for meaning, rather than characters—in the more conven-

---

by setting up an identification with an implied questioner (*Jaz, Big Shoot, Misterioso 119*).

tional psychological understanding of the term. Always the symbolic medium for rituals, bodies, not unlike in Beckett's theater, concentrate the public's attention.[13] But unlike Beckett, Labou Tansi and Kwahulé do not obsess over temporal decay. Rather, their bodies exist in an environment of social filth and political decadence. In Labou Tansi's *Moi, veuve de l'empire* (1987), the bodies are even ornamented with personal vomitoriums. Libertashio's family members are disfigured and violated because they get in the way of the military machine. Libertashio himself is imagined as a floating head. Before Bintou is excised, she flaunts her body and its powerfulness in frenetic moments of "exotic" dancing in which her exposed belly button becomes not only the passage for her birthing of herself, but also for the male characters' phantasmatic regression into wholeness.

In Kwahulé's *Jaz*, a short piece that resonates with *Bintou's* kaleidoscopic imagery, the central character, Jaz, has been raped in the communal toilets of a housing project. Her rape—as well as Bintou's mutilation, Labou-Tansi's tortured, beaten bodies (for example, the prostrate, bleeding, twitching Mallot of *Je soussigné cardiaque*)—might be understood as means of figuring the plundering and dismemberment of postcolonial Africa and African peoples and the ever-threatening violence closing in on their existence. No worthy authority figure—nation or father—prevails. But danger looms everywhere, as play after play implies: from France's sale of 15,000,000 handcuffs to control 30,000,000 citizens (*La parenthèse de sang*), to the "américasseurs" (Americancrushers) developing the mineral wealth of African nations to the detriment of their peoples (Labou Tansi, *Monologue d'or et noces d'argent*, posthumous publication, 1998), to victims who embrace their position of victims because if there are torturers, there have to be victims (*Big Shoot*).

This excessive cruelty takes, I submit, the form of ritual exorcism—my conjecture being prompted by Congolese scholar and writer, Pius Ngandu Nkashama. Taking the cue from Labou Tansi himself, Nkashama finds clear traces in Labou Tansi's work of the traditional rituals of the Kongo people, Labou Tansi's ethnic group.[14] Nkashama ref-

13. For insights into the intersection of the body and ritual and an analysis of how the body functions as part of a ritual enactment in Labou Tansi's novel *La vie et demie*, see Eileen Julien, "Rape, Repression, and Narrative Form in *Le devoir de violence* and *La vie et demie*," Lynn A. Higgins and Brenda R. Silver, eds., *Rape and Representation* (New York: Columbia University Press, 1991), 160–81.

14. Pius Ngandu Nkashama, "La mémoire du temps . . . le temps de la mémoire dans

erences, in particular, a ritual form banned by the colonial power structure, known as "the theater of madmen" (or *kingizila*), one of the manifestations of psychodramatic rituals prevalent in much of central and western Africa. A healing ritual in which mentally ill people perform assigned roles, *kingizila* realizes healing through enactment. Nkashama sees Labou Tansi as the conductor of performances of social madness through theater work, performances meant to help purge the public of the mental sickness brought on by dictatorship. In like fashion, I believe, Kwahulé engages in healing rituals in his theater, attempting to help exorcise the negative effects of marginalization, dislocation, and poverty by giving form to broken mental structures and violent social life.

To return to the question of endings, or resolutions, I suggest that while there is no resolution to the problems of dictatorship, alienation, and violence posed in their plays, the ritual nature of the work addresses the emotional impact of these situations. Rather than resurrect heroes in which the public can believe, or that provide models for action, as do the acknowledged founding texts of what might be called the first phase of African Francophone theater, most specifically Aimé Césaire's *La tragédie du Roi Christophe* (1963) and Bernard Dadié's *Béatrice du Congo* (1970), Labou Tansi's and Kwahulé's theater presents the possibility of an on-stage transgressive performance that highlights a visceral truth and puts into movement its evacuation.

There is something of the "cannibalistic," metaphorically speaking, in this operation of exorcism. The horror and the absurdity are registered and ingested by the audience and then transformed into something lighter, less awful in the process of the play's emotional voyage. As is true of the conceptualization of cannibalism in many cultures, the play thus becomes a vehicle of growth and change. Indeed, throughout his corpus, Labou Tansi offers up multiple images of cannibalistic behavior, an ongoing metaphor for him of how to take on and deal with a grotesque universe. This operation of ingesting, digesting, and giving back something altered is precisely what both authors do through their lexical and syntactical creativity. Such linguistic behavior may even be Labou Tansi's revenge for having to wear as a

---

le théâtre de Sony Labou Tansi," *Notre Librairie* 102 (juillet-août 1990) :31–37. For a longer development of the ritual quality of Sony Labou Tansi's work, see also Jean-Michel Devesa, *Sony Labou Tansi: écrivain de la honte et des rives magiques du Kongo* (Paris: l'Harmattan, 1996).

schoolboy a sack full of excrement around his neck every time he made a mistake in French.[15]

While I am not equipped to demonstrate how their French texts are traversed by Labou Tansi's Lingala or Kwahulé's Baoulé, I can use their fellow playwright Kossi Efoui's metaphor of *marronnage* (or run-away slavery) to talk about the way these African playwrights use the French language.[16] Words and phrases never show up where you expect them, but rather always dodge and feint. Sony Labou Tansi's verbal fulsomeness takes the form of invented words, spoonerisms, syntactical inversions, and code switching. To indict the collusion between international bankers and local leadership, he creates, for example, the verb *pognoniser* (to dough up), a construction built on slang for "money" (*Qui a mangé Madame d'Avoine Bergotha*, 1999). He personifies body parts, objects, and abstract ideas, reifies humans, and uses oxymorons to recast previous images: "My hands have drunk enough blood. I want to wash them in audacious silence" (*Moi, veuve de l'empire*, 7). In *Qui a mangé Madame d'Avoine Bergotha*, people "bark" (11), life "bites" (15), the police are "always in erection" (13), and independence is both a "being without balls" (16) and "wearing out as soon as you start to use it" (14). In *Parenthèse de sang*, Martial is condemned to die by "regions" (43), guns have "eyes" (69), Libertashio will be "provisionally definitively found" (21), Sergeant Marc confuses "urine" with voting "urns" (23), and the Doctor falls in love over "short-wave skin" (50).

Kwahulé's language is less coarse—though his sexual imagery can be brutally frank—and his farcical malapropisms less frequent than Labou Tansi's. His lyrical flights, however, are just as exuberant and his personifications as pungent: Bintou dances "like an unleashed poem" (16), "Death stalks in the fever of embraces and pleases itself by picking the green before the ripe" (8). Bintou's gang of "wild beasts" circulates in a frenzy of "snapping jaws" (19) and "muzzled sexes" (12). In *Bintou*, Kwahulé also embeds a string of African-inspired proverbs that trap Bingou within the logic of necessary control and surveillance: "When the hand isn't big enough, the forked stick will gather the fruit" (30) or "Even drunk, the egg knows better than to dance on gravel" (33). That Kwahulé undercuts a model of traditional African knowledge by

15. Quoted in Bernard Magnier, "Entretien avec Sony Labou Tansi," in Sony Labou Tansi, *Qui a mangé Madame d'Avoine Bergotha* (Brussels: Lansman-Editions Promotions Théâtre, 1989): 129.

16. Quoted in Chalaye, *L'Afrique noire et dramaturgies contemporaines: Le syndrôme Frankenstein*, 35.

using it to shore up the authority of a perverse father figure proclaims his commitment to question not only the operation of the French language, but also that of African discourse.

Reflecting on how playful, disruptive, even wild language contributes to making these texts so stunning, so exhilarating, leads me to the ways in which Kwahulé's texts diverge from the proposed model of African stage textuality. For his use of rhythms and sonorities is, in fact, quite different from Labou Tansi's and confers on his texts a musicality that Labou Tansi's texts do not have. Furthermore, this musicality relates to a referential field that takes his public beyond Labou Tansi's allegorical African nation.

Kwahulé worries that certain forms of Francophone African theater, notably in their use of traditional movement and percussion, continue to give audiences, and particularly international audiences, the picture of Africa they already have in their head, of a kind of "whore in the window."[17] Such anxiety has helped him develop a form of diasporic consciousness. He writes from a space of exile, from the longing born out of the forced deportation and movement of African peoples. While we see this yearning in Francophone plays of the Caribbean, where it frequently takes the image of flying off to Africa or of zombification (a metaphor for the enslaved soul, as in Simone Schwarz-Bart's *Ton beau capitaine*, 1987), in Kwahulé's plays, longing becomes a form of split consciousness reinforced by a pattern of musicality. In *Jaz*, for instance, the character Jaz dialogues with a musical instrument as a projection of her shattered self.

Kwahulé incorporates jazz as a counterpoint to images of a world of blood and detritus. In stage directions, he calls for the introduction of themes from Coltrane, Monk, and Parker as a way of giving memory to what is absent. He uses jazz in his titles (*Cette vieille magie noire*, *Misterioso 119*); and his syncopated rhythms, bold use of refrains, and repetitive riffs project an Africa that has extended to the Americas, an Africa with which Euro-blacks can also identify. It is this "musical blackness" that becomes, in Kwahulé's work, the launching pad for an expression of universal malaise and a point of reference for curing cultural myopia.

Kwahulé displays a jazzman's ability to descend to "hell" and re-emerge bereft but alive. Labou Tansi, like the Fool in many of his plays and like the *atalaku*, or on-stage orchestrator of pop music concerts in

---

17. Quoted in Chalaye, *L'Afrique noire et son théâtre au tournant du XXe siècle*, 133.

the Brazzaville and Kinshasa of the 1980s, shakes things up and communes with a higher force by his carnivalesque resourcefulness. Both theater men, emblematizing today's African theater from within their engaged theater practice—a constant in Francophone African literature from its inception—employ a stage textuality that foregrounds linguistic invention as a form of resistance, as well as a pattern of articulation, a conceptualization of space, and a focus on the staged body that contribute to an overall experience of theater as ritual. Kwahulé also marks through musicality his preoccupation with shattered identities and with what it means to be an African in the world, not just on the continent.

This sketch of Francophone African stage textuality should doubtlessly be taken with a grain of salt. It is very tricky to propose a set of criteria for a body of work still in the making. Furthermore, at this point, the ubiquitous Francophone African theater is not at all what has been described, but rather "theater for development," inspired by the work of Brazilian militant Augusto Boal.[18] In every corner of western and central Africa, funded by NGO's and government agencies, theater for development teaches about safe sex, good nutrition, necessary medical practices, and, in a roundabout way, democracy.

New technologies, moreover, are even now transforming Francophone African theater. It may not be long before video theater and what that represents in terms of dramatic structure, acting technique, and language replace altogether (as has happened in Nigeria) many forms of live theater. Finally, as Kagni Alem tells us, while much of the financing for Francophone African theater, and particularly for the all important cross-fertilization made possible by theater festivals in Africa, still comes from France, more and more money is now available from services within the European Union.[19] We might, then, wonder what impact the European cultural project will eventually have on Francophone African stage textuality.

18. François Campana repertories over eighty productions in 1993 at the annual theater for development festival in Burkina Faso. There is no question that the number of groups doing theater for development has grown since then. François Campana, "Des festivals pour rapprocher les hommes," unpublished report for the Agence Intergouvernementale de la Francophonie, 2002.

19. Kagni Alem, "Notes sur les pratiques théâtrales en Afrique noire: dramaturgies contemporaines et logiques festivalières," in Suzie Suriam, ed., *L'annuaire théâtral* 31 (Ottawa: University of Ottawa Press, Printemps 2002).

SYLVIE CHALAYE

Contemporary Francophone Drama: Between Detours and Deviations[1]

"Never seek direction from someone who knows the path. Otherwise,
you shall not be able to go astray."
—Rabbi Nahman de Braslav[2]

In the past few years, Francophone theater from Africa and the French
Antilles witnessed profound changes that greatly transformed the landscape of Francophone theatrical expression. At the end of the 1980s,
African theater was represented by figures such as Sony Labou Tansi,
Werewere Liking, or Souleymane Koly, whose theatrical practice relied
on a return to African rituals and traditions. Similarly, Caribbean playwrights such as Maryse Condé or Vincent Placoly sought to define a
West Indian identity through the use of the Creole language and a thematic concern with the historical commemoration of slavery. However, an important transformation occurred in the early 1990s when a
new black theater emerged that defined itself on the global scene, encompassing the diaspora, embracing hybridization, and transforming
colonial history into a site of invention and renewal. Beyond the need
to return to origin, the playwrights of this generation of rupture, nick-
named "the *enfants terribles* of Independences,"[3] did not know each

1. Translators' note: Among its many meanings in French, the word "détour" can
imply detour, deviation, roundabout means, circumvention, or circumlocution. Throughout the essay, we have generally used the word deviation to evoke departure from an established norm or course, but also occasionally used circumvention and detour as a stylistic choice.
2. Koffi Kwahulé uses this epigraph in *Blue-S-cat. Misterioso-119* followed by *Blue-
S-cat* (Montreuil-sous-bois: Éditions Théâtrales, 2005).
3. Sylvie Chalaye, "Les enfants terribles des Indépendances: Théâtre africain et

YFS 112, *The Transparency of the Text*, ed. Donia Mounsef and Josette Féral,
© 2007 by Yale University.

145

other: Kossi Efoui came from Togo, Koffi Kwahulé from the Ivory Coast, Koulsy Lamko from Chad, Caya Makhélé and Léandre Baker from the Congo, and Michèle Rakotoson from Madagascar. The event that brought them together and allowed them to discover their aesthetic affinities was a series of interviews entitled *Dramaturgies 93,* conducted in Paris by Caya Makhélé and subsequently published by Lansman Publishers. This new generation of dramatissts included José Pliya and Ousmane Aledji from Benin, Kagni Alem, Rodrigue Norman, and Gustave Akakpo from Togo, Marcel Zand and Kouam Tawa from Cameroon, as well as Jean-Claude Ismar, Alain Foix, Gaël Octavia, and Yoshvina Medina from the Caribbean.

FROM COLONIAL CIRCUMVENTION
TO THE RETURN TO THE SELF

It is well known that in Africa (and other areas), colonization imposed with it a cultural and artistic agenda. Since the spread of colonial influence in the 1930s, western theater was exported to Africa and performed in the context of educational institutions such as William Ponty's public schools in West Africa (Senegal, Ivory Coast, etc.), or the missionary schools in equatorial Africa (Congo, Cameroon, etc.). Molière and other classical plays were adapted and performed in Africa and the Antilles throughout the colonial period making theater, along with education, a powerful ideological instrument of indoctrination and brainwashing.

On the islands where theater was at first a matter of entertainment for the whites, the settlers would bring their slaves to performances of French plays as a way to introduce them to the culture of metropolitan France while imposing on them an ethos of French society and customs. Even after the abolition of slavery, theater continued to be a tool of assimilation: imported Vaudevilles and melodramas were performed on the islands from the end of the eighteenth century and throughout the nineteenth century. At the beginning of the twentieth century, many dramatists, such as Gilbert de Chambertrand in Guadeloupe, wrote plays in French interspersed with Creole, a language that sought to better translate Caribbean reality. But the 1950s saw a strong revival of French repertory theater with the troupe of Jean Gosselin, who adapted the Parisian *pièces de boulevard* to the Caribbean context.

When the call for independence resonated across Africa in the early

---

identité contemporaine," *L'Afrique noire et son théâtre au tournant du siècle,* coll. "Plurial" (Rennes: Presses Universitaires de Rennes, 2001), 19–26.

1960s, a theatrical neo-Negritude movement united dramatists around
the need to express an African identity that could free the stage from
European conceptualization. The search for a theater that could recon-
struct national and cultural identity and rewrite the history of Africa
from an African perspective became paramount. Many plays that
championed powerful characters emblematic of black resistance became the hallmark of this era; characters such as Samory Touré, Chaka
Zouou, Toussaint Louverture, Lumumba, and others were celebrated
on stage. Other examples of plays with similar pan-African concerns
include Aimé Césaire's *La tragédie du Roi Christophe* (1963) or *Une
saison au Congo* (1966), Edouard Glissant's *Monsieur Toussaint* (1961),
Jean Pliya's *Kondo, le requin* (1966), Bernard Dadié's *Île de tempête*
(1971) or *Béatrice du Congo* (1970), Seydou Badian's *La mort de Chaka*
(1961), and Cheikh N'Dao's *L'exil d'Alboury* (1967). Theatrical creation became synonymous with pan-Africanism.

But the various African independence struggles would not come
without their disenchantment: the 1970s witnessed a kind of artistic
withdrawal into the self and a concern with individual rather than collective identity. African playwrights expressed their dissatisfaction
with failed collective and national projects by creating a satirical theater denouncing African dictatorships that emerged from the ashes of
colonialism. With his *Monsieur Tôgho-gnigni*, Ivory Coast playwright
Bernard Dadié inaugurated this new trend of a dark, comic, and often
abrasive theater that denounced immorality and corruption. Many
authors contributed to this comedic genre in which Africa cruelly
mocked itself; among them Maxime Ndébéka from Congo-Brazzaville
with *Le Président* (1979), Zadi Zaourou with *L'oeil* (1974), Guillaume
Oyono Mbia from Cameroon, with his famous comedy *Deux préten-
dants, un mari* (1969), and particularly Jean-Evina Mba, also from
Cameroon, with *Politicos* (1972), and Sylvain Bemba's *L'homme qui
tua le crocodile* (1972). Correspondingly, in the Antilles, "departmen-
talization" yielded disillusionment expressed with a militant and politically engaged theater. Arthur Lerus founded the Théâtre du Cyclone
in 1972, Robert Dieupart launched Poulbwa, and Alex Nabis created
the Théâtre du Volcan. Alongside this Creolophone theater of protest,
a profoundly satirical theater emerged, that of José Jernidier in Guadeloupe and Georges Mauvois and Daniel Boukman in Martinique. However critically daring it was in content, in form—both in Africa and the
Antilles—this political theater continued to subscribe to classical
models inherited from colonial times.

The 1980s theater brought about a much desired transformation that called for a complete rupture with western European models of psychological realism. Niangoran Porquet from the Ivory Coast, whose work championed the *griot* tradition, was among the most vocal in calling for "a more African theater." The Cameroonian playwright Werewere Liking explored the indigenous rituals of the Bassa ethnic group while Zadi Zaourou (Ivory Coast) rediscovered the traditional forms of the Didiga people. Similarly, Souleymane Koly introduced the "Kotéba," a Bambara ritual, into his theatrical practice. In a different way, but driven by the desire to write theater informed by African aesthetic and affect, Sony Labou Tansi (Congo) created a theater in which the senses reigned supreme. He invented new words, structured an unprecedented syntax, endowed the language of the body with new meaning with sounds and movements belonging to the sensual and natural worlds (barks, grunts, heavy breathing, and so on). Despite this assault on realist language, the themes of this "new theater" remained somewhat conventional: the denunciation of political decay and dictatorship and the critique of state-sponsored violence. However, this theater enjoyed international recognition due to the support of various Francophone theater festivals, such as the Limoges Festival of International Francophone Theater and the Ubu Repertory Theater in New York. Such organizations gave international visibility to unknown Francophone drama and the opportunity for performance before an enthusiastic audience moved by this African cultural novelty.

THE NECESSITY OF DEVIATION

Fanning the flame ignited by Sony Labou Tansi, the 1990s brought about a much more profound transformation both in themes and in forms. An entire new generation of playwrights challenged Western realist theater by refusing linear narrative structure, coherent dialogue, and fully developed characterization in favor of disjointed narrative, experimental language, and figure-like characters. The themes also moved away from a "nativized," "Africanized" reality to a more individualized destiny of characters grappling with urban life who "ingested the evils of the city and the shock of cultures,"[4] as the Congolese

---

4. In 1995, Caya Makhélé collected the words of authors from the generation inspired by Sony Labou Tansi for a special issue of *Alternatives théâtrales* (no. 48) and opened the issue with the article, "Les voies du théâtre contemporain en Afrique," which would serve as a manifesto.

Caya Makhélé declared. These playwrights drew inspiration from other global theatrical traditions: the Japanese Noh theater and spaghetti westerns in Werewere Liking's work, South American literary influence in Kossi Efoui's plays, American cinema and jazz in Koffi Kwahulé's work, Greek myths in Caya Makhélé's work, and the French literary influence of Hugo, Rimbaud, and Claudel in José Pliya's work. In various ways, they all advocated an avant-garde chimerical theater of collage where forms and ideas are borrowed and transplanted to reflect postcolonial hybridization; what one may call a form of "Frankenstein" theater.

As the time of withdrawal into the self came to an end, "Africa," as Kossi Efoui would say, "has an appointment elsewhere."[5] "No more feather skirts or tom-toms!"[6] African reality opened its borders to globalized culture. So much so that at first the European public was disconcerted by this theater that no longer acknowledged the reassuring and customary Africanness. Certain critics would go so far as to suspect the authenticity of such a theater that, according to them, abandoned its African origins. Such theatrical deviations were as geographic as they were cultural. In 1992, Koffi Kwahulé took a detour to America and wrote *Cette vieille magie noire*, which takes place in New York in the world of boxing and black music. José Pliya also crossed the Atlantic, both in his life and in his work, with *Négrerrance* (1998) and *Nous étions assis sur le rivage du monde* (2004), both set in the Caribbean, and he did not shy away from more incongruous European detours such as Hamburg during World War II in *Une famille ordinaire* (2004), or the mythical lands of the Old Testament in *Parabole* (2003), and even, surprisingly, the great distance between Uruguay and Germany in the 1900s in *La soeur de Zarathoustra* (2005).

But these "circumventions" could also pass through Africa itself. For example, Rodrigue Norman, originally from Togo, explores the Mandinka culture in *Trans'sahélienne* (2004) and Koulsy Lamko, born in Chad, sets *Comme des flèches* (1996) in West Africa. In this theater, the detour is not a quest for a faraway horizon or a fantasized "elsewhere"; on the contrary, it demonstrates the necessity to engage with a complex and dynamic world made of differences, and encounters with

5. Chalaye, "Interview with Kossi Efoui," in *Afrique noire: Écritures contemporaines d'expression française, Théâtre / Public* 158, (Gennevilliers, 2001).
6. "Le théâtre de ceux qui vont venir demain," preface to *L'entre-deux rêves de Pitagaba* (Paris: Acoria, 2000), 3.

otherness. The idea of place as a transitory space in these plays conveys a sense of fracturing, represented by the crossroads in several plays by Kossi Efoui, the airport in *Aterrissage* (2002) by Kagni Alem or *L'exilé* (2002) by Marcel Zang, the elevator in *Blue-S-Cat* (2005) by Koffi Kwahulé, and the public parks in *Cannibales* (2004) by José Pliya.

In the Caribbean, a similar movement made its appearance at the beginning of the 1990s. Gerty Dambury traveled to distant places and addressed social and emotional problems that affected different island communities. Instead of setting his drama in the Caribbean, he chose a far away location such as Reunion. Meanwhile, Simone Schwartz-Bart turned to Haiti to stage ordinary lives and the daily constraints of exile instead of focusing on her native Guadeloupe. Ina Césaire and Julius Amédée Laou also created theater based on the drama of the in-dividual grappling with the struggles of alterity and difference. The same friction between the individual and collective is present in Alain Foix's theater, where the "news in brief" overlaps with history's well kept secrets, as in *Venus et Adam* (2007), in which the investigation re-garding a human torso discovered in the Thames in London overlaps with the Venus Hottenttot investigation.

DEVIATIONS OF/IN LANGUAGE

In addition to deviations on the geographic and thematic levels, it is structural and linguistic deviations that give a signature of originality to this theater. Each author asserts an independent identity that tran-scends artistic movements or schools. For example, Kossi Efoui's the-ater privileges lack, holes, and absence, where dialogues are con-structed as ellipses, with great sections of history missing, making it impossible to follow a direct path. The structural detours reflect in this sense the diversions and tribulations of memory itself. The diegetic flow of Efoui's theater by-passes these absences constructing layers of history like archeological strata. In *Io (tragédie) (2006)*, for example, Anna is a sort of reincarnation of the character Io and, through her, all of the voices of mothers who haunt history. This theatrical palimpsest, which connects physical and temporal wandering, is even stated ex-pressly in the play by the character Masta Blasta:

> Io
> It is written
> You understand
> That she was seen passing through Antioch

Someone saw her
Or perhaps a crowd
In Ankara
She was seen near Adana, Tripoli, Byblos
Io seen
her silhouette
to disappear and reappear
to disappear until Tyr
and reappear in Sidon
cities of the magnificent Phoenecians
It is written, inventors of the alphabet used to capture
    in the clay-imprinted slate
her passage to the deep Ethiopia of black people whose
    soft banks we inhabit

To the unfolding of the layers of Io's identity, Anna responds:

The setting is called the faraway land
The land where the sun lost its memory.[7]

Not unlike Efoui, Koffi Kwahulé uses a polyvocal, polysemous expression as another deviation of speech. He challenges the powerlessness of a single voice to articulate the unspeakable by appropriating plurality and constructing the whole through fragments. Kwahulé claims that nothing can ever give itself as a whole; reality is one of fragments, wreckage of history scattered, pulverized, vaporized, always to be reconstructed. In all his three major plays, *Jaz* (2002), *Blue-S-Cat*, and *Misterioso-119* (2005), meaning coalesces gradually through the combination of voices, utterances, and memory. A different type of deviation occurs in the theater of Caya Makhélé—that of mistaken identity, where characters are compelled to change their appearance and their identity, donning mask upon mask until they reach a sort of vertigo. This is the fate that awaits the character Picpus in Makhélé's *La danse aux amulettes* (1995), who, in a gesture similar to Oedipus's plucks out his own eyes so as not to recognize himself anymore. In José Pliya's plays, deviation takes on a performative value; speech is articulated through multiple ellipses. However, unlike Makhélé's characters, who become strangers to themselves to the point of self-annihilation, Pliya's characters are estranged from one another even when they speak the same language. The exchange between them is governed by the

7. *Io (tragédie)* (Solignac: Le bruit des autres, 2006), 38–39.

rules of business transactions and haggling. In *Le complexe de Thé-nardier* (2001), recalling the relationship between Cosette and the Thé-nardiers in Hugo's *Les Misérables*, Madame—the mistress of the house—makes demands of Vido, her servant who has come to Madame's house after escaping genocide. The master-slave narrative joins force with a critique of class struggle. One day Vido decides to leave, and the play stages her farewells; a cursory moment stretched over an entire lifetime. The two characters remain trapped in their own trauma, completely impervious to one another, each one following her own path, as Vido herself confirms in a retort that constitutes a *mise en abyme* of the entire play:

> We misunderstand one another. A war is not enough for us to realize it. We've lived in the same house without really knowing one another. Side by side. Two figures of solitude in the noise of the cannons. A very long, barely fragmented monologue. We misunderstand one another. I came to you with deference, which you took for greed. I wished for your blessing, you offered me a bargain. We misunderstand one another.

Pliya shows us this abyss of communication between beings, which structures the majority of his plays.

A similar incommensurability haunts the epistolary theater of Gerty Dambury and Simone Schwartz-Bart who, in *Lettres Indiennes* (1993) and *Ton beau capitaine* (1987) respectively, resort to a working of voice and absence. The letter in the case of Gerty Dambury, and the recorded cassette in the case of Simone Schwartz-Bart challenge the assumption that dialogue is possible in theater. Similar interrogations are present in the work of Ina Césaire, particularly in her play with the evocative title *Mémoires d'île* (1983). The memory of the Caribbean islands is made up of holes, gaps, absences, variance that transform theater into a site of emptiness, a void imposed by multiple histories and fissured memories. For it is "in the absent body that the real tragedy begins," as one of the voices of Kwahulé's play *Blue-S-cat* says in an elevator.[8] Even the title of *Blue-S-cat* refers to the interweaving of voices,

---

8. "Skin broken scattered dispersed it is laid out end to end and makes a body. The body is found there. Even a head even an arm even a toe makes a body. Mourning can happen. Because those who stayed in New York in the buildings those who had no other choice than to stay, well, they were vaporized. Vaporized. Vaporized. No body to honor. And impossible to mourn. They pretend so as to make a good impression but this isn't mourning. And it is at that moment of the absent body that the real tragedy begins." K. Kwahulé, *Blue-S-cat*.

as "blue" refers to musical blues intercepted with "scat"; a mixing of genres and modes of expression.

Francophone Afro-Caribbean theater is profoundly marked by this ontological disappearance linked to the history of the slave trade. It is the tragic and foundational void of the *entre-deux*, the "in-between." It even resonates within some titles of plays: Efoui's *L'entre-deux rêve de Pitagab*; Rodrigue Norman's *Entre deux battements*—or in theatrical locations: between two floors of an elevator in motion in *Blue-Scat*; in the fugitive space of in-between, a "corner of dawn" in *Le complexe de Thénardier*; and "just before daybreak" at the fetish market that comes to life in *Io (tragédie)*. The detour becomes a spatio-temporal circumnavigation imposed by Black history. For, as Jean-Pierre Sarrazac recalls in his groundbreaking essay on the parable, "deviation, the art of variation, does not only belong to the realm of geometry"; according to him, "it is equally present in the domain of music."[9]

This writing is a form of syncopation, off the beat, in other words, a rhythmic experiment, as defined by Gilles Deleuze: "rhythm that falls between two spaces, or between two interspaces, as between two bodies of water, between two hours, between day and night."[10] It is the art of discrepancy, of sudden and controlled swerve, a magical leap across the void, a "changing of place unexpectedly" (Deleuze, 385).

THE DREAM OF TWISTS AND TURNS

Deviation is not only associated with a negative absence or lack, it is not simply an ellipsis of being colonized; it is an inventive process that turns theater into a productive domain. At the heart of this theater of deviation one finds the essence of orality itself, of the fable, of griotic storytelling. Koffi Kwahulé's work explores this dimension through characters such as Ikédia in *P'tite-souillure* (2002), of Bintou or El Mona, along with many other fantasized characters, fashioned entirely by the imagination. José Pliya's characters are also born out of similar strokes of the imagination: the blue-haired soldier who triggers Vido's departure and insubordination in *Le complexe de Thénardier*, and whom she undoubtedly dreamed or invented; the missing baby in *Cannibales* (2004) who never really existed; or Caya Makhélé's Motéma,

9. Jean-Pierre Sarrazac, *La parabole ou l'enfance du théâtre*, (Paris: Circé-Poche, 2002), 28.

10. Gilles Deleuze and Félix Guattari, *Mille plateaux: capitalisme et schizophrénie*, (Paris: Minuit, 1980), 385.

the woman to be saved from Hell and who in the end is revealed as a figment of the little girl's imagination in *La fable du cloître des cimetières* (1995). Similar fabulous creations inhabit Gerty Dambury's and Simone Schwartz-Bart's plays, through the improbable addressee of the letter and the impossible return to Haiti.

As such, orality and the powers of invocation could be seen as the link between Africa and the Caribbean. Linguistic detours carry breath from writing to utterance, from the page to the stage; a suspended breath, a rhythm carried by the voice of the actor, resonating outside scriptural determinism, reinvesting the rhythms of music, the origins of jazz as a sundry form. The force of orality surges up and is expressed in the parables used in these plays. The fables told have a double signification, a second meaning that is presented to the spectator as an enigma. For example, the excision in *Bintou* is depicted not simply as a traditional African practice, but also as a helpless attempt of a society that tries to repress the desire of its youth instead of channeling it. In the same way, in *La fable du cloître . . .* , the descent into hell by Makiadi to bring Motéma back from the world of the dead, refers to the impossible return to ancestral Africa, an imagined continent, a testimony to the lack of a single truth.

Even one of José Pliya's plays carries the suggestive title *Parabole* (2003). Stating the return of the prodigal son, the play functions as a *mise en abyme* of the figure of deviation. The journey of the youngest son, who goes off to lose himself at the ends of the earth, is the voyage necessary for the completion of the concept off the self. Not unlike this necessary voyage in *Parabole*, the detour into the unknown becomes a condition through which the character can understand his destiny, as is the case of Io's flight after her metamorphosis into a cow:

> Outside father's home
> outside the country
> beast devoted to the gods to the ends of the earth[11]

In her trans-substantiation, she encountered Prometheus, the fire chief, in one of his many wanderings, and it was only at the end of her journey that she regained her human form to be able to give birth to Epaphus.

The choice of the parable, a form that Sarrazac defines as the ruse of Perseus (Sarrazac, 20–21), becomes the sidestep necessary for the

---

11. *Io (tragédie)*, 15.

playwright to avoid the need to represent reality. The parable pushes theater into a constant state of becoming that exploits discord and doubt, that learns to look into the abyss, to live with the emptiness of origins.

FOR A RETURN TO THE HUMAN

> Here we are at the foot of the wagon
> that opened its doors to death in the days of old.
> Painful wound
> of a tragedy beyond all understanding.
> Here we are at the foot of the wagon
> where man reified man,
> horrible testimony in the face of which memory
>   prefers to rock softly
> on one leg,
> then on the other,
> blinking its eyes,
> and pouting.
>
> —Koffi Kwahulé, *Le masque boiteux.*[12]

"The return constitutes the vanishing horizon of the detour. And the detour is not the art of losing oneself but, by overcoming the test of the labyrinth, what gives value to having found one's own way" wrote Sarrazac regarding the art of the parable (24). In other words, one must know how to lose oneself in order to find oneself, to rediscover the individual in the collective, the particular in the universal. The deviations in today's African and Caribbean Francophone theater show that human suffering concerns all human beings. This theater makes us accountable for the graveless dead of the past. As such, the Holocaust is not only a Jewish tragedy, the Rwandan genocide is not only an African tragedy, and slavery is not exclusively an American horror—these abominations are ours, those of humanity, and only humanity as a whole can fight them. The theatrical experiments of Africa and the Antilles have, first and foremost, the ambition to bring us back to the human, and to lift us from the narrow confines of self-absorption that blinds us and takes away our sense of responsibility. Nourished by difference and otherness, such a theater transforms human complexity into a poetics. It is no longer a question of scratching the wounds of one's own group, but instead, of reinventing an identity against and with others. This theater summons all the horrors of our time: illegal

12. Koffi Kwahulé, *Le masque boîteux* (Paris: Théâtrales, 2003), 29.

immigration, urban violence, civil wars, child soldiers, genocidal exe-
cutioners, *double peine* laws, excision, incest, rape, drugs, consumer-
ism. Makhélé's mistaken identity theater, Efoui's theater of collage,
Pliya's back-to-back theater, Kwahulé's polyvocality, or Gerty Dambury's epistolary theater: all, in different ways, attest to the necessity
of the reinvention of the self that can survive tragedy, than can emerge
from the abyss of history. In other words, they express the necessity to
construct new paths without ignoring the rifts, to invent detours that
can transcend obstacles. The theater of the new generation is one of
burial and resurrection, where art becomes the burial ground and participates in mourning. The incredible force of this theater is precisely
its capacity to teach us to be reborn as human once again.

This is the meaning of the vision conjured up by Kwahulé in *Le
masque boîteux* (2003), where a woman's body looms up in the night
from the "yellow wagon," a "body-in-which-all-bodies-were-buried,"
and which the stage directions describe as "a black woman," "nude in
the frame of the door," "her body covered with ash as though she'd
emerged from a dumping ground," who has come to say something to
the audience in a "bloodless voice":

> A question?
> One word.
> One single word . . .
> A trepidation.
> An enigma.
> Barely whispered.
> So be silent and prick up your ears. (29–31)

—Translated by Donia Mounsef and Christy Wampole

PHILIPPA WEHLE

Lost in Translation, or Why French-language Plays Are Not Often Seen on American Stages[1]

American theater has long been firmly rooted in a tradition of realism. Our audiences clearly enjoy a good traditional play with a clear story line, naturalistic representation, believable characters, plot, suspense, climax, and denouement. Our mainstream theater is interested in the customs and behavior of middle class or working class families and more often than not, sets are exact replicas of familiar rooms.

In France, on the other hand, where realism and naturalism were born in the 1870s with Emile Zola and in the 1880s with the pioneering theater of André Antoine and the plays of Henri Becque, interest in surface authenticity and objective case studies of lower or middle class conduct, as revolutionary as it was at the time, did not last long. After Becque's *Lex corbeaux* and *La Parisienne*, naturalism seemed no longer to appeal to French playwrights. As Joseph Chiari pointed out in his *Contemporary French Theatre, Flight from Naturalism*, the French seem allergic to naturalism in the theater.[2]

It was not until the 1970s that realism once more appeared in serious French theater thanks to the authors belonging to the Théâtre du Quotidien (Daily Life Theater, or Theater of the Everyday). This school of writing sought to record moments in the ordinary lives of working class and lower middle class people and to give a voice to their concerns and fears.

Michel Vinaver, considered the leader of this movement, had in fact been centering his work on the everyday since the 1950s and has con-

---

1. Parts of this article were first presented at a Theater Colloquium sponsored by the French Interdisciplinary Group, Northwestern University, October 29, 2004, as part of Chicago's 2004 Playing French Festival.
2. Joseph Chiari, *The Contemporary French Theatre: The Flight from Naturalism* (London: Camelot Press, 1958).

YFS 112, *The Transparency of the Text*, ed. Donia Mounsef and Josette Féral, © 2007 by Yale University.

tinued to do so to this day. Richard Maxwell, a 38 year-old American playwright/director from Fargo, North Dakota, who began his career in Chicago in the early 1990s as one of the founders of the Cook County Theater Department, also centers his theater on the everyday. Like Vinaver, he takes his inspiration from the daily lives of average people, and like Vinaver he goes beyond the surface banality of the everyday, transcending this banality to create an extraordinary, hyper-real theater.

While Vinaver enhances the everyday by creating dramas composed of disparate fragments of conversation and snippets of lives, juxtaposed and arranged in such a way as to keep us guessing, Maxwell writes original plays about ordinary people in familiar situations and stages them himself with an anti-theatrical approach to directing that favors poker-faced delivery and stiff, unnatural movements that contradict his texts. Both authors are avid listeners. Vinaver enjoys recording the banal phrases of typical conversations overheard between office managers, secretaries, or business executives. Maxwell prefers exchanges captured on subways, buses, and city streets. Both go beyond the surface banality of these trivial phrases in order to create an original theater.

A comparison of Vinaver's chamber play *Dissident, il va sans dire* (*Dissident, goes without saying*)[3] and Maxwell's *Drummer Wanted*,[4] intimate plays with remarkably similar subjects, as examples of how these two playwrights dramatize the mundane, may shed some light on the question of why their theater, despite being ostensibly based in "real life," has not been widely produced in the United States where the tradition of realism continues to reign. Is Vinaver, like so many other important contemporary French-language playwrights, the victim of preconceived ideas in this country about a certain kind of current French playwriting, i.e. too abstract, too intellectual, too difficult to stage? Or is it because he, like Maxwell, is seen as an experimental writer and therefore by definition given a minority status?

Michel Vinaver, one of France's leading contemporary playwrights, has written epic-scale pieces, with casts of twenty or thirty as well as short plays for small casts. While his large plays deal with corporations, his intimate pieces tell simple, "ordinary" stories with few characters. They concern familiar situations such as a man fired from his job in *La demande d'emploi;* two bachelor brothers whose lives are disrupted when a young girl comes to live with them (*Nina, c'est autre chose*), or

3. Michel Vinaver, *Dissident, goes without saying,* trans. Paul Antal, *Performing Arts Journal* (1986).
4. Richard Maxwell, *Drummer Wanted,* first produced at P.S. 122, New York City, November 2001.

two neighbors, both raising children as single fathers, in *Les voisins*, or the strained relationship between a mother and her son, as in *Dissident, goes without saying*, the play that interests us here.

Dissident, goes without saying is a two-character play composed of twelve short scenes, separated by blackouts. In it we quickly learn that Philip, a teenager, lives with his mother Helen, that she is divorced from his father, a successful businessman, and that she works as a statistics clerk, analyzing invoices by sales districts. As expected of a typical teenager, Philip prefers to lie around listening to records or hang out with his friends rather than look for a job. Helen, a typical mother, urges Philip to find meaningful work. As the play proceeds, Helen loses her job to computerization, the absent father increases his alimony payments and Philip announces that he has found a job, working on the assembly line at the Peugeot factory. Mother and son share moments of closeness followed by periods of withdrawal. One minute Philip gives Helen a box of her favorite chocolate-covered truffles or compliments her on her new dress. The next, he has disappeared for weeks at a time, leaving Helen with no idea of where he's gone.

Months go by as Philip grows thinner and his cheeks become hollow. Helen learns that her son had left his job after only three weeks because, as he says, he couldn't bare to be stuck on an assembly line with its intolerable noise level and repetitive moves at the conveyer belt. It finally becomes clear to Helen that her son has taken up drugs and crime. In the final scene, while the police are knocking at the door, Helen and Philip share a brief moment of closeness, a genuine coming together, before he is arrested.

As this brief synopsis of the play's story suggests, *Dissident*, the most naturalistic of Vinaver's plays, could be mistaken for a "slice of life" domestic drama. On the surface, the material is ordinary, straightforward, and flat. There is an apparent throughline and a strong sense of the familiar reality of a naturalist drama. Helen's and Philip's dialogue, with its unfinished sentences and changes of subject in midstream, could be mistaken for the stuff of commonplace conversations. At closer look, however, it becomes evident that these are not ordinary exchanges but snatches of conversation, captured and purposefully reorganized in such a way as to form a mosaic composed of carefully selected phrases and fragments of speech.[5] It is this process of re-assembling and re-arranging words and phrases to form a montage that keeps

---

5. For a complete study of Vinaver's theater practices, see David Bradby, *The Theater of Michel Vinaver* (Ann Arbor: The University of Michigan Press, 1993).

us on our toes. Clearly his is a theater of poetic possibilities rather than a theater of the every day. This artistic practice allows for meanings to emerge, not from the banal remarks of Helen and Philip's conversation, but indirectly, in the intervals and spaces between the words and in the blackouts between the twelve scenes. "What is unsaid weighs more than what is said,"[6] as Vinaver points out in his Author's Notes to the play.

Richard Maxwell's plays, on the other hand, have a clear plot and a solid structure, beginnings, middles, and ends. They deal with familiar American subjects "A-1 steak sauce . . . , Florida State coaches . . . (and) toast,"[7] according to his description. Indeed, in the many plays he has written and directed since the early 1990s, Maxwell's subjects have ranged from the problems of the dissatisfied workstaff of a Burger King, to the personal concerns of three cross-country furniture movers, the strained relationship between a mother and son, and a love story between an addict in need of rehabilitation and a counselor at the rehab center.

Consider his play *House,* for example, for which he won an Obie in 1999. On the surface, it seems to be about a family of first generation immigrants living in a Chicago suburb and the strange things that happen to them. The opening dialogue is anything but catchy. Mother, Father, Son walk out onto the stage, line up and stare out at the audience. Mother serves toast. Father and son munch, staring into space. "Hello" says the Mother to the Father in a flat tone. He does not answer. She continues: "I was at a ah . . . a ah . . . meeting. Do you know? It's for this group."[8] The father goes on munching and staring, arms hanging loosely at his side. It is a while before anything else happens. The three young women in *Showy Lady Slipper* are less catatonic and more talkative, but they are equally strange. They ramble on mindlessly about boys, horses, gossip, jewelry, and clothes. Their conversation, sprinkled with "Ohmigod" and "you guys," is as empty as the vacant stares of the players.

Clearly, Maxwell's originality does not reside in his dialogues or his subject matter. It is what he does with these conversations and situa-

6. Vinaver, Author's Note to *Chamber Theater,* trans. Paul Antal, *Performing Arts Journal* (1986): 62.
7. Richard Maxwell, "Remarks" made in Philippa Wehle's class on Contemporary Theater Experiments, Purchase College, State University of New York, February 16, Spring 2004.
8. Richard Maxwell, *House,* script sent to Philippa Wehle, February 13, 2000.

tions and how he directs his actors that make his theater unique. What matters to him is to break down the conventions of traditional realistic theater and explore the boundaries of the form, without the help of sophisticated technology or novel effects. To achieve this, he is totally engaged in all aspects of the production process.

As director, Maxwell works to help his actors get rid of all artifice. Instead of portraying or becoming the character, they must resist the urge to perform, to portray or become the characters. Using a modified version of LeCoq's neutral mask techniques, Maxwell gets his actors to focus on the task and resist the impulse to interpret or define a character emotionally. They practice moving without any tension in their bodies or stand motionless in front of the others, stripped of all props, forced to get rid of what Maxwell calls the "actor face," in order to be real. For this reason, Maxwell likes to cast nonprofessional actors along with trained actors who may find it hard to acquire this neutral acting style.

In Maxwell's theater, gestures are limited and laughter is mechanical, not jovial. His "ha ha ha"s, delivered loudly but without emotion, have become legend. Sometimes his characters let out a yell that might indicate anger, frustration, or the eruption of some feeling. In general, however, his characters speak with a flat, emotional disconnect. His settings are urban or suburban (a boxing ring, a room in a house or a shelter). The set for *House*, for example, doesn't even attempt to create the illusion of the interior of a house, while other pieces have very realistic sets. *Good Samaritans* plays in an exact replica of a room in a shelter for recovering addicts, while *Drummer Wanted* takes place on a unit set that allows for the players to evoke different locations by simply moving clockwise around the space when the dialogue suggests a change of place (from piano to car to bar).

Costumes, appropriately described by theater critic Ben Brantley as "low-end K-Mart recycled by the Salvation Army,"[9] are the typical jeans, tee shirts, and sweat jackets of most average Americans—unless of course his characters are security guards, as in *The End of Reality*, his latest show, and have to wear a uniform.

Maxwell writes songs and music for his shows, which he considers to be musicals rather than dramas. His characters often break into solos that are not so much sung as croaked off-key. The effect is both amusing and disarming. At times there is live music, at others a char-

9. Ben Brantley, *New York Times*, review of *House*, December 8, 1998.

acter takes out a hand-held tape recorder, switches it on, and sings a love ballad or some other piece with quirky lyrics that may tell us something about the character's inner feelings. But since the timing is off and the actors sing standing stiffly in one place, the effect is often comical rather than serious. Clearly on all levels, Maxwell is not really interested in the emotional psychology, personal history, or motivation of his characters. He does not want to replicate the reality of life. "I'd rather accept the reality of the stage," he says. "The reality is that we're doing a play; I just put the actors on the stage, have them say their lines and let the audience fill in the blanks" (Maxwell, "Remarks").

As with his other plays, *Drummer Wanted*, billed as a personal lawsuit musical, tells a simple story. It is a two-character play, about a mother and her 29 year-old son Frank, forced to live together when Frank breaks his leg, the result of a motorcycle accident. There is no father, and mother and son do not enjoy the best of relationships. She is proper and overly polite. He is rather coarse and needy. Both are musicians, so-called. She plays the piano; he hammers on the drums. Clearly, he has little if any musical talent even though he has recorded 5,000 miles of songs on tape over the past fifteen years, and he plans to set up his own recording studio with the insurance money he hopes to get for his accident. They both like to go to karaoke bars and sing. But there their connection ends. At first the mother is solicitous of Frank's predicament; she brings him ice and props him up on a pillow, but soon their bickering begins. He yells at her not to touch him. She sings him a lullaby, an odd choice for a grown man. She wants him to get a job; he wants her to leave him alone even though he is afraid she will. Her response is delivered with little feeling: "I never left you and now you won't leave." This is a rare moment of truth. Most of the time, mother and son are afraid to say what they really feel. If the mother allows herself to come close, Frank counters with brutal rejection, cursing or chortling maliciously. If she plays Bach, he wildly bangs on the drums to drown her out. When she cries, however, he does try to console her, but it is an awkward moment. It is only when they sing that we hear their true feelings. "I feel so helpless when you're not around," he croons. "I can't find my way, on my own." And she replies: "Baby, I love you, what can we do?" By the end of the play, we have watched a tenuous relationship deteriorate. The mother sits motionless, staring into space. "I've gotten really good at not feeling anything," she tells us. We wonder if she is even listening to Frank as he rants on about letting go, singing "Can I let go? Go with the flow? I want to let go."[10] He removes his leg brace, a sign that he is healed, but will he move on?

Without Maxwell's special brand of mise en scène, this mother/son crisis would be of passing interest. As usual, his set is spare, a basement rec room, perhaps, with wall-to-wall carpeting and wood paneling (that immediately situates the characters as middle class), a piano stage right, and some chairs. Frank lies against the rear wall, his broken leg stretched out before him. His drum set, the focal point of his rage as well as his hopes, stands center stage, behind him. Mother and son never move outside of this enclosed space. When they speak of driving to the karaoke bar, the set does not change; they simply move from center stage to two chairs, which become car seats, and from there they move on to the bar. It is a constant reminder of Frank's impotence, both physical and psychological, and of the mother's entrapment as well. While the mother delivers her lines with a studied politeness that never varies, Frank regularly changes volume as well as pitch, from strident shouts to muttered phone conversations sprinkled with "Man" and "Dude."

In both Vinaver's and Maxwell's plays, the surface stories and situations contain familiar clichés of mutual dependence between mother and son, single mothers raising their children, rebellion, and so on. Both feature divorced, working mothers (Helen is a statistics clerk, Maxwell's mother a real estate agent) and fathers that are either absent or rejected. Philip is passively non-conformist, following his friends on the path of crime and drugs with an attitude of "what else is there?" Frank is an angry young man taking his rage out on his mother. Of course there are obvious differences as well. Frank and his mother's situation is concentrated in one critical moment. Frank is literally immobilized for most of *Drummer Wanted*, forced to depend on his mother to drive him to the karaoke bar, or get his painkillers at the pharmacy, and she is equally caught in a co-dependent trap. In contrast, Helen and Philip have lives outside the home. References are frequently made to what is going on between the scenes. Helen has an accident and sells the car, she has fainting spells, and uses a dating service to find a partner. Philip's friends come and go, he gets a job, steals money from his mother, and sells drugs. There is talk of buying a new car, and of the

---

10. Richard Maxwell, *Drummer Wanted*, script sent to Philippa Wehle, Fall 2004; all quotes from *Drummer Wanted* are from this script.

economic realities of a woman living on unemployment and a son selling drugs. Helen and Philip are more sympathetic than the mother and Frank, and their relationship is more ambiguous in terms of their closeness. But these are perhaps only surface points.

What matters, in both Maxwell's and Vinaver's plays, is what is left up in the air, or simply left out. There are many loose ends, many unanswered questions. What do we really know about these characters? Do they have an inner life? Although more is known of the lives of Helen and Philip, still we get only small doses of their moments together. As for Frank and his mother, we are left in the dark beyond the surface banality of their small talk and their conflictual relationship. Clearly meaning lies elsewhere.

We have seen that with Vinaver what matters is not the meaning of the anecdote so much as the structuring of the material in a way that disorients the audience and allows it to draw its own conclusions. What also matters to him is the larger social, economic, and political context within which the story takes place and the impact this has on the characters and their day-to-day lives. Helen and Philip are not just a mother and son, working on their relationship; their lives and attitudes are profoundly influenced by the problems facing young people and working people in France at the time *Dissident* takes place, issues that arise from computerization, joblessness, what to do when unemployment compensation runs out, or the monotony of life on the conveyor belt, a job Philip describes as "Plop in pedal plop." No wonder he prefers to rebel, albeit passively.

Maxwell, on the other hand, insists that the subjects he chooses to write about are decidedly irrelevant, non-topical, and unimportant. "There might be political, social, and economic meanings going on," he says. "But I refrain from imparting some message about that."[11] Even though Maxwell has begun to notice the political resonances of his work, he still insists that it is up to the audience to decide what they might be. His main interest is in exploring and exploding the boundaries of theater. The story, the text itself is not what matters to him; he sees it as a manual, a tool that he must bring to life in a new way, using deftly placed pauses, distorted delivery, and songs, especially songs, to disrupt and break the rhythms of the text. Despite his claim to remain above politics, however, there is no doubt in the au-

11. Richard Maxwell, phone interview with Philippa Wehle, October 23, 2004.

dience's minds that Maxwell's theater speaks to them of the issues they face on a daily basis. Because his actors are not acting out their emotions, the audience gets to have the emotional response and despite our laughter, a defense mechanism perhaps in this case, we feel deeply moved.

We have seen how both of these singular artists capture actual heard patterns of speech, how both tell familiar stories, and how both work in the realistic vein, while subverting the realistic elements in their plays. Why then is Vinaver not better known in our country and why is Maxwell's work supported and appreciated by the French more than in the United States? Using Vinaver and Maxwell as our guiding examples, we may find some answers to these questions.

Keeping in mind that it is not an easy task to get contemporary American playwriting on our stages much less foreign plays, and that there is no one clear explanation for the scarcity of contemporary French plays in our repertories, it seems fair to say that part of the reason can be found in a prevailing view held by a number of producers, presenters, critics, and audiences in this country that contemporary French theater is too wordy, too cerebral, too abstract, and for these reasons, too disconcerting. There is no storyline, we're told, no easily recognized characters. Even though there is great diversity among current French-language playwriting, there is still a tendency to see contemporary French playwriting as art theater, in other words, elitist, and therefore foreign to American audiences that want plays that are immediately comprehensible. It is just such stereotypes that have kept audiences from discovering the work of Olivier Cadiot, Valère Novarina, Philippe Minyana, José Pliya, Marie Ndiaye, and Michel Vinaver. When we do get the opportunity to see their work, it is thanks to a few dedicated university professors and translators, and to special events such as Chicago's 2004 Playing French festival and New York's 2005 Act French season of contemporary French-language theater, but these are short runs in mostly small theaters or on university campuses. Bernard-Marie Koltès, whose work has been produced here more often than others, may well be the exception, but even his plays are not standard fare in American regional theaters much less on or off Broadway. Even when Patrice Chéreau's outstanding production of Koltès's *In the Loneliness of the Cotton Fields* was presented at BAM in 1996, in French, one reviewer referred to it as "an uphill slog, . . . its ideas presented so slathered in overripe or not especially apt similes that you feel as if you are being force fed the world's largest, fruitiest, nuttiest all day Sunday."[12]

In the case of Vinaver, his plays are anything but wordy and they certainly are not abstract. He captures our attention with either familiar domestic situations or plays about the world of business and marketing, surely subjects of interest to American audiences. Interestingly, Vinaver actually sees many of his plays as "American": "Not just with American characters but about American business practices."[13] His play *11 septembre/September 11*, written by him in English in the weeks immediately following 9/11, using words taken from daily newspapers, personal accounts, and other sources, is one of the most important French dramas in recent years, clearly a play to be seen and discussed by American audiences. It was given an excellent production by CalArts in April 2005 with American actors and a French director, yet it has not been seen in the rest of America.[14]

As "American" as it may be, still Vinaver's theater has an unmistakable Frenchness to it.[15] What does this mean? Vinaver explains: "It is true that my theater contains a constellation of precise objects connected to French life at a given time and in a given place, in the most concrete sense."[16] References to the new Renault 5, with the double-welded frame, in *Dissident, goes without saying*, for example, to Helen losing her job to computers, strikes at the Peugeot factory, computer dating, unemployment compensation, and Philip's talk of the Algerians at the factory, are indeed objects that are localized in time and space. Could this "Frenchness" date Vinaver's work and be a reason for his plays not being widely produced in this country? Edward Baron Turk, Professor of French and Film at M.I.T., doesn't think so: "the amazing thing is how prescient his plays are, content-wise, since the problems he raises about big business are simply exacerbated to-

12. Vincent Canby, *New York Times*, review of Patrice Chéreau's production of Bernard-Marie Koltès's *In the Loneliness of the Cotton Fields*, presented at BAM, February 1996.

13. Michel Vinaver, remarks made to Philippa Wehle, July 19, 2006, Avignon, France.

14. New York City was deprived of the CalArts production of Vinaver's *11 September 2001*, scheduled to be part of the "Act French" festival, because the French government withheld part of its promised support for the project out of a concern over the way the play gives equal time to documented statements by President Bush and Osama bin Laden.

15. Bradby writes of this Frenchness in Vinaver's work in *The Theater of Michel Vinaver*.

16. Michel Vinaver, remarks made to Philippa Wehle, July 19, 2006, Avignon, France.

day; to call him 'outdated' is like saying that Balzac's descriptions of Paris and money speculation are dated because the city and the financial system have changed radically."[17] The question for Vinaver is whether or not an author is engaged in the world he lives in at the time he is writing. These details, this "out-of-dateness" (his term in English) are signs of a past that enrich the present; they add to the pleasure of the experience of his theater. "Such details of time and place in my theater do not prevent my work from being produced widely today."[18]

The issue of translation is of course crucial to finding directors and producers who will be interested in reading a French play; give them a poor translation and you've lost your battle before you've started. With Vinaver, this is not a problem; translations of his plays are excellent and available. Generally speaking, however, finding good, accurate, and sensitive American English translations of contemporary French authors is a challenge. When French cultural attaché Yannick Mercoyrol took up his post in Chicago and began to plan Playing French, Chicago's First Festival of Contemporary Plays from France, he stated the situation very clearly. "The contemporary French repertory rarely goes beyond the usual names—Ionesco, Genet—for a simple reason: a lack of translations."[19] Accordingly, to jump start the festival, he distributed more than seventy translations of contemporary French-language plays to Chicago theaters interested in participating and asked them to choose those that best fit their aims and facilities. A number of these were recent commissions, and did not necessarily exist in published form. The fact remains that English translations of French contemporary playwrights are difficult to find in the United States because they are not published.[20] Theater director and translator Marion Schoevaert, who co-produced the Koltès festival in New York City in 2003 and translated and produced the work of Olivier Cadiot during the Act French Festival in 2005, has found this to be distressingly true. "Yes, there are translations of French contemporary playwrights in English published in the U.K.," she writes, ". . .but the written language of the-

17. Edward Baron Turk, remarks made to Philippa Wehle in an e-mail sent September 6, 2006.
18. Vinaver, remarks made to Philippa Wehle, July 19, 2006, Avignon, France.
19. Yannick Mercoyrol, statement made to the Chicago Tribune, September 12, 2004.
20. Other than the Performing Arts Journal Publications volumes of translations of contemporary European theater, and the volumes of contemporary French-language plays published by Ubu Repertory Theater, it is rare to find published translations of contemporary French-language plays in the United States.

ater is meant to be spoken and pronounced in action . . . and British translations sound foreign in the U.S."[21] Indeed, the question of "foreignness" is an interesting one for the translator, when it comes to appropriate word choices as well as fidelity to the original. When Vinaver was asked if a translator should keep the specific French references in his plays or look for contemporary equivalents, update them or explain them, his answer was unequivocally no. "Does a translator translate Francs into Euros? No, he keeps Francs."[22] These "objects" are signs of a past that enrich the present and accordingly they must be kept. Vinaver has been fortunate in finding excellent, compatible translators for his plays in this country and because he is bi-lingual, he can work closely with them so that nothing is "lost in translation," but how many others can say as much?

Pockets of solutions exist and have existed here and there, to be sure: the Koltès Festival in New York City based on new translations of his plays worked on by a translator team of writers, poets, and theater artists and presented over a four week period at the Ohio Theater; or a similar festival devoted to introducing the work of José Pliya through readings of new translations of his plays and a full production in French of one of them brought from Paris with the author present; the Ubu Repertory Theater, which for twenty years introduced New York audiences to the work of contemporary French playwrights, through full productions, readings and published translations of their work, to mention but a few.[23] Such experiences are commendable and they are not limited to New York City: CalArts with its Vinaver project and Atlanta's 7 Stages theater's sponsoring of a fruitful collaboration between a French director (Arthur Nauzyciel), American actors and a French playwright (Bernard-Marie Koltès), are cases in point. But what is the follow-up? It seems that despite so many efforts, they are destined to be shortlived.

And what about Richard Maxwell, beloved of the French and other Europeans, but so uniquely American? His portraits are portraits of today's urban America, portraits that chronicle the ills of contemporary urban life, security guards confronted with violence, addicts trying to be rehabilitated and failing time and again, ordinary American types

21. Marion Schoevaert, remarks made to Philippa Wehle in an e-mail sent September 6, 2006.

22. Vinaver, remarks made to Philippa Wehle, July 19, 2006, Avignon, France.

23. Most unfortunately, Ubu Repertory Theater no longer exists. It provided American audiences with a wealth of new French and Francophone playwriting.

trying to connect but unable to communicate. Maxwell captures their numbness and their isolation by subverting the realistic elements in his plays with lines delivered with no emotion, movements stiff and sluggish, pauses that startle and unexpected jumps in time. At a time when the American musical is in deep trouble, with not much happening but revivals, big production numbers, and over-miked spectacles, Maxwell offers up his special brand of musical theater for the new century. Off key, out of sync, and as such, indicative of our current society. Why then, we may ask, must he—with few exceptions—continue to open his latest plays either in the small, underfunded venues of downtown New York City, or in arts centers rather than in regional theaters, or depend on European festivals, and particularly Paris's Festival d'Automne, to provide his work with the financial support and the larger audience it deserves?

Why is Vinaver, France's leading active playwright, whose plays are regularly produced in his country's important subsidized theaters (this year alone three of them were presented in Paris in April, May, and June), not widely known in this country?

Must we conclude that Maxwell and other experimental American authors will forever be relegated to minority status along with their French counterparts? Because, on the one hand, Americans go for spectacle; they want sensationalism, a thrill, stimulation, and need to be shocked, as if the terrifying moment we live in, with its distorted information, manipulation, and lack of caring for other people, weren't enough of a challenge. Or, on the other hand, because American realistic plays, still the preferred form of theater in mainstream America, still follow a structure with lengthy exposition, clear plot, recognizable characters, and logical resolution, and neither Vinaver's poetic theater of multiple possibilities or Maxwell's anti-theater fit this model, as we have seen.

If indeed American theater is on the decline as Frédéric Martel argues in his recent study *Sur le déclin du théâtre en Amérique (et comment il peut résister en France)*,[24] then there is little hope for a theater that speaks to us of our fears and hidden realities in a language that is not an exact reproduction of everyday speech and situations. The reasons for this decline are many, of course. As Martel points out, however, it is not just the obvious situation of a lack of government fund-

---

24. Frédéric Martel, *Sur le déclin du théâtre en Amérique (et comment il peut résister en France)* (Paris: Editions La Découverte, 2006).

ing, withdrawal of foundation monies, and a system where show is business and the market rule; it also has to do with America's insularity, its isolation, its disconnect from the rest of the world, culturally and politically, along with an increasingly conservative audience that is afraid to take risks. An audience that won't take risks on its own theater is not going to take risks on French plays and authors they've most likely never heard about.

Tom Sellar, editor of *Theater Magazine*, agrees: "American drama, at this moment, mostly corresponds to our national politics: smug, self-satisfied, and often willfully ignorant of the precedents, standards, and developments of the rest of the world. And New York theater is in an equally fallow moment, with everyone waiting for the Next Big Thing while looking for cash and watching an art form decline in the face of conservatism (in its audiences and institutions)."[25]

It seems that we are forced once more to conclude that writers like Vinaver and Maxwell are first and foremost experimental writers who must by definition surprise us with original plays and production techniques; they may tell stories of ordinary people in ordinary situations, but they tell them in a highly compressed language; a language that is heightened, stylized, stripped down. Even though Vinaver speaks to us of our business practices, of our corporate world, of human relationships and society's ills shared by both cultures and Maxwell addresses the apathy and numb response of so many to the terrifying moment we live in, there is nothing explicitly sensational or shocking about their theater; it is an innovative theater that challenges the very stage conventions that commercial American theater promotes. It is not safe; it is uncomfortable. These writers are the exceptions; we look to them to jolt us out of our complacency. Yet, as Sellar suggests: "It may well be that our theater is condemned to wait "for the Next Big thing while looking for cash and watching an art form decline."

25. Sellar, remarks delivered at the "Act French" Festival, final session at the Public Theater, New York City, January 16, 2006.

Contributors

Tom Bishop is Florence Gould Professor of Modern French Literature and Professor of Comparative Literature at New York University, where he also directs the Center for French Civilization and Culture. He chaired NYU's French Department from 1970 to 2003. He is the author of *Pirandello and the French Theater; From the Left Bank: Reflections on the Modern French Theater and Novel; Le passeur d'océan*. He edited *Avant-Garde: French Theater Since 1950; Sartre's Huis clos; Les anti-américanismes; Roland Barthes: Thirty Years Later*, and co-edited the Cahier de l'Herne *Beckett*. He was the co-Artistic Director of the Festival International Paris-Beckett 2006.

Bernadette Bost is Professor of Theater Studies at the Université Stendhal (Grenoble 3). A drama critic for *Le monde* and other newspapers, she is chiefly concerned in her research with contemporary dramaturgy (she has written on Bernard Chartreux, Michel Deutsch, Jean-Christophe Bailly, Valère Novarina, and Michel Vinaver, among others) and the relationship between various artistic disciplines as they interact on stage.

David Bradby is Professor of Drama and Theatre Studies at Royal Holloway, University of London. His books include *Modern French Drama 1940–1990* and *Beckett: Waiting for Godot* (Cambridge UP, 1991 and 2001 respectively), *The Theater of Michel Vinaver* (University of Michigan Press, 1993) and (with Annie Sparks) *Mise en Scène: French Theater Now* (Methuen, 1997). He has translated Lecoq's *The Moving Body* (Methuen, 2000) and translated and edited plays by Michel Vinaver and Bernard-Marie Koltès. With Maria M. Delgado, he edits the *Contemporary Theatre Review* and published *The Paris Jigsaw: Internationalism and the City's Stages*

YFS 112, *The Transparency of the Text*, ed. Donia Mounsef and Josette Féral,
© 2007 by Yale University.

(Manchester UP, 2002). He is general editor of the Cambridge University Press series "Cambridge Studies in Modern Theatre."

SYLVIE CHALAYE is Professor of Theater Studies at the Université Rennes 2. She is the author of several works dealing with the theater of French-speaking Sub-Saharan Africa: *Dramaturgies africaines d'aujourd'hui en 10 parcours* (Lansman, 2001), *L'Afrique noire et son théâtre au tournant du XXe siècle* (Presses Universitaires de Rennes, 2001), *Afrique noire et dramaturgies contemporaines: le syndrome Frankenstein* (Éditions Théâtrales, 2004). She edited *Nouvelles dramaturgies d'Afrique noire francophone* (Presses Universitaires de Rennes, 2004). Her other publications include *Du Noir au nègre: l'image du Noir au théâtre de Marguerite de Navarre à Jean Genet (1550–1960)* (L'Harmattan, 1998); *Le Chavelier de Saint Georges de Mélesville et Beauvoir* (L'Harmattan, 2001); *Nègres en images,* (L'Harmattan, 2002), *Les Ourika du boulevard* (L'Harmattan, 2003).

ARIANE EISSEN is a lecturer in Comparative Literature at the Université de Poitiers. Her dissertation focuses on the reception of mythology and national imaginings, both in France and Great Britain from the end of the nineteenth century to the early twentieth century. She is the author of *Mythes grecs* (Belin, 1993), has written entries for the *Dictionnaire des mythes littéraires* (Éd. du Rocher, 1994) and the *Dictionnaire des mythes féminins* (Éd. du Rocher, 2000), and co-edited a collection on *La dimension mythique de la littérature contemporaine* (La Licorne, 2000).

JOSETTE FÉRAL is Professor and Chair of Theater Studies at the Université du Québec in Montréal. She has published widely on the theory of theater and has edited many books: *Mise en scène et jeu de l'acteur,* volumes 1, 2 and 3 (1997, 1999, 2007), *L'école du jeu, former ou transmettre* (L'Entretemps, France, 2003), *Theatricality* (special issue of *Substance,* 2002), *Les chemins de l'acteur* (Montréal, 2001), *Rencontres avec Ariane Mnouchkine* and *Trajectoires du Soleil* (Paris, 1999). She has written extensively on theater in Canada, the United States, and Europe.

CLARE FINBURGH is Lecturer in Modern Drama at the University of Essex, UK. She has written on various aspects of twentieth-century and contemporary French and Francophone theater, notably on Jean Genet, Kateb Yacine, and Michel Vinaver. Her essays have appeared in *Théâtre/Public, Theater Journal, French Forum, French Studies, Research in African Literatures* and *Paragraph: The Journal of Mod-*

ern Critical Theory. She has co-edited a book entitled *Genet: Performance and Politics,* and is currently completing a monograph on *mise en scène* in Jean Genet's theater and conducting a research project on representations of terrorism in theater.

JUDITH MILLER is Chair and Professor of French and Francophone Theater in the Department of French at NYU. She has published widely on French and Francophone theater, both text and production. Among her recent publications are "Tony Kushner and Ariane Mnouchkine: New Forms for New Conflicts," *Contemporary Theater* (spring 2006) and *Ariane Mnouchkine,* a study of the French director for Routledge's series on key performance practitioners (2007). She is also bringing out, with Christiane Owusu-Sarpong, the French version of *Women Writing Africa: West Africa and the Sahel,* a compilation of texts: fiction, documents, letters by African women writers (Karthala, 2007).

DONIA MOUNSEF is Associate Professor of French and Theater Studies at Yale University. She is the author of *Chair et révolte dans le théâtre de Bernard-Marie Koltès* (L'Harmattan, 2005) as well as articles on contemporary French theater, performance theory, film theory, and politics and performance. She edited a special cluster of articles on text and performance for the *Yale Journal of Criticism* (2003). She is currently co-editing a collection on *Theaters of Global Suffrage: The Plays, Performance and Protest of Women's Rights* and completing a manuscript on the theories of the body at the intersection of theater and film.

DONALD NICHOLSON-SMITH has translated works by Henri Lefebvre, Guy Debord, Thierry Jonquet, and Paco Ignacio Taibo II. Born in Manchester, England, he is a longtime resident of New York City. At present he is translating books by Artaud and Apollinaire.

MARY NOONAN is Lecturer in French at University College Cork. She completed a doctoral thesis on voice in the theaters of Sarraute, Duras and Cixous (Royal Holloway, University of London), and has published widely on their work. She is currently researching the work of writers for the contemporary French stage. In 2005, she organized an international conference—*The Contemporary French Theatre: Writing, Performing, Teaching*—at University College Cork, and is now preparing a book on this topic.

JEAN-PIERRE RYNGAERT is Professor of Drama Studies at the Université de Paris III-Sorbonne nouvelle, and is, with Jean-Pierre Sarrazac, the moving spirit behind the research group "Poétique du drame moderne et contemporain." Among the books he has written are *Intro-duction à l'analyse du théâtre* (Bordas, reprinted at Armand Colin) and *Lire le théâtre contemporain* (Dunod, 1993, reprinted at Armand Colin). He recently edited *Nouveaux territoires du dialogue* (Actes Sud-Papiers, 2005) and wrote, with J. Sermon, *Le personnage théâtral contemporain* (Théâtrales, 2006). He recently staged in Switzerland Daniel Danis's play, *Celle-là*.

CHRISTY WAMPOLE is a graduate student in French and Italian at Stanford University. Her interests include nineteenth-, twentieth-, and twenty-first century French and Italian novels and the Franco-Italian avant-garde.

PHILIPPA WEHLE is Professor Emeritus of Contemporary French Language and Culture and Drama Studies (Purchase College, State University of New York), Chevalier in the Order of Arts and Letters, author of *Le théâtre populaire selon Jean Vilar* (Actes Sud, 1991) and *Contemporary Drama: France* (PAJ, 1986), as well as of numerous articles on contemporary theater and performance. She is a noted translator of contemporary French-language plays by Marguerite Duras, Nathalie Sarraute, Philippe Minyana, José Pliya and others. She is also artistic program advisor to festivals and cultural centers in France.

LESLIE WICKES is a translator and a Doctoral Candidate in the Department of English at McGill University, Montréal, Canada. Her research focuses on crime and gender in eighteenth-century literature. She has given papers on criminal writings and Jane Barker, and worked on the Juvenilia Volume of The Cambridge Edition of the Works of Jane Austen (2006). She is currently in the final stages of completing her dissertation, titled "Con-texts': Gender and the Criminal Narrative in Eighteenth-Century Fiction."

The following issues are available through **Yale University Press,** Customer Service Department, P.O. Box 209040, New Haven, CT 06520-9040. Tel. 1-800-405-1619. yalebooks.com

69 The Lesson of Paul de Man (1985) $22.00
73 Everyday Life (1987) $22.00
75 The Politics of Tradition: Placing Women in French Literature (1988) $22.00
Special Issue: After the Age of Suspicion: The French Novel Today (1989) $22.00
76 Autour de Racine: Studies in Intertextuality (1989) $22.00
77 Reading the Archive: On Texts and Institutions (1990) $22.00
78 On Bataille (1990) $22.00
79 Literature and the Ethical Question (1991) $22.00
Special Issue: Contexts: Style and Value in Medieval Art and Literature (1991) $22.00
80 Baroque Topographies: Literature/History/ Philosophy (1992) $22.00
81 On Leiris (1992) $22.00
82 Post/Colonial Conditions Vol. 1 (1993) $22.00
83 Post/Colonial Conditions Vol. 2 (1993) $22.00
84 Boundaries: Writing and Drawing (1993) $22.00
85 Discourses of Jewish Identity in 20th-Century France (1994) $22.00

86 Corps Mystique, Corps Sacré (1994) $22.00
87 Another Look, Another Woman (1995) $22.00
88 Depositions: Althusser, Balibar, Macherey (1995) $22.00
89 Drafts (1996) $22.00
90 Same Sex / Different Text? Gay and Lesbian Writing in French (1996) $22.00
91 Genet: In the Language of the Enemy (1997) $22.00
92 Exploring the Conversible World (1997) $22.00
93 The Place of Maurice Blanchot (1998) $22.00
94 Libertinage and Modernity (1999) $22.00
95 Rereading Allegory: Essays in Memory of Daniel Poirion (1999) $22.00
96 50 Years of *Yale French Studies*, Part I: 1948-1979 (1999) $22.00
97 50 Years of *Yale French Studies*, Part 2: 1980-1998 (2000) $22.00
98 The French Fifties (2000) $22.00
99 Jean-François Lyotard: Time and Judgment (2001) $22.00

100 FRANCE/USA: The Cultural Wars (2001) $22.00
101 Fragments of Revolution (2002) $22.00
102 Belgian Memories (2002) $22.00
103 French and Francophone: the Challenge of Expanding Horizons (2003) $22.00
104 Encounters with Levinas (2003) $22.00
105 Pereckonings: Reading Georges Perec (2004) $22.00
106 Jean Paulhan's Fiction, Criticism, and Editorial Activity (2004) $22.00
107 The Haiti Issue (2005) $22.00
108 Crime Fictions (2005) $22.00
109 Surrealism and Its Others (2006) $22.00
110 Meaning and Its Objects (2006) $22.00
111 Myth and Modernity (2007) $22.00

ORDER FORM   **Yale University Press,** P.O. Box 209040, New Haven, CT 06520-9040
I would like to purchase the following individual issues:

_____

_____

For individual issues, please add postage and handling:
Single issue, United States $2.75   Each additional issue $.50
Single issue, foreign countries $5.00   Each additional issue $1.00
Connecticut residents please add sales tax of 6%.

Payment of $_____ is enclosed (including sales tax if applicable).

MasterCard no. _____ Expiration date _____

VISA no. _____ Expiration date _____

Signature _____

SHIP TO _____

_____

See the next page for ordering other back issues. Yale French Studies is also available through Xerox University Microfilms, 300 North Zeeb Road, Ann Arbor, MI 48106.

The following issues are still available through the **Yale French Studies Office**, P.O. Box 208251, New Haven, CT 06520-8251.

19/20 Contemporary Art $3.50	42 Zola $5.00	54 Mallarmé $5.00
	43 The Child's Part $5.00	61 Toward a Theory of Description $6.00
33 Shakespeare $3.50	45 Language as Action $5.00	
35 Sade $3.50		
	46 From Stage to Street $3.50	
39 Literature and Revolution $3.50	52 Graphesis $5.00	

Add for postage & handling

Single issue, United States $3.85 (Priority Mail)   Each additional issue $1.25
Single issue, United States $1.90 (Third Class)   Each additional issue $ .50
Single issue, foreign countries $3.75 (Book Rate)   Each additional issue $3.00

YALE FRENCH STUDIES, P.O. Box 208251, New Haven, Connecticut 06520-8251
A check made payable to YFS is enclosed. Please send me the following issue(s):

Issue no.   Title   Price

_____

_____

Postage & handling _____

Total _____

Name _____

Number/Street _____

City _____ State _____ Zip _____

The following issues are now available through Periodicals Service Company, 11 Main Street, Germantown, N.Y. 12526, Phone: (518) 537-4700. Fax: (518) 537-5899.

1 Critical Bibliography of Existentialism	19/20 Contemporary Art
2 Modern Poets	21 Poetry Since the Liberation
3 Criticism & Creation	22 French Education
4 Literature & Ideas	23 Humor
5 The Modern Theatre	24 Midnight Novelists
6 France and World Literature	25 Albert Camus
7 André Gide	26 The Myth of Napoleon
8 What's Novel in the Novel	27 Women Writers
9 Symbolism	28 Rousseau
10 French-American Literature Relationships	29 The New Dramatists
11 Eros, Variations...	30 Sartre
12 God & the Writer	31 Surrealism
13 Romanticism Revisited	32 Paris in Literature
14 Motley: Today's French Theater	33 Shakespeare in France
15 Social & Political France	34 Proust
16 Foray through Existentialism	48 French Freud
17 The Art of the Cinema	51 Approaches to Medieval Romance
18 Passion & the Intellect, or Malraux	

36/37 Structuralism has been reprinted by Doubleday as an Anchor Book.
55/56 Literature and Psychoanalysis has been reprinted by Johns Hopkins University Press, and can be ordered through Customer Service, Johns Hopkins University Press, Baltimore, MD 21218.